THE HISTORY
OF THE SAS

Also by Chris Ryan

Non-fiction
The One That Got Away
Chris Ryan's SAS Fitness Book
Chris Ryan's Ultimate Survival Guide
Fight to Win
Safe

Fiction
Stand By, Stand By
Zero Option
The Kremlin Device
Tenth Man Down
Hit List
The Watchman
Land of Fire
Greed
The Increment
Blackout
Ultimate Weapon
Strike Back
Firefight
Who Dares Wins
The Kill Zone
Killing for the Company
Osama

In the Danny Black Series
Masters of War
Hunter Killer
Hellfire
Bad Soldier
Warlord

In the Strikeback Series
Deathlist
Shadow Kill
Global Strike
Red Strike

Chris Ryan Extreme
Hard Target
Night Strike
Most Wanted
Silent Kill

CHRIS RYAN

THE HISTORY OF THE SAS

CORONET

First published in Great Britain in 2019 by Coronet
An Imprint of Hodder & Stoughton
An Hachette UK company

1

A CIP catalogue record for this title is available from the British Library

Hardback ISBN 9781529324648
Trade Paperback ISBN 9781529324655
eBook ISBN 9781529324662

Typeset in Bembo Std by Hewer Text UK Ltd, Edinburgh
Printed and bound in Great Britain by Clays Ltd, Elcograf S.p.A.

Hodder & Stoughton policy is to use papers that are natural, renewable
and recyclable products and made from wood grown in sustainable forests.
The logging and manufacturing processes are expected to conform
to the environmental regulations of the country of origin.

Hodder & Stoughton Ltd
Carmelite House
50 Victoria Embankment
London EC4Y 0DZ

www.hodder.co.uk

To Geordie Doran

Contents

INTRODUCTION

To Dare Is to Win

Sixty years ago, the modern SAS was fighting for its very survival.

Back then, the guys in the Regiment were only just beginning to establish themselves after the original Special Air Service Brigade had been disbanded at the end of the Second World War.

Founded in 1941 by David Stirling, the men in 'L' Detachment operated deep behind enemy lines in the desert of North Africa, attacking German airfields, carrying out port operations and terrorising Axis forces. They were phenomenally successful, destroying hundreds of aircraft on the ground. One legendary SAS soldier, Paddy Mayne, accounted for more planes than any single RAF fighter pilot. Stirling was captured in early 1943 and spent the rest of the war in prison, but under Mayne the unit (now reduced in size and renamed the Special Raiding Squadron) saw action in Europe, taking part in the Allied landings in Italy.

In 1944, they were dropping into France and linking up with various elements of the French resistance, gathering intelligence, harassing German forces and disrupting lines of communication. By that time the SAS had reverted to its original name and had been brought up to brigade strength, numbering over two thousand men including Belgian and French elements. They ended the war in Germany, pushing ahead of the main invasion force and hunting Nazi war criminals.

At the end of the war, the SAS Brigade was officially disbanded. Senior figures in Whitehall, never big fans of the concept of

Special Forces units, believed that they had no place in the conflicts of the future.

They were wrong.

The unit was revived at the beginning of the 1950s to help take on the gangs of ruthless Communist guerrillas operating in the jungles of Malaya. It performed brilliantly, disrupting the enemy and patrolling in some of the harshest conditions imaginable.

Conventional military wisdom suggested that a soldier could last no longer than a week in the jungle. The SAS regularly sent out patrols that lasted for three months. Some guys survived even longer, spending well over a hundred days below the canopy. They tore the rulebook up and went toe-to-toe with the Communist terrorists, dominating the ground and putting them on the defensive.

But while the Regiment was out there doing the business, there were individuals in the War Office who viewed the unit with hostility. Some saw the SAS as a bunch of rogue operators, a law unto themselves with little regard for the traditional chain of command. Jealousy also, probably, played a part: some didn't like the fact that these scruffy, bearded individuals were going out and getting to grips with the enemy, using unorthodox military tactics that had little in common with the conventional approach of the regular 'green' army.

Many of the tactics the SAS first devised in the jungle have stood the test of time and are still used today. But it was only by proving themselves in the campaign in Malaya, and later in Oman, that the unit was finally assured of its future. Up until that point, there were no guarantees about the long-term survival of the Regiment.

Today, it's no exaggeration to say that the British Army could not function without the fighting skills of 22 SAS and its support elements.

Whenever it has been called upon, time and again the Regiment has shown that it has the capability to deploy and dominate in any type of environment. Whether it's a long-range patrol in the desert, a counter-insurgency operation or a hostage rescue, the

SAS has got what it takes to get the job done. And that flexibility makes it a priceless asset in today's world of hybrid warfare and international terrorism.

What makes the Regiment the success story it is today? There are many reasons, but I would argue that it comes down to two key factors.

One is the standard of training. SAS Selection is without a doubt the best and toughest Special Forces selection course in the world. I should know, because I was an instructor on Training Wing for several years. Selection lasts for five months, and candidates are expected to prove themselves in a variety of punishing environments, from the hills of the Brecon Beacons to the sweltering jungle. Quite simply, there is no other military course that demands as much from a soldier – mentally as well as physically.

The other reason is the unique quality of the British soldier.

The average soldier in this country is resourceful and highly motivated and doesn't give up easily. Above all, he or she can more than handle themselves in a fight. In my experience, our soldiers are capable of dominating any other conventional military force. There is just something about the Brits that makes us formidable warriors.

The SAS has also been fortunate to have been kept almost continually busy since it was re-formed in the 1950s. In late 1958, towards the end of the Malaya campaign, one of the squadrons went straight out to the Middle East to help put down a revolt against the Sultan of Oman. Some of the guys involved had little or no previous experience of fighting in the desert and they had to learn everything from scratch: navigation skills, patrolling, and desert warfare. In January 1959 the second remaining Sabre Squadron arrived in Oman and the soldiers stormed the rebels' mountain stronghold, the Jebel Akhdar, a position that no military force had conquered since the Persians back in the tenth century.

After a rare period of quiet the guys were back in the jungle a few years later, operating in Borneo during the Confrontation with Indonesia in the early 1960s. During this time the SAS's resources were stretched to the limit, with the unit also taking part in a campaign in Aden. In one disastrous mission in the Radfan Mountains in 1964, two soldiers were killed after their patrol was compromised. The severed heads of the two dead men were later displayed on posts in a Yemeni town, a grisly reminder of what can happen when an operation goes badly wrong. The SAS also practised counter-insurgency warfare in an urban environment for the first time in Aden, going out undercover on the streets to look for targets.

In 1970 the guys were back in Oman, helping to combat a Communist-backed insurgency against the Sultan. On 19 July 1972, the Regiment fought one of its most heroic engagements, when a nine-man team (backed up by a force of Omani gendarmerie and Askari tribesmen) found itself under attack from a force of more than two hundred determined rebels. Despite the overwhelming odds, the soldiers managed to hold off the enemy until airstrikes and reinforcements could come in and drive the rebels back. Victory came at a cost: two brave SAS men, Talaiasi Labalaba and Tommy Tobin, lost their lives.

In 1976, a few months after the final defeat of the Omani rebels, the guys were sent into a European theatre for the first time since 1945 when they deployed to Northern Ireland. They had to adapt yet again, learning a set of new tactics and operating within strict rules of engagement in their war against the terrorists of the Provisional IRA. In 1980 they stormed the Iranian Embassy at the end of a six-day siege, a hostage-rescue op that was, tactically, a million miles away from anything they had done before.

Two years later they went back to a more traditional type of warfare in the Falklands, using Klepper canoes to run ashore and launch a night-time raid on an enemy airfield. The Regiment also suffered its largest single loss since the Second World War during the Falklands conflict, when a Sea King helicopter crashed into the ocean, killing twenty men. Despite this tragedy, the soldiers recovered to play an instrumental role in retaking the Islands.

In the late 1980s, during my time in the Regiment, we were ordered to go to Colombia and train up the Jungla commandos, the country's counter-narcotics unit, teaching them the skills they needed to take on Pablo Escobar and the Cali cartel. That was the big deal at that time.

In 1991 we were off to the Middle East, targeting Scud missiles and military installations during the Gulf War. A lot has been written about what happened to our patrol, but what's less talked about is that the guys in A and D Squadrons did an incredible amount of damage in the desert of western Iraq, directing airstrikes, blowing up communication towers and ripping up convoys. Their actions took the Iraqis by surprise: they couldn't believe that British Special Forces teams were operating so far behind enemy lines. It got to the point where the high command had to order the squadrons to go static because there was simply nothing left for them to destroy.

A few years after we came back from Iraq, the Bosnian War kicked off, so some of the lads were sent out under the guise of UN inspectors, acting as the eyes and ears of the commanders. The Regiment helped to map out the disputed territories, nego-tiating with all three warring sides and assessing the morale and strength of their respective forces. By the same token, they were ideally placed to carry out a forward-observation role in the besieged Muslim enclaves, helping to bring in Coalition aircraft to bomb various Serbian positions and providing cover so that vital UN food convoys could get through.

In 2003, the Regiment went back to the desert to take part in the Iraq War. The years after the invasion saw a revolution in coun-ter-insurgency warfare as the SAS took on a very different role from previous conflicts. Working in small strike teams as part of a joint US–UK task force, the guys were getting briefed on targets, going out to lift them, gathering intelligence and sometimes doing multiple raids in a single evening. The workload was more demand-ing and intense than ever before, but it did the trick: the SAS played a key role in the eventual defeat of al-Qaeda in Iraq.

In the more recent conflict with ISIS, the Regiment evolved

its approach yet again, taking on a more proactive role, going out in squadron-sized formations with the aim of hammering the enemy. This time, there was no interest in taking any prisoners or making hard arrests as they had been doing in Iraq, and later on in Afghanistan. Now they were just going in hard and blasting targets, wiping out the insurgents. Some of the missions the Regiment has pulled off in Iraq, Syria and elsewhere are gobsmacking. If the general public knew even half of what the soldiers have achieved, they would be deeply impressed.

This ability to constantly reinvent themselves is what it's all about for the lads in the SAS: adapting to whatever environment they're fighting in, changing their tactics, experimenting with new techniques and skillsets. Doing whatever it takes to destroy the enemy.

Today the unit is in demand more than ever. In the fight against Isis, they have been going out on constant rotations in Iraq, Afghanistan and Syria, with barely time to catch their breath between operations. With their typical black humour, the guys refer to it as the 'Circle of Death'.

Even as the nature of war changes, there will always be a role for the SAS, because no one else can do what they do. Other SF units might have superior equipment or support, but their operators don't match up to the fighting capabilities of our lads. They have to go further and train harder than anyone else, and that makes them extremely resilient.

After I came back from the Gulf War, I remember going over to Fort Bragg in North Carolina to brief the Americans on my escape. Arriving at the airport, I was greeted by a US Army Ranger, who was there to drive me to the base. As I climbed into his car the Ranger turned to me, obviously having been briefed on the reason for my visit.

'So are you talking about your escape?' he asked.

'Yeah,' I said.

The guy nodded. 'How long were you on the run for, buddy?'

'Seven,' I replied.

The Ranger said, 'Oh, I did seventeen with my patrol.'

I spun round in my seat and stared at the Ranger in disbelief. '*Seventeen* days?' I spluttered.

The Ranger started shaking his head. 'No, I meant seventeen *hours*,' he said. 'Why, what the hell are you talking about?'

So I told him what I'd done in Iraq. After I'd finished speaking, he looked at me and frowned. 'I don't get it,' he said. 'Why didn't anyone come to pick you up when you were on the run?'

'Because we didn't have any helicopters to spare at the time,' I replied matter-of-factly. 'How about yourself? Did you get picked up?'

The Ranger nodded. It turned out that from the moment their patrol made contact with the Iraqis, and during their subsequent escape, the Ranger and his mates had thirty-seven friendly aircraft circling in the air above. This guy could not get his head around the idea that we had only three Chinooks in the desert and the head shed wouldn't send them for us immediately, so we had to make our own way back after our patrol was compromised. To him, it beggared belief that we were effectively abandoned. But that's the situation. If there are no assets, then there are no assets. That's it. That's how the guys in the Regiment work.

Some Special Forces units become dangerously kit-reliant. Which is fine when you have access to the best kit, until you don't. Then you suddenly realise that you've forgotten how to soldier. Whereas the guys in the SAS would simply shrug and go, 'Okay, the situation isn't great, but we'll just get on with it.'

That's the attitude of the lads in a nutshell. They're very resourceful, driven and excellent at solving problems. Ever since their first deployment in the Malayan Emergency, the SAS has been reinventing the wheel in terms of military tactics. They're still doing it to this day, pushing the envelope whenever they're confronted by a dangerous new enemy, doing the unexpected.

At the heart of the SAS are the soldiers themselves – the 'Blades'. More so than anyone, they are what make the unit what it is today.

History is made of generals' accounts and war memoirs written by senior officers. But the unique nature of the Regiment demands a different approach. For that reason, this history focuses on SAS operations from the ground up. The careers of various COs and the administrative life of the Regiment have been told in other excellent military histories. The aim of this book is to tell the reader how it felt to be a soldier in the SAS, fighting in often testing circumstances against some of the most feared enemies in the world.

Although the wartime SAS and the modern Regiment share a common name and heritage, they are distinct entities. The 'Originals' primarily operated as raiders and shock troops in conventional theatres of war involving massive armed forces – the North African desert, the beaches of Italy, Nazi-occupied France. Whereas 22 SAS has developed into a much more diverse unit, often operating in places where it has been politically inconvenient to deploy regular forces. In terms of personnel and tactical principles, they have a shared DNA, but today's SAS works to a much broader remit than its wartime predecessor.

Whether it's training up foreign militias, running OPs on terrorist camps or snatching targets in the middle of the night in Baghdad, the guys have transformed their tactics to keep pace with their enemies. Today, the SAS is running very different operations from the type of raiding actions pioneered in the Second World War. As we have seen, this evolution can be traced right back to its origins in the jungle, when the unit was revived to deal with the threat of Communist terrorists in Malaya. That is where the modern story of the Regiment begins, and for that reason, I have chosen to focus on the current SAS in this book. The history of the wartime unit is another story – one told brilliantly in many other popular titles.

The story of 22 SAS is a great British success story. From its humble beginnings, the Regiment is now a highly professional, well-oiled machine – one that the British Army simply cannot do without. It has survived, above all, because of the soldiers who have served and died in its ranks, fighting in the furthest-flung corners of the world, in the face of seemingly impossible odds.

This is their story.

CHAPTER 1

The Malayan Emergency

Malaya, 1950–59

The birthplace of the modern SAS was the Malayan jungle. For nine years, the men of the reconstituted unit learned how to fight a new type of war, radically different from previous conflicts. Operating in deep jungle, they went out in small patrols for months at a time, hunting down bands of elusive Communist guerrillas. Many of the Regiment's current tactics can be traced back to those early days in Malaya, when a cadre of hard, committed men rewrote the rulebook on how to soldier. They formed the bedrock of the SAS as an elite fighting unit.

The history of the Malaya campaign dates back to the Second World War, when Singapore and Malaya fell to the Japanese. In response, Britain sent over commandos and supplied equipment and weapons to the various guerrilla movements to fight against the occupiers. Among the most effective of these groups was the Malayan People's Anti-Japanese Army (MPAJA), the de facto military wing of the Malayan Communist Party.

The MPAJA drew most of its support from the ethnic Chinese minority, which made up almost forty per cent of the population. Half a million of them lived in shanty towns on the fringes of the jungle, providing the guerrillas with food, recruits and intelligence, allowing them to wage a series of deadly offensives. With the defeat of the Japanese in 1945, the Communists were fêted as heroes, but it wasn't long before trouble started brewing.

1

At the end of the war, the Malayan economy was in tatters. Unemployment was high, there was crippling inflation and food was increasingly scarce. After Mao's revolution in China, the Communists sensed an opportunity to exploit this discontent, wresting control of Malaya and its lucrative tin and rubber exports. The Malayan National Liberation Army (MNLA), the successor to the wartime Communist guerrilla force, returned to the jungle and unearthed the thousands of weapons they had greased and cached at the end of the war.

Supported by thousands of Chinese non-combatants, known as the Min Yuen, in April 1948 they began a murderous offensive, burning villages to the ground, attacking police stations and carrying out gruesome public executions. Communist gangs emerged from the forest and captured supervisors and foremen working at the plantations, shooting them dead in front of the rest of the terrified workforce before fleeing back into the forest. Such brutal tactics were designed to intimidate the local population, letting them know what would happen to anyone who dared to work with the Brits.

The crisis came to a head on the morning of 16 June 1948, when a gang of Communist Terrorists (CTs) raided a rubber plantation near Sungai Siput and killed the British manager, A.E. Walker. Later that same morning, the manager of another nearby plantation and his assistant were tied up and executed by a gang of up to a dozen Chinese guerrillas. The murders of the three Europeans shocked the authorities. Up to that point, the guerrillas had restricted their attacks to local non-Communists, but now the British could no longer ignore the situation and declared an emergency.

Whitehall officials deliberately avoided calling it a war for insurance purposes. The underwriters in London, who covered the country's tin and rubber manufacturers, would not have been liable for any losses that occurred as a result of war. To get around this problem, the government always referred to the conflict as the Malayan Emergency. But it was a war all the same.

Early attempts to tackle the CTs were largely unsuccessful.

About eighty per cent of the Malay peninsula is dense primary jungle, giving the enemy the ideal place to base itself and launch attacks. From the safety of their camps the Communists carried out ambushes on roadsides, railway lines and plantations, retreating back under the canopy before the Malay police or infantry could close with them. Led by Chin Peng, a Communist fighter who had fought alongside the British during the war, the CT gangs terrorised the domestic population, murdering hundreds of civilians, police and soldiers. In 1950, more than a thousand civilians were killed or injured during this campaign of terror.

By now it was abundantly clear that the security situation was rapidly deteriorating. Clearly, something needed to be done to restore order.

In response the military chiefs came up with a plan to seize the initiative from the CTs and put them on the back foot. Brigadier 'Mad' Mike Calvert, a former CO of the wartime SAS Brigade who had fought with the Chindits in Burma, was instructed to make a report on the situation. He spent six months travelling around Malaya and made a number of recommendations on how to deal with the insurgency. His findings became the basis of a plan to defeat the Communists by cutting them off from their food supply.

The CTs relied heavily on the hundreds of thousands of Chinese squatters living on the jungle edge for their supplies. By resettling these villagers, the authorities could deprive the guerrillas of their support network, denying them much-needed food, recruits and intelligence and driving them deeper into the jungle. This programme of food denial and resettlement became known as the Briggs Plan, after the Director of Operations, Lieutenant-General Sir Harold Briggs. The second phase of the plan involved hunting down the enemy and forcing them out into the open, where the security forces could close with them. Around five thousand CTs were believed to be operating from their bases in the jungle. There could be no peace until they were captured or destroyed.

The second part of the plan required a specialist new unit to be raised, since the existing infantry lacked the training or skills to conduct long-range, deep-penetration patrols into the jungle. Two months later, Calvert was given permission to raise this unconventional new fighting force.

At this time the SAS existed only as a Territorial Army unit. The SAS Brigade had been disbanded at the end of the Second World War, stabbed in the back by cost-cutting Whitehall officials, who were sceptical of its function as a peacetime unit and saw no role for Special Forces in the emerging conflict with the Soviet Union. By October 1945, the Belgian and French regiments had returned to their national militaries and the brigade had been fully dissolved.

That might well have been that, but fortunately several far-sighted officers came to the forefront in the years immediately after the war. Among them were Calvert and Brian Franks, the former CO of 2 SAS. Perhaps inspired by the principles and hero-ics of the 'Originals' such as David Stirling and Paddy Mayne, they fought to keep the idea of the SAS alive in one form or another. When the opportunity arose to form a specialist unit for the Malaya campaign, Calvert was determined to give it a name that forged a link between the new force and the exploits of the wartime brigade.

It was against this background that the Malayan Scouts (SAS) was established in 1950 – the unit that would later become 22 SAS.

Calvert scoured the Far East for potential recruits. A hundred volunteers initially came forward to bring the new force up to strength, drawn from other green army units. Some of these men were hardened veterans of the Burma campaign; others had been part of the clandestine Special Operations Executive (SOE) during the Second World War. From these recruits, A Squadron was formed, along with a HQ element. There was no Selection process for the first intake of SAS soldiers. Leaflets were sent out to every unit in the British Army asking for recruits; successful applicants were sent out to the base camp at Kota Tinggi, near Johore, to undertake a jungle training course, doing runs and learning the basics of jungle survival.

A month later they were joined by B Squadron, comprising reservists from the TA unit, known as 21 SAS (Artists Rifles). Soon after that, C Squadron was drawn up from a selection of volunteers from the Rhodesian armed forces. They were later joined by D Squadron, made up of recruits from regular units back in the UK.

Each Sabre Squadron had a fighting strength of around forty guys, plus support elements and attached personnel. Squadrons were divided into four Troops, with each Troop containing between six and twelve soldiers. At that embryonic stage of the Regiment, the Troops did not have the separate identities they have today, distinguished by specialist insertion methods such as Air Troop or Boat Troop, and the individual skills of each soldier on patrol were not yet set in stone.

This diversity of backgrounds, with recruits being drawn from different units and countries, is something that later became hard-wired into the ethos of the Regiment. When you have got a mixture of guys thrown together from a bunch of different army units, they're going to bring contrasting ideas about how to solve problems. That way you avoid military groupthink.

Soldiers from an infantry unit, even a highly trained one, will generally propose the same solution to an obstacle, because they've all come through the same system. Whereas in the SAS, because volunteers can apply from any British Army unit, you'll have one guy who served in the Royal Engineers, and another who has come across from the Pathfinder Platoon, and they'll each have very different ways of thinking.

It is like thoroughbred dogs. A pure breed dog will inevitably have a mountain of health problems throughout their lifetime. Get a mongrel, however, and you'll probably never see the vet's door. That's exactly what the SAS should aspire to be – mongrel squadrons, a mixture of guys from across the board who have come through differing systems and have contrasting mentalities.

Some of the early pioneers in A Squadron gained a reputation as troublemakers, fighting and drinking heavily and lacking in professional discipline. There were lurid stories of guys coming out of the jungle and raising hell, going out and getting wrecked in the bars of Kuala Lumpur.

It's undoubtedly true that there were a few wild characters in the first intake. The recruits didn't have to pass any rigorous Selection process, and some of the officers in the regular army may have seen the formation of the Malayan Scouts as an opportunity to get rid of any bad apples in their own ranks. But in Calvert's defence, he was a man in a hurry, having to raise an elite force from scratch – much like David Stirling had done in the North African desert. There was no time to assess properly each and every volunteer.

There are no stories of any problems with the men while they were out on operations. The trouble seems to have only begun when they emerged from the jungle at the end of a three-month tour, having worked up a serious thirst. After several weeks in almost total isolation, living in a highly stressful environment, some of the soldiers couldn't resist the temptations of the outside world and allowed themselves to get carried away. The rest of the squadron ended up getting a bad rap as a result.

Either way, the misfits didn't last long in Malaya. Those men who couldn't handle the demands and stress of long-range jungle operations were soon weeded out of A Squadron. The remainder proved to be highly skilled operators, and many went on to enjoy stellar careers with the Regiment.

The initial intake had to teach themselves everything. Before they went out, the soldiers undertook a brief training programme at their base camp at Kota Tinggi. Soldiers were taught the principles of moving through the forest without alerting the enemy, moving stealthily and noiselessly. The men practised these skills when they hunted one another in the jungle, armed with air rifles. At other times Calvert had them train using live rounds and hand grenades. They also learned how to set booby traps and how to track the enemy through the jungle by reading signs. Other than that, they would have to learn on the job, literally making it up as they went along.

The first patrols were undertaken in August 1950. Few contacts were made during those early operations, but they were vital in terms of getting to grips with the jungle itself.

We have a saying in the Regiment: 'If you can soldier in the jungle, you can soldier anywhere in the world.' There's a common misconception that learning to operate in the jungle is all about tactics. That is wrong. Living in the jungle is very physically and mentally demanding. Anyone who survives in it must be made of strong stuff.

There are three kinds of jungle: primary, secondary and bamboo. Malaya has all three types. Primary means any area of forest that hasn't been logged or otherwise disturbed by humans. In primary jungle the canopy can be anything up to two or three hundred feet high, and the ground beneath it is relatively clear. It's airy and pleasant and in places it can almost feel as though you're walking through an English forest.

Secondary or 'dirty' jungle is where the primary has been cut down at some point and the undergrowth has been opened up to the sunlight, allowing it to flourish. It can be very dark and damp in there, and it's much harder to move through secondary jungle because of the heavily tangled undergrowth. You also get a lot of bugs, ticks and mosquitoes, especially near to the river-beds.

Bamboo jungle is the worst kind. It's awful stuff, solid as a wall and almost impossible to move through, because of the way it grows in massive clumps. I once spent a day on a training patrol in Malaysia, navigating through a patch of bamboo. We tried to push our way through, but it kept getting thicker and thicker. It ended up with each of us having to take off our Bergen rucksack, passing it to the next guy in line before picking our way through the growth. The next guy in line would slide the first man's Bergen through ahead of him and then follow the same route. Over the course of that day, we ended up covering about two hundred metres. It's a nightmare.

Whatever kind of jungle a soldier finds himself in, everything quickly begins falling to pieces: your kit, your clothes, your belt, your boots. It's as if the jungle wants to fight you. Every living thing seemingly wants to bite you, attach itself to you or bury itself in you. But there's no point in fighting back. You have to accept the jungle for what it is and deal with it. That's the only way to survive.

The early SAS patrols faced a bewildering number of challenges. The average temperature in present-day Malaysia is in excess of 82 degrees Fahrenheit, or 28 degrees Celsius. Under the trees it can feel hotter than that, because of the humidity and the lack of a breeze on the jungle floor. It is extremely difficult to move in that kind of heat: the guys were sweating constantly, even at night when lying down in their hammocks, and if they weren't careful, they could come down with heat exhaustion.

Much of the terrain is broken and hilly, so they were either going uphill or downhill, or ploughing through swamps. The men lost a tremendous amount of weight on patrol. It rains nearly all the time, especially during the wet season, so they had to get used to the fact that they were living in soaking wet clothes and moving on slippery ground covered in leaf mould. After a while some of the guys developed sores from the straps on their heavy rucksacks, which could get infected unless properly treated. Many others came down with fevers or diseases. Apart from the radio carried by the signaller, they were isolated from the outside world, far from the comforts of civilisation. And then, of course, there's the vegetation.

'Wait-a-while' creepers are a constant menace in the jungle. These are covered in sharp barbs that snag on your skin or clothes as you're passing through. When some soldiers get caught on a wait-a-while, they'll thrash about wildly, but that will only cause the thorns to snap off, giving you an infection. The trick is to be slow and deliberate, carefully unhooking the thorns before working your way round the obstacle.

Even worse is the bastard tree, so-called because of the vicious six-inch spikes protruding from the bark. One of the first rules of the jungle is that if you're on patrol and you slip, you never reach out to grab anything. The reason for this is that you're likely to impale yourself on a bastard tree.

I learned this the hard way during SAS Selection. I was getting ready to jump over a gully, so I reached out and planted my hand against a nearby tree to support myself. An agonising pain instantly flared up in my hand, and when I looked across, I saw a long spike jutting out of my palm. It had gone right through.

I was able to plough on, but the wound later turned septic. If that had happened in the middle of an operation, I would have been in serious trouble.

Insects and animals were another problem facing the SAS in Malaya. Leeches were impossible to avoid. They'd crawl along the ground or fall from the canopy above, attaching themselves to the soldiers' arms, legs, necks and armpits – even their privates. Sometimes at the end of a day's patrol a soldier would change out of his kit and find his legs covered in leeches.

Some of the guys burned them with cigarettes or flicked them off. Others left them alone, waiting for the leeches to drop off once they'd had their blood meal. Salt was used to remove them, and mozzie repellent was also effective: a quick squirt and the leeches would fall to the ground. The thing never to do was to pull them off, because you'd leave parts of their mouths in your skin, which could get infected.

Much more painful were the tiger leeches, also known as the painted leech. They caused a sharp stinging sensation when they bit into your skin. You'd soon know about it when a tiger leech attached itself to you.

There were other nasties to look out for in Malaya. Scorpions would find ways of crawling inside unattended rucksacks or soldiers' boots at night, even finding their way up shirt sleeves. The guys quickly learned to watch where they put their hands and took extra care to secure their kit at the end of each day. They also had to look out for bamboo snakes, a venomous pit viper native to the region.

Mosquitoes were everywhere in Malaya, along with sandflies. The latter are nasty little creatures that suck your blood, leaving itchy red bumps on the skin. The only way to stop sandflies from biting you is to lather yourself in mozzie repellent. In later jungle campaigns, the men learned to keep their OG (Olive Greens) shirts buttoned up to the neck, and they rolled their sleeves down,

9

in spite of the stifling heat and humidity. When your sleeves are rolled up to your elbows, all you're doing is exposing more skin for the hordes of bugs and ticks to feast on.

Malaria was a constant threat to the soldiers. So was leptospirosis. 'Lepto' is transmitted through rat urine, although monkeys and dogs can also spread it. You can catch it by drinking water that has been contaminated with rat urine, or through contact with an exposed wound. A person suffering from severe leptospirosis will quickly come down with a high fever, muscle pains and crippling headaches, and will start urinating blood. In the worst cases it can lead to kidney failure, lung disease and even death. Any soldier coming down with lepto needs urgent medical treatment.

In the tribal villages there was also the risk of contracting scrub typhus, also known as bush typhus. This is commonly found near areas of human waste, such as the communal toilets used by the villagers. These places attract bugs carrying all sorts of nasty diseases. If you get bitten, you'll come down with a fever, aches and rashes. It gets to the point where you can't soldier, because you're so ill.

To combat the threat of infection, the guys were given a daily dose of Paludrine anti-malarial pills. Consumption of Paludrine is part and parcel of life as an SAS operator. Whether you're deployed in the African savanna or the jungles of East Asia or South America, you're popping these pills. In fact, the all-ranks bar at Hereford was named the Paludrine Club as a result – and it's still called that to this day.

Because it made you drowsy, the old type of Paludrine doubled up as an effective sleeping pill. In fact, I used to pop a couple at last light in the jungle to guarantee myself a good night's kip. Later on, somebody changed the formula and they stopped making you sleepy. The tablets are still good for preventing you from itching, though – helpful when you're covered in bites.

The guys in Malaya also took salt pills, to replace what they had lost through sweat. Soldiers who came down with heat exhaustion were given Oxo cubes washed down with water for the same reason.

The SAS also had to watch for man-made traps such as punji pits. These involved digging a massive hole in the ground and driving sharpened bamboo stakes into the bottom of it. Then the enemy would cover the pit over with sticks and sprinkle leaves on top. Any soldier who walked across would plunge into the pit, impaling his foot on the pointed stakes. The CTs were in the habit of smearing the tips with human excrement, so the wounded soldier would quickly develop an infection.

A common tactic was to leave something obvious near the site of the pit, such as a discarded water bottle. The bottle would catch the eye of the passing soldier, who would automatically assume that it had been left behind by the enemy and move towards it to investigate – neglecting to examine the ground around the bottle and drawing his attention away from the trap in front of him. The soldier wouldn't see the pit until it was too late.

The Viet Cong used punji pits to great effect in the Vietnam War. They were so effective that the Americans started inserting stainless-steel plates in the soles of standard-issue jungle boots, to stop the stakes from puncturing the soldier's foot.

Pig traps were another CT favourite. This involved binding four sharpened bamboo stakes to the length of a long bendy branch, preferably also cut from bamboo. The branch was pulled back into an arc and attached to a trigger device, usually two pegs held together under pressure, connected to a thin metal wire running across a track.

To disguise the trap, whoever was setting the ambush would look to see where the sun shone through the canopy, making sure that the wire was set up in a shaded area so it wouldn't catch the light. Leaves would also be scattered around the site of the trap. When the soldier's boot brushed against the wire it released the wooden peg and the branch came swinging towards the victim's legs, doing all kinds of damage. Even if the spikes missed the target, the strength of the bamboo and the speed at which it was moving could still shatter bones.

The pig trap wasn't designed to kill. Its main purpose was to maim a soldier, slowing the patrol down and causing panic among the others. A soldier blundering into a trap needed immediate medical treatment. It also made the rest of the team much more cautious going forward. If the CTs were really cunning, they would set more traps to the left and right of the first one, knowing that the soldiers' first instinct would be to abandon their current route and head on a new bearing instead. That way the guerrillas might wound two or three guys instead of one.

The aboriginal tribes used crude traps such as these to catch wild pigs, but the Communists found them highly effective at targeting soldiers, too. In the early days there was no immediate hope of getting casevaced, as helicopters had yet to be deployed. For the wounded SAS man, it was a long and agonising journey out of the jungle.

The Communists were not the only ones laying booby traps. SAS patrols used to set them as well, rigging up explosives around enemy camp sites. Once a target location had been established, the patrol would send a signal over the radio set, requesting an engineer to be sent forward from base camp. The traps were set, and the guys retreated and waited for the enemy to arrive.

If nobody showed up, the engineers had to be brought back in again to dismantle the booby traps, sometimes months after the explosives had originally been rigged. This was very dangerous work. The demolitionist had to have an excellent memory on him, taking notes on exactly where each trap was placed. Otherwise he could very easily get blown to pieces.

CHAPTER 2

On SAS Patrol

On 6 October 1951, the British High Commissioner, Sir Henry Gurney, was on his way to Fraser's Hill, a highland resort in the mountainous area north of Kuala Lumpur, when the convoy he was travelling in suddenly came under attack. Dozens of guerrillas poured down fire from the surrounding slopes, hammering the armoured scout vehicle and the commissioner's black Rolls-Royce. In the first few moments of the ambush several police officers were injured, and the commissioner's chauffeur was killed. Gurney himself was shot dead as he stepped out of the car to draw fire away from his wife, who was still trapped in the Rolls-Royce along with the other passengers. Several minutes later, the road fell silent as the guerrillas melted away into the jungle and made their escape.

The attack stunned the British establishment, demonstrating that the Communist bandits were still a force to be reckoned with. But they were also suffering their first setbacks of the campaign as the SAS made real progress against the CTs. By early 1952, the lads were beginning to forge a reputation as an elite unit when it came to long-range jungle warfare. Tactics were honed as the patrols spent more and more time living in the jungle, getting to grips with both the environment and their Communist foe.

The SAS deployed into the jungle in full squadron-sized formations of approximately forty men before breaking down into their individual Troops to clear their designated areas. Soldiers would normally patrol in four-man teams, although they would sometimes go out in smaller formations or in full Troop strength of up to a dozen guys, depending on the nature of their mission and the terrain they were operating in. Each patrol had a dedicated commander and a signaller, as well as someone who could speak the local language, laying the foundations for the classic four-man patrol that would become the bedrock of SAS operations in the decades to follow.

At the same time the guys were constantly experimenting with different ideas for insertion and resupply. They trialled the use of mule trains to deliver supplies to patrols into the jungle and came up with new lightweight ration packs designed to allow a soldier to survive for up to fourteen days between each resupply. They even invented a new method of insertion into areas of operation, an approach unique to the Regiment called tree-jumping.

The idea behind tree-jumping was to deploy the guys close to the CT camps, cutting the guerrillas off before they could retreat deeper into the jungle. This was in the days before abseiling from helis became a standard method of insertion, so the soldiers came up with the next best thing: jumping out of the side of an RAF transport aircraft and steering towards the treetops, in the hope of ensnaring their chute on a sturdy branch.

Each parachutist wore a 'bikini' seating harness with a steel ring fixed to the front of it. The trick was to aim for a large tree, getting your chute snagged on a branch. Then you'd take a two-hundred-foot length of webbing line, pass it through the D rings on the front of the bikini harness and tie one end of the webbing to a secure branch. The other end of the line was fastened to the Bergen. Once that was secure, you'd slowly lower the rucksack to the ground, before descending the line to safety.

In theory the system worked. In practice it was extremely dangerous. Steering the chute was practically impossible, and where the guys landed was more down to luck than skill. If the chute worked its way loose from a weakened branch, that soldier was going to fall and hit the ground hard, breaking an ankle or his back, or worse. If they were really unlucky, they'd land in a patch of bamboo and get cut to pieces. The radio set would sometimes get damaged during the descent, which meant that the patrol couldn't send for medical assistance over the comms to treat the injured soldiers. When help did finally arrive, it was sometimes too late to save them.

Three SAS men lost their lives tree-jumping. By the end of the Malaya campaign the practice had been discontinued. It was incredibly dangerous, but it shows how committed these guys were to the job, that they were willing to risk using this method of insertion.

The first SAS recruits were free to carry a variety of weapons. Anything they could get their hands on at the armoury was considered fair game. As a result, there was a fair amount of experimentation at the start as soldiers tried out different weapons to see which best suited the jungle conditions. Many soldiers favoured the American M1 carbine; others opted for the Australian-manufactured Owen submachine gun (SMG), shotguns, light machine guns or even two- and three-inch mortars. Many of the heavier weapons were ditched as the men got to grips with the demands of soldiering in the forest, and by the mid-1950s patrols had settled on a standard weapon system.

On patrol, lead scouts carried the Remington twelve-gauge pump-action shotgun. The reason for this was simple. They needed a weapon that would give a good spread in the event of a sudden contact, allowing them to squeeze off a round that would put the enemy down and give the rest of the patrol a chance to react. The Remington, at the time, was deemed the best weapon to have for that kind of contact. The barrel was sometimes sawn down several inches, giving the operator an even wider arc of fire. On a longer barrel, the ball bearings would shoot out in a spread of about five inches. With the barrel cut right down, the spread would cut down anything in a ninety-degree arc.

After a few years, the Remington was put to one side and the scouts migrated to the SLR (Self-Loading Rifle), the UK version of the FN FAL battle rifle.

There were several benefits to the SLR. It was chambered for the 7.62x51mm NATO round, which has a lot of stopping power and won't get deflected off the undergrowth. The downside is that the SLR is a big hunk of metal, heavy and long, which impedes the movement of the operator. The ammunition, when carried in bulk, is very heavy, and if you're taking a couple of hundred rounds it can really make a difference to the overall weight you've got to carry. SLRs also had a tendency to rust up quite easily in the jungle. Soldiers had to stay on top of their weapon maintenance all the time, more so than any other weapon, frequently field-stripping it to keep it clean.

In the 1960s the SAS would move on to the M16 rifle, a much lighter weapon, shorter and more dependable in the jungle, with a thirty-round magazine capacity. It was also fully automatic, which meant that if the lead scout ran into a contact, he could put a long burst down in the direction of the enemy and then bug out. Accuracy isn't a priority in that kind of engagement – it comes down to instinctive firing, aimed in the general direction of the target. The enemy would naturally go to the ground, giving the lead scout a valuable second or two to bug back, while the rest of the guys in the patrol put down a series of aimed shots at the enemy targets in front of them.

The only issue with the M16 is that it takes a smaller 5.56mm round, which fires at a higher velocity and is more susceptible to being deflected when it hits vegetation. But the lighter ammunition had an advantage, in that you could carry more rounds without being weighed down – vital when going out on long-range patrols. The M16 also had a reputation for being more reliable in the jungle than the SLR.

Other kit the guys carried in Malaya included water bottles, morphine phials and compasses. Their ration packs were designed to last two weeks and consisted of hard tack biscuits, corned beef, rice and soup, as well as tea, condensed milk, Oxo cubes, chocolate, matches and Hexamine blocks, solid-fuel tablets used to cook food.

In the later years of the campaign, the Regiment developed a ration pack that lasted even longer, allowing a soldier to survive for twenty-eight days without resupply. Eating curry every day for a month quickly gets boring, so some of the lads traded their tinned goods for the pungent dried fish carried by the aborigines, which was considered a local delicacy. The men also took to carrying an onion or garlic in their Bergens to add some flavour to their meals.

Garlic had several uses in the jungle. Several guys used it as a natural stimulant by chewing on it during patrol, keeping them alert. It was also considered an effective natural mosquito repellent. There was a theory at the time that the scent would get into your bloodstream and seep out of your pores, preventing the mozzies from nipping at you. Of course, this had to be balanced against the risk of the smell of the garlic carrying through the air, potentially giving away their location to the enemy.

Soldiers also carried a heavy knife called a parang, a smaller version of a machete. Using parangs in the jungle could be a dangerous business. Soldiers had to learn the difference between softwood and hardwood trees when cutting wood. If they tried chopping through a hardwood tree, the parang would simply bounce off the surface. Using a parang in that situation is about as effective as hacking through a metal girder – and even experienced SAS veterans can sometimes forget this.

I once watched a Training Wing instructor demonstrating to students on Selection the proper way to use a parang. This guy proceeded to swing his blade against a hardwood tree without realising it. The blade promptly ricocheted off the trunk and struck him, opening up a huge gash on his leg. The next thing the instructor knew, his trouser leg was soaked with blood. That blade gave him a hell of a cut.

In 1952 the unit was renamed 22 SAS Regiment. For the next three years, the lads dramatically stepped up their operations in Malaya. At the same time, hundreds of thousands of Chinese and Malay were resettled in new villages surrounded by barbed wire, as part of the overall strategy of denying food, manpower and other goods to the Communists. SAS teams also helped to construct forts in fringe areas of the jungle and then handed them over to the Malayan police and infantry, enabling the security forces to protect the aborigines from the CTs. Responsibility for the protection of the squatters' villages was later delegated to the Home Guard, a locally raised force of Chinese and Malay auxiliaries, numbering over a hundred thousand men.

These new villages were a big improvement on the ramshackle settlements these people had been living in before, providing them with electricity, clean water and schools, as well as fertile land to grow their crops. Many of the squatters who moved to the new villages ended up staying put, even after the areas around their original homes had been cleared of guerrillas.

Cut off from one of their most dependable sources of food and intelligence, the CTs retreated deeper into the jungle. The Regiment pursued them, using their experience and knowledge of the terrain to hunt them down.

A typical patrol would insert by parachute, or on the ground at a road-head; later on, helicopters were used as well. Teams also inserted by train. The soldiers would ride open-topped wagons from Kuala Lumpur station to the countryside, then debus from the train at a certain point on the tracks and slip stealthily into the treeline, waiting until dawn before moving on.

The Regiment was tasked with patrolling areas of 'black' jungle. These were sections of the forest that had not yet been cleared by the security forces. 'White' jungle had been cleared of CTs and was considered safe. In Malaya, the SAS always operated in 'black' jungle. Patrols were accompanied by aborigine porters, local tribespeople who came from the villages. They were in charge of carrying the spare batteries for the radio set and did various chores around the camp, such as cleaning out mess tins. Once inside the jungle, the soldiers' first task was to establish a forward mounting base. This would typically be in friendly territory, somewhere safe from enemy ambush, where the guys could receive resupply by air between patrols.

Arriving at the base camp, each soldier selected a site to basha up. 'Basha' is a Malayan word describing a type of hut with a thatched roof. In the Regiment, it means anywhere a guy is going to sleep. The men constructed raised shelters, using their parangs to cut down softwood trees and fixing a pair of logs between two large A-frames. The logs were then threaded through a stretcher, a long piece of material that served as the soldier's bed. A poncho sheet was then mounted above the stretcher and tied to the trees with para cord to act as a roof, protecting the soldier from rain.

The men learned not to leave anything on the jungle floor at night. Soldiers would plant sticks on the ground next to their shelters before last light and hang their boots from the top. Not only did this help to dry their boots out, but it stopped all kinds of nasties such as scorpions from crawling into them.

While out on patrol from the base camp, the men would basha up on hammocks tied between two stout trees, with a poncho above it. Sleeping on the ground was avoided, because the soldier would leave too much sign and he'd wake up covered in bite marks and sores. When constructing a hammock, strips of hessian were wrapped around the trees before tying the para cord over it, to stop the cord from leaving tell-tale marks.

Weapons had to be cleaned every night to stop them from rusting. Rifles were stripped down, wiped down with linseed oil and dried off. The men kept their weapons next to their bashas while they slept, never leaving them further than an arm's reach away. That rule still applies today: any student who leaves his rifle and wanders off during the jungle phase automatically fails Selection.

To dry their clothes, the men used to take off their OG shirts and trousers and hang them up on a washing line after they returned from a patrol. The jungle was still warm late in the evening and by the time the men had sorted out their A-frames and basha'd up for the night, their kit had dried out. Their clothes would then go back on before the men hunkered down for the evening.

Despite these privations, there were advantages to living in the jungle. For a start, the men were guaranteed a solid eight hours' sleep. In Malaya the chorus starts at dusk, when the wildlife goes berserk until it gets dark. Then it is pitch black and more or less silent, apart from the odd creature making a noise.

The soldiers were also generally safe at night. There was no movement after last light in the jungle, since it was too dark beneath the canopy and impossible to navigate. Anyone trying to slog through the forest at night would either walk straight into something and cut themselves or get bitten and come down with a serious infection. This worked both ways, however, and the CTs avoided night-time movement for the same reason.

An hour before first light, the wildlife chorus starts up again as all the animals and insects high up in the canopy burst into an ear-splitting cacophony. It's beautiful in its own way, but very noisy and impossible to sleep through.

The soldiers at base camp would wake up with the pre-dawn chorus. Each man did his 'stand-to' before first light, getting up in total darkness, putting his kit on and waiting for daybreak with his Bergen packed and his rifle ready at his side. Stand-to is always done before first and last light, because those are the most likely times for a patrol to get bumped by the enemy. Dawn would come up and once it was considered safe, the guys would get a brew on. Then they had a briefing, known as 'morning prayers', before going out on patrol.

A standard light order patrol could last anything from a couple of days to three weeks. The size of the team depended on the type and length of operation the guys were undertaking. For long patrols, with the aim of confronting the enemy, they might go out in larger formations, since they'd need the numbers to carry all the food and kit. For shorter observation-type ops, a patrol might comprise only three or four guys.

They were sometimes accompanied by a Chinese liaison officer or an SEP (Surrendered Enemy Personnel). The latter were former CTs who had either been captured and flipped by the security services, or who had voluntarily given themselves up. Many of these individuals came forward in response to the government's rewards-for-surrender programme, which offered cash sums to guerrillas who wished to come over to the other side, or gave information leading to the capture of their fellow terrorists. It was the job of the ex-CTs to guide the SAS to their former comrades' camp sites in the hopes of ambushing the enemy.

Patrols were resupplied by air at their base camp at regular intervals: once every fourteen or twenty-eight days, depending on their ration packs. Setting up a DZ (drop zone) involved identifying a suitable location, usually on a ridgeline, before cutting down the trees with their parangs. If the team was operating close to the enemy, they might decide to use a natural DZ instead, such as an open field or a bend in the river. This avoided creating unnecessary noise and potentially giving away the soldiers' presence to any CT gangs lurking in the area.

Explosives were sometimes used to clear DZs in friendly areas. The size of the DZ depended on the type of aircraft coming in. When the SAS later had access to a few Sycamore helicopters in Malaya, the clearing had to be extra-large to accommodate its distinctive long tail boom. When no natural clearing was available, the resupply was simply dropped through the canopy, with the location of the DZ marked with a balloon tethered to a long cord. The balloon was inflated by mixing a chemical powder with water to produce hot gas. The chemical was highly toxic and had to be handled with care; the same substance could also be used to catch fish by pouring it into a river or stream, instantly killing the oxygen in the water.

Resupplies could go wrong. Sometimes the chute would snag on the branches and hang two or three hundred feet above the jungle floor. On these occasions the patrols retrieved the package by firing a signal flare at the chute, causing it to burst into flames – a typical example of the Regiment's ability to improvise. If that didn't work, one of the aborigines would step up. These guys were fantastically agile and could climb up almost any tree, unhooking the chute from the branches.

Along with new rations, the men received fresh sets of jungle boots, plus shirts and slacks to replace their rotting gear. Bread, eggs, fresh meat, fruit and vegetables were among the luxuries

21

dropped with the packages. Steak sandwiches, called banjos, were a big favourite on resupply day. Mail from loved ones back home would come in, as well as reading material.

For the lads on the ground, resupply day was a huge morale booster. The fresh food was a welcome change from their dreary ration packs – and it was essential to their health, because the army-issue rations had a tendency to bung the guys up. Which is hardly ideal when they're on a long-range patrol.

The day after resupply, the SAS would clear up their base camp and move on to another site, usually at a distance of at least ten thousand yards from their previous location. Nothing was left behind for the enemy to discover. Everything had to be binned, buried or burned. Then the team would establish a new base camp from which to carry out further patrols.

This went on for two or three months until the team returned to the main SAS camp. When patrols came out of the jungle, their comrades were often shocked at their appearance. The men were gaunt and dishevelled, thickly bearded and pale from the lack of sunlight. Their clothes were reduced to slimy pieces of cloth that reeked of ammonia. Nobody was smiling.

Soldiers had one or two weeks of leave, which was usually spent gorging themselves on steak, eggs and chips, and pints of Tiger beer. There was a brief period of retraining, which the SAS used to keep their knives sharp, updating their kit and working on their weapon skills down on the ranges. This was also an opportunity for new arrivals to be integrated into the patrol, finding out their strengths and weaknesses and making sure they understood what the patrol commander liked to do in the event of contact with the enemy. The last thing you needed to be doing was teaching the new tom the Troop drills in the middle of a firefight.

Then it was back to the jungle again for another three-month rotation.

The Regiment had it tough in Malaya. They were required to move stealthily through dense, unforgiving terrain that has few distinguishing features, carrying Bergens and kit that weighed anything up to 120lbs, engaged in a constant struggle for survival while searching for a cunning enemy. It was an incredibly stressful job that tested the soldiers to the very limits of their ability.

Jungle navigation is a skill in itself. In the forest, you are constantly surrounded by a thick green blanket. A soldier can be standing on a ridgeline, but he might not be able to see the next hill or river junction. In places you can't see any further than twenty or thirty feet in front of you. It gets to the point where some guys start to feel as if the jungle is closing in on them.

The maps in Malaya were unreliable and of a poor standard. They were based on photographs taken by RAF aircraft flying overhead and as a result, smaller features such as streams were sometimes hidden below the tree canopy. In other places the terrain was obscured by cloud cover. These white patches were left blank on the map, which meant the lads often had to patrol blind. Most of the time the soldiers navigated by the contour lines and heights of certain features on the map.

In some places the ground was broken with steep hills and lots of ridgelines. In other areas there were swamps, where the depth could vary from a few inches to several feet, depending on the season. Mangrove swamps especially were a nightmare. They are dark and smelly, and in the wet season the soldiers would be submerged up to their waists in water, slowing the pace of the patrol down to a crawl.

This could be dangerous: if the soldiers ran into the enemy while wading through swampland, they couldn't break contact very quickly or get very far away. Water seeped through the holes in the soldiers' boots, breaking down the skin on their feet. Foliage could be so thick that it resembled a bowl of spaghetti. Mangrove trees are almost impossible to cut, so the only option was to crawl through the slight gaps between the branches. In fact, the only advantage to patrolling through swampland was knowing that the enemy was having to slog through the same horrible terrain. That, and the ready availability of water.

Once a patrol got bogged down in a swamp, the priority was

to get out of there again and back on to dry land before the end of the day, so they could basha up. In the dry season, the team might find a patch of land nearby and tie up their hammocks between a pair of mangrove trees, but it is far from ideal and their best bet would be to clear that area as quickly as possible.

River crossings could be treacherous. A soldier could easily lose his footing on the muddy banks either side of the river or slip on the rocks scattered along the river-bed. After locating a fordable point in the river, the soldiers would throw a couple of sticks into the water to estimate the current. Then each man eased himself down to a sitting position and slid down the bank to the edge of the water.

If the current was gentle, they could simply walk across to the other side. For fast-flowing rivers, the soldier would wade across at an angle, letting the water take the weight of his rucksack, aiming for a point about two hundred metres downstream. Once he reached the opposite bank, he'd haul himself up using an over-hanging branch or fallen log. The first man would then secure the far side of the river, covering the ground while the rest of the patrol made their way across.

Patrols never followed the course of a river. There's a very good reason for this: rivers do not go in a straight line. They zig and zag, and if you try to follow one, you'll end up walking five times further than if you had plotted a straight line on a map. River routes will also take you into areas where it's boggy, damp and dangerous. Following one is never a good idea.

The lads stayed away from man-made tracks and roads. Even animal tracks were best avoided. If they had to cross a road, they would form up into a horizontal line in the trees and watch it carefully, looking for any sign of movement. Once they were satisfied that the coast was clear, they would cross simultaneously, rushing over to the far side of the track in a single group. Moving this way meant there was less chance of the team being spotted by a sentry. For patrols of six or eight men, two of the guys would form an advance party and scuttle across to recce the opposite side of the road. Then they would give the signal and the rest of the patrol would rush across in a single line.

The lead scout on patrol kept a round up the spout of his weapon at all times, ready to engage the enemy. His job wasn't to navigate, but to watch for targets ahead of the patrol. If he encountered a contact, the scout would discharge two shots from his shotgun at the target in quick succession. The first shot stunned the target, making him pause for a split-second; the second shot put him down. Then the men would start pulling back.

Meeting the enemy head-on was rare, but not unheard of: one officer in D Squadron, Sergeant Major Bob Turnbull, bumped into an enemy lead scout while on a routine clearance patrol. Turnbull, one of the finest jungle soldiers the Regiment had ever produced, was part of a Troop who had been tasked with patrolling a designated 'black' area of jungle. Leaving the rest of the Troop behind in an all-round defence, Turnbull and two other soldiers moved forward to recce a track adjacent to the base camp.

As he scanned the track in the fading light, he spotted a glimpse of movement amid the trees. Realising he had spotted an enemy lead scout, Turnbull concealed himself behind a tree, with the two other guys a short distance to his rear.

Once the CT was close enough, Turnbull stepped out from behind cover and emptied two blasts from his trusty Remington at the CT before the latter could squeeze a round off. As the target lay squirming on the ground, Turnbull moved forward with the other soldiers, ready to drop the rest of the enemy patrol, but found no other targets to engage. The man Turnbull had killed later turned out to be a notorious senior Communist, Ah Tok. The authorities had been hunting him for years.

CHAPTER 3

Masters of the Jungle

On operations in Malaya, it was the job of the patrol commander and the rest of the team to direct the lead scout, watching for tracks and signs of CT presence. Aside from a signaller and a linguist, SAS patrols were accompanied by specialist Iban trackers: tribespeople brought in from northern Borneo who had a reputation for collecting human heads as trophies.

The Ibans were the true masters of the jungle. They had a unique talent for identifying footprints and spoor and passed on their secret knowledge to the Regiment. From the Ibans the SAS learned about vegetation, what to eat and what to avoid, how to distinguish different noises in the jungle, and what the various animals sounded like.

They also taught the SAS how to look for signs. These could be anything from a cigarette butt to an overturned leaf. When, for example, someone walks through the jungle their boots will inevitably disturb the undergrowth, flipping dead leaves over, crunching twigs and loose stones underfoot. The damp side of a leaf facing upwards was a sure sign that someone had recently passed through that area. Likewise, the lighter side of the leaves on a bush or plant pointing upwards indicated that a stranger had brushed against it.

Recent CT camp sites could be identified by ground disturbance. A fire would leave marks on nearby trees, while scorch marks on the jungle floor were evidence of someone making a brew using a burner block. Toilet pits were another sign of habitation. If the enemy took a dump somewhere and wiped their arse on a leaf, that would be a red flag. Clothing might get torn or shredded on a wait-a-while bush, leaving behind fragments for a sharp eye to detect.

In a muddy area the patrol looked for footprints. A good tracker could estimate the age of a depression based on the amount of moisture around it, and whether the sides had collapsed. Footprints filled with water indicated that whoever they belonged to had passed through before the most recent bout of rainfall. On the other hand, older footprints will harden and become less distinct as the muddied soil dries out.

Soldiers also learned to distinguish between animal and human tracks. If it was the latter, he would be able to determine what type of boots the person was wearing, or if they were barefooted, as well as the size of the enemy formation. All of this helped the soldiers form a picture of the ground, giving them an idea of how many enemies they were dealing with and how recently they had been in the area.

By spending long periods living in the jungle, and working closely with the Ibans, the SAS became experts in identifying signs. Reading the jungle soon came to them as naturally as someone walking down a street, reading the road signs around them. Upturned leaves, snapped branches, scuff marks on the ground – these are your double yellow lines and stop signals. Then you have more subtle signs such as the smell of cigarette smoke or soap, which could drift for miles below the canopy. Cigarette smoke in particular is a big giveaway. During my time on the run in Iraq, there was one night when the civilian population was actively out looking for me. These people were all smoking, which meant that I could smell them before I saw them. Their cancer stick habit saved my life that night.

The SAS in Malaya also learned to distinguish between animal and human signs. Wild pigs, for example, love to root around on the ground. The holes they leave look as if they've been dug with a spade, and only an experienced eye can tell the difference.

But the SAS weren't the only ones practising these techniques.

As guerrillas with long experience of jungle warfare, the CTs were also skilled at tracking and evading traps.

As the war progressed, a deadly rivalry ensued between the SAS and their Communist prey, with each side hunting the other while taking care to leave as little sign as possible. Movement through the jungle was therefore slow and deliberate. The guys never rushed anything, making sure they didn't kick up dead leaves or snap any twigs underfoot. Tracks could be covered by brushing over them with a leafy branch, then sprinkling foliage on top. Teams might also move towards their target at an angle, setting a false trail by approaching it indirectly. Anyone following that patrol would not know what target they were heading towards.

Soldiers on patrol had to remain vigilant at all times, making sure that they were concealed from the guerrillas by following the basic military rules of why things are seen. In the jungle, anything that is an unusual shape, anything that shines or presents a silhouette or casts a shadow, or any evenly spaced objects, will immediately draw the attention of the enemy. The men had to camouflage themselves, blending into the background of the forest, moving in shaded areas wherever possible to avoid creating long shadows, and keeping irregular distances from one man to the next.

Everything shiny had to be cammed up or hidden away. Jewellery was taken off before a patrol, watches were covered up and mess tins were stowed away in the soldier's rucksack, only to be brought out when in a safe area. When nearing a suspected enemy camp or staging post, they perfected a technique of walking silently by placing the heel down first, then rolling the foot softly onto the ground before moving off again.

The men avoided any cutting while on patrol. They navigated around obstacles such as bamboo rather than hacking through it and leaving obvious signs for the enemy to discover. If the soldiers thought that there was an enemy patrol in front of them, or if they encountered an open area they didn't want to cross, they would 'box the target' by pulling back and moving on a new bearing at a ninety-degree angle to the target area, then walking parallel to it for two hundred metres. Once they had passed the target, they would box in again and resume their original bearing.

The guys didn't shave or use soap. Washing was strictly limited to having a 'dhobi' in a river or stream bed. A soldier with his wits about him would use this opportunity to give his clothes a good scrub as well: sweat-stained clothing can get rough and starchy from the ammonia, chafing against the skin and causing painful sores. Use of toothpaste was forbidden. Teeth were cleaned by brushing them with a salt solution.

Water was never taken from standing water, because of the danger of contracting lepto. Instead the men would locate a section of bamboo in a safe area (preferably close to the base camp), cut it and drain the fluid trapped inside the stalk. This normally provided a soldier with enough water to fill his bottle. If there was no bamboo available, soldiers located a nearby river or stream, preferably one that was clear and fast-flowing. As long as there were no dead animals within three or four metres of the bank, it was probably safe. Fish in the river was another reliable indicator of clean water.

Once he had located a source, the soldier filled up his Millbank bag, a wartime canvas sack designed by the British Army for use in the tropics. Water drips through the sack, which removes any debris. The water is then poured into the soldier's bottle. Once the bottle is full, the soldier can either boil the water for five to ten minutes or put iodine or sterilisation tabs in it and leave it for thirty minutes until it's safe to drink. The tabs give the liquid a horrid taste, but it kills anything nasty.

The soldiers in Malaya could never rest. They were having to continually stay aware of their surroundings, making sure they didn't fumble about or disturb the ground. At night they had to take meticulous care of their weapons and kit and their bashas. All while lugging a heavy Bergen around, wearing slimy clothing and covered in leeches and tick bites. It's a job that required total concentration, because the moment the guys switched off, they'd get walloped.

★   ★   ★

Hunting down the CTs in Malaya required patience, skill and discipline. Most of the time the Regiment was looking for a handful of enemy guerrillas in an area of many hundreds of square miles. Targets were usually discovered by following tracks or footprints for days on end, by observing old enemy camp sites for signs of activity, or through intelligence gleaned from captured CTs or friendly aborigine tribes.

The SAS would also target the dead letter boxes used by CT units to communicate with one another. Chinese couriers would stash messages and money near a river junction or inside the hollow of a tree. Patrols would then sit and watch the drop location, waiting for someone to come along and either collect or drop off a message.

When the team located an enemy position, they would recce it closely before establishing a lying-up point (LUP). This would be anywhere up to three hundred metres from the ambush location. It was the job of the patrol commander to select a suitable site for the LUP. He would be looking for a densely wooded area, well away from any tracks, roads or ridgelines. Ideally, he wanted somewhere another human would be unlikely to walk through.

Areas near to rivers were usually a good bet, although it was important not to basha up too close to the banks in case there was a thunderstorm at night. In the wet season there are frequent flash floods, caused by the water level rising during periods of heavy rainfall. If a soldier is sleeping close to a river on a steep slope, and he gets caught in a flash flood, a tsunami of water will come crashing down on him and surge through the valley, sweeping everything away.

Once the LUP site had been identified, the team would loop round it, carrying on past the site for twenty or thirty metres before breaking off to the side and looping back round in the shape of a fish-hook. They'd spend half an hour lying up, watching the route to make sure they weren't being followed. If anyone walked past, the soldiers were in an ideal position to launch a counter-ambush.

Once it was safe, the patrol went into the LUP and put up

all-round defence to secure the area against possible ambush. The guys would set up according to points on a clock face, with the Bergens stashed in the middle. One man would position himself so that he was facing out to the twelve o'clock position, with the other members of the patrol looking out at their three, six and nine o'clock. This ensured that arcs of fire covered every approach to the LUP. The patrol commander and one or two others would then move forward to select the ambush site, before returning to brief the rest of the patrol.

If the enemy was away from their camp at the time, the team might booby-trap the location. They could also plant explosives on the other side of the target, in case any of the CTs tried legging it during the firefight.

Ambush tactics in Malaya were strictly ad hoc and depended on the nature of the ground and the size of the SAS team. A four-man patrol would establish a kill group at the ambush location, with two guys on stag (guard duty) and the other two dossing up back at the LUP with the kit. The men rotated every eight hours. Larger patrols would position cut-off teams to the left and right of the kill group, ready to shoot any fleeing targets. The cut-offs doubled up as the early warning group, watching for a sign of the enemy.

With the ambush set, the signaller sent a last scheduled message on the radio – the sets had no voice capability and all communication was done via Morse code. Then they settled down to wait.

At this point they were on hard routine. This meant no fires, no smoking, no warm drinks or cooked meals. Everything was eaten cold. Communication was done by hand signs and whispers. The guys would relieve themselves in plastic bags, or in a hole in the ground further back from the LUP. The men on watch had to lie perfectly still, weapons at the ready, knowing that the slightest movement might compromise the operation.

The pressure they were under at this time was unbelievable. If they shifted slightly, or if they weren't properly cammed up, there was a risk of being spotted by the troops of monkeys that lived high up in the canopy. The larger monkeys tended to keep to themselves, but the smaller breeds would go wild if they caught sight of a human, screeching and chucking down sticks and clumps of their own excrement, blowing the op.

Sometimes the men had to wait two or three weeks in the driving rain for the enemy to arrive. On other occasions, the CTs simply failed to show up. Maintaining this routine required strict discipline. If the average civilian had to lie absolutely still in the jungle for fourteen days, they'd create an incredible amount of disturbance – if they didn't go mad first. Out of sheer boredom they'd start pulling at leaves and snapping branches or twigs. It's just human instinct. Whereas the SAS man had to stay switched on the whole time, keeping his eyes focused on the target.

Imagine waiting in your house and watching the front door, knowing that somebody is going to come crashing through it at some point in the next fortnight. And then having to sit there and not move a muscle for that whole time. That's what the Regiment was having to do in Malaya.

When enemy movement was finally spotted, the team on stag (or the cut-offs, in larger ambush groups) would signal to the rest of the patrol. This was done either by crawling back to the LUP or by tugging on a length of string running between the guys in the main kill group – the men tasked with initiating the attack – and the smaller cut-off teams positioned to the left and right of the kill group in a linear ambush.

As the CTs passed in front of the main kill group, the patrol commander gave the order to open fire and the group initiated the ambush. If explosives had previously been set these were also detonated. As soon as it went noisy, the soldiers would start shouting at one another, pointing out targets in front of them, dropping anything that moved.

Everything was over very quickly. There were no large-scale engagements or lengthy firefights in Malaya. It was small groups of men, fighting one another at very close range. From opening fire to the last round being loosed off was no more thirty seconds, and often much less than that.

Once the last targets were down, the patrol commander would

wait a moment before shouting for his men to cease fire. Then he'd order a search party to move forward, yelling the order so that everyone in the patrol knew that the guys crossing into the killing zone were friendlies and nobody accidentally opened fire on them. The search party's job was to go in and dispatch anyone who was still breathing, dispose of enemy weapons and then retreat towards the kill group.

All dead enemy CTs had to be taken out of the jungle, either carried on a stretcher or lifted out on a chopper, before being handed over to Special Branch for formal identification. Every item of kit had to go out with the bodies, down to the cigarettes they carried: the guerrillas were known to hide messages secreted on the inside of the rolling paper.

Ambushes in Malaya didn't always go according to plan, however. One patrol in A Squadron spent two weeks lying in wait for a gang of four insurgents to return to their staging post. After almost two weeks the enemy at last showed up. The patrol had rigged explosives beneath the bamboo floor of the hut, but when these failed to detonate due to the rain, one of the troopers on watch improvised and dropped two of the CTs with his rifle. The other guerrillas managed to escape, but one of the victims turned out to be a senior official in the Communist ranks. His death was a major coup for the British army.

Contacts with the enemy were rare. For every single CT they killed, it was reckoned that the SAS spent 1,800 hours patrolling the jungle. During the later years of the Emergency, most patrols ended without catching sight of the enemy. But this didn't mean that such missions were a failure. By actively operating in areas that the terrorist gangs had previously considered safe from attack, the Regiment forced them onto the defensive, making them think twice about what they were doing. The Communists were never able to rest or stay in a single location for very long. As a result, their ability to plan and conduct offensive operations was severely disrupted.

The CTs went from being a proactive force, ambushing civvies, to hiding out in the remote jungle. Never safe, always on the move, living in fear.

By the mid-1950s the writing was on the wall for the insurgents. Their leaders had legged it across the border to Thailand and their numbers had dwindled to a hardcore element of two thousand or so.

In response the Regiment evolved its tactics, going out on longer patrols and targeting small groups of CTs using a combination of intelligence on the ground and the tracking skills of the Ibans. The relentless pressure applied by the SAS forced the remaining terrorists deeper into the forest, driving them closer to the border.

At the same time, the SAS needed to win the hearts and minds of the indigenous population. As the Communist guerrillas retreated deeper into the trees, they bullied the poor native Malayan tribes, forcing them into handing over food and other supplies, as well as providing them with intelligence. It was the job of the SAS to make contact with these tribespeople, win them over and protect them from the Communists. This is where the hearts-and-minds campaign came into its own.

The SAS applied themselves to the idea of 'hearts and minds' like no other fighting force had done before, laying down a template for future ops in Borneo and Oman. Soldiers with basic first aid training went out into their villages, known as *kampongs*, providing assistance to tribes who had never come into contact with Western medicine.

Making contact with the tribespeople carried its own risk. Some of these tribes were 'lost' or uncontacted peoples, who had never seen a white face before. The soldiers had no way of knowing how they might react or where their loyalties lay. But in this case, their fears were unfounded: the soldiers shared meals with the tribespeople and studied their languages and their customs. Gradually, a sense of mutual respect began to develop between the Regiment and the aborigines.

By the late 1950s, the Emergency was all but over. The Regiment's success in disrupting CT operations was beginning to have a real impact on the ground and the number of civilian deaths from terrorist attacks had declined from a high of 344 to 60 or 70 a year. At this point 22 SAS had five operational squadrons in Malaya, bringing its strength up to a total of 560 men including HQ and support elements. One squadron from New Zealand had been raised to replace the Rhodesians in C Squadron, who had returned home in 1953. The 140-odd recruits from New Zealand included a number of Maoris. They were joined by a fifth squadron made up of volunteers from the Paras, simply called the Parachute Regiment Squadron.

The Regiment was fast becoming a more professional machine. In 1952, a basic Selection course had been established for potential recruits at the Airborne Forces Depot in Aldershot. As part of their training, volunteers were taken on a series of gruelling endurance marches in the Brecon Beacons. By 1957 this had evolved into a comprehensive Selection course based at Dering Lines, an old wartime camp near the town of Brecon, in Wales. Students tackled an assault course and were instructed in the basics of map-reading before facing a series of cross-country navigation exercises in the hills. The men undertook these in pairs and individually, carrying rucksacks weighed down with bricks.

Those who passed this early version of Selection – sometimes no more than half a dozen men – flew out to Singapore and then took a train to the main SAS camp. Recruits then had to undergo a month of serious training before they became fully badged members of the Regiment. (Getting 'badged' refers to that moment when the soldier is finally awarded the famous SAS beret, when he earns the right to wear the winged dagger.)

The first week was spent on general fitness and basic survival, followed by three weeks on a training patrol. Veterans taught the 'crows' (a slang term referring to new recruits) about jungle navigation, air resupply procedures, Immediate Action (IA) and contact drills, knowing where to find clean water, how to spot enemy sign and traps.

It was down to the Regiment NCOs (Non-Commissioned Officers) to inform the CO whether the individual volunteers were good enough for the SAS. Then, at the end of the training programme, students were told by the CO of 22 SAS whether they had passed or not. Those men who made it through the jungle phase were then sent out on operations more or less immediately. Many of these later patrols were fruitless in terms of confirmed kills, but their presence helped to maintain the pressure on the few CT gangs left in the jungle.

None of the tactical breakthroughs the Regiment developed in Malaya came about by magic. They were earned the hard way, by soldiers on the ground, asking themselves questions about the best way to tackle their enemy. How do we soldier here? What kit do we need when we're on a long-range patrol? Who's going to sort out a bullet wound if one of us gets hit during a contact? How are we going to find the CT camps? How can we use our expertise to help win the trust of the aboriginal tribes? Through hard graft, experimentation and experience, the SAS assembled a knowledge of jungle warfare unrivalled by any other elite fighting force.

In their efforts to defeat the CTs, the soldiers left no stone unturned. Throughout the war they continued to experiment with new tactics, entry and resupply methods. In one trial, the SAS tested the idea of using elephants to resupply the troops at their base camps. This isn't as far-fetched as it might sound – elephants can carry huge loads, making them ideal for transporting large quantities of rations, hardware and kit. Unfortunately, they made too much noise tramping through the forest and the trial had to be abandoned.

The SAS even tried patrolling with dogs at one point, taking Labradors out into the jungle with them. The idea was to use them to sniff out the enemy and to guard camp sites against potential ambushes. This was many years before canine units became standard within SF units. The experiment failed, mostly because the soldiers lacked the veterinary knowledge and dog-handling skills needed to properly train the animals. The extra

36

weight the guys were having to carry in pet food didn't help. But the concept itself was sound.

This spirit of reinvention and experimentation still exists in the SAS today. I know of a Training Wing instructor who had the idea of taking nothing more than an umbrella and a belt kit with him into the jungle. Long-range patrols have to carry a hefty amount of kit on their backs, which can be debilitating. The instructor's reasoning was that instead of taking all the equipment needed to set up a basha each night, he could sleep against a tree, keeping the umbrella over him to stay dry.

The instructor wouldn't need to carry a poncho or a hammock or lengths of para cord, or plenty of other gear besides. He could in theory just live out of his belt kit, with no need to lug an eighty-pound Bergen through the sweltering hot jungle.

He managed to last three or four days before he came down with exhaustion. It turned out that he wasn't getting any proper rest, because sleeping against a tree isn't nearly as comfortable as a raised hammock. To make matters worse, he was getting stung and bitten by all the ticks and living things that live on the floor in the jungle.

To soldier effectively in the jungle, you need to be dry at night and get a full eight hours of kip. If you don't get that, you're going to struggle, as this guy found out. But the main thing was that he was willing to give it a try. This is what the SAS is all about: dedication to the job, going further than the next guy, pushing yourself and redefining the art of what is possible.

By late 1958, SAS operations in Malaya were beginning to wind down. Several months earlier, the Regiment had captured several CTs, including Ah Hoi, a notorious rebel who had brutally executed the pregnant wife of a suspected informant. Three Troops from D Squadron had been patrolling in the Telok Anson swamps, searching for an enemy camp, when they spotted a pair of CTs.

In the ensuing contact one enemy was killed and the other, a woman, fled into the jungle. D Squadron followed her tracks and with the net closing the woman eventually came out to negotiate the group's surrender. The authorities refused to discuss terms and two nights later, the group gave itself up. Among them was the 'Baby Killer' himself, Ah Hoi. His capture, and the subsequent discovery of a substantial weapons cache, proved to be the final nail in the coffin of the insurgency.

Although the squadrons still patrolled the area close to the Thai border, searching for the few remaining CTs who had fled there, the enemy no longer had the stomach to fight and the campaign was effectively won. Operations finally drew to a close in 1959, with the newly independent Malayan government declaring the end of the Emergency twelve months later.

The counter-insurgency campaign in Malaya succeeded for a variety of reasons. A combination of separating the rural population from the guerrillas, reward-for-surrender programmes and winning the hearts and minds of the indigenous people all contributed to the defeat of the CTs. Another factor was undoubtedly the lack of popular support for the Communists among the locals. The insurgents only enjoyed the sympathy of the ethnic Chinese and lacked the domestic manpower and overseas resources that the Viet Cong could draw on during the Vietnam War. But none of this would have been as effective without the military capability to hunt down the guerrillas and flush them out into the open.

Although other units in the British Army and its Commonwealth allies did most of the fighting, the Regiment was at the tip of the military spear. For nine years, they fought against a ruthless and determined enemy who knew the jungle much better than they did. They took on the CTs in their own back yard, mastering the terrain and learning how to fight and survive deep in the jungle.

They used this knowledge to hunt down and destroy the terrorist gangs, ambushing them in their camps and cranking up the pressure with constant patrols, achieving a better contact-to-kill ratio than any other unit. Then they went out and won the support of the aboriginal tribes, protecting them from the CTs and simultaneously depriving them of badly needed supplies. They did all this from scratch, inventing a completely new way of soldiering that formed the basis of SAS operations for decades to come.

In my opinion, the guys who soldiered in the early days in Malaya do not get anywhere near enough credit for what they did. What they achieved in the jungle was nothing short of incredible.

Although they accounted for only a tiny number of the CTs killed during the war, with 108 confirmed kills, the real contribution of the SAS was in developing a radical new type of unconventional warfare that ultimately led to the defeat of the Communist forces. They had demonstrated that small-sized patrols of elite operators, trained to a very high level, could survive and operate for long periods of time, in the toughest conditions on the planet. Not only that, they had achieved tangible results, disrupting CT operations and forcing the guerrillas into a defensive posture from which they never recovered. In the process, they laid the foundations for the modern SAS.

What makes this even more astonishing is that they did this with weaponry, rations and technology that were far inferior to the equipment used by the Regiment today.

In the 1950s, the average SAS man's kit was far worse than ours. Everything from their uniforms down to their boots was poorer. Some of the soldiers even used to put holes in their boots to let the water out and stop the skin from peeling off their feet. Their canvas rucksacks weren't as good. Their rations were mostly tinned goods, which added to the overall weight they had to carry, unlike the lighter boil-in-the-bag rations that we were given decades later in the Gulf War.

Their radio systems and weapons were heavier than ours, and their means of transportation were limited. The process of gathering intelligence on the enemy was a million miles away from the technology-driven methods of today, too. In the second Gulf War, the SAS and their American counterparts could locate and track targets through mobile phone signals analysis. No such technology existed back in Malaya. Everything had to be done by guys on the ground, either by talking to the locals, questioning captured CTs, or tracking footprints and signs. Even their knowledge of the ground was limited to some poor-quality maps and aerial photographs.

The end of the Emergency ushered in a period of uncertainty for the SAS in Malaya. Despite its achievements, there were question marks over its long-term future. Sceptics at Whitehall viewed it as a specialist jungle warfare unit and were unsure about its ability to perform elsewhere. There was also an element of jealousy at work. The Regiment's critics in the War Office hated the fact that a bunch of guys were going around wearing their Winged Daggers with pride, pioneering a new type of warfare while displaying scant regard for rank. Some officers from a conventional military background viewed the Regiment as a threat – one that had to be stamped out.

It was a bad time to be making enemies in Whitehall. After the disastrous Suez campaign, the government had started taking a scalpel to the army. In 1957, the SAS was cut down from five Sabre Squadrons to just two, A and D, and there were rumours of the entire Regiment being disbanded once operations in Malaya had drawn to an end.

The future of 22 SAS hung in the balance. Now it would have to fight for its survival once more – and this time in an environment dramatically different from Malaya.

CHAPTER 4

The Jebel Akhdar

Oman, 1958–59

In November 1958, the forty-odd men of D Squadron, one of the two remaining SAS squadrons in Malaya, were urgently recalled from their patrols near the Thai border and ordered to assemble in Kuala Lumpur. From there, they were ferried across to Singapore, where they boarded a flight to Ceylon (present-day Sri Lanka), stopping briefly to refuel before heading on to the RAF base at Masirah, a small island located off the eastern coast of Oman. At this point, none of the lads knew exactly where they were going or what they would be doing. All they had been told was that they would be taking part in a top-secret operation, somewhere in the Middle East.

Shortly before they boarded the transport aircraft waiting for them on the runway at RAF Masirah, they finally learned of their destination: Muscat, the capital of Oman.

D Squadron arrived in the country on 18 November 1958. In the space of less than three months, they would achieve something no fighting force in Oman had attempted since the Persians almost a thousand years earlier: storming a virtually impregnable mountain fortress, held by a well-armed enemy.

It was to be the first of two legendary campaigns the Regiment fought in Oman.

There is a long-standing history between Great Britain and Oman. In 1798, the two countries had signed a Treaty of

Friendship, under which Britain guaranteed the Sultan's rule. Then in 1891, Oman had officially become a British Protectorate, reliant on British military funding and support.

In the 1950s, the Sultanate of Muscat and Oman was still a feudal backwater ruled by an autocratic despot, Said bin Taimur. By every measure, the country the Sultan presided over was stuck in the Dark Ages. Hospital services and schools were non-existent. Farming methods were primitive. There were no telephones, books or radios. There were practically no cars or motorbikes and only a few miles of paved road in the entire country. The justice system was medieval: adulterers were stoned to death and thieves had their hands cut off. Smoking and alcohol were forbidden, and nightly curfews were imposed across the country.

When the SAS landed in Oman, the Sultan was struggling to put down a rebellion against his rule by the grizzled tribes that inhabited the remote interior of the country. In 1954, the long-standing enmity between the fiercely conservative mountain tribes and bin Taimur had reached a crisis point. The tribal representative, Imam Ghalib Ibn Ali, revolted against the Sultan's rule and declared independence from Muscat.

The Sultan's Armed Forces (SAF), a locally raised force staffed by British officers, managed to put down the rebellion, but Ghalib's brother Talib escaped to Saudi Arabia and raised a militia force of roughly two hundred men, drawn from the Omani expatriates living there. He returned to Oman three years later and, together with Ghalib and Sulaiman ibn Himyar, the sheikh of one of the largest tribes in the mountains, launched another insurrection against the Sultan. Backed up by Saudi weapons and money, they had come close to defeating bin Taimur's troops, and in July 1957 the desperate Sultan turned to his British friends for help in crushing the rebel threat.

Under its long-standing agreement with the Sultan, Britain was in no position to refuse. Oman was believed to be sitting on potentially vast oil deposits and British companies wanted a piece of the action. Which meant keeping the repressive Sultan on his throne. The introduction of RAF Venom and Shackleton aircraft and infantry soon had the rebels on the defensive, driving them back from the lowlands to their stronghold on the Jebel Akhdar: the 'Green Mountain'.

The Jebel is a steep-sloped mountain range that rises like a fist from the desert floor to over six thousand feet above sea level, covering an area of around thirty square miles. In the summer the terraced hills of the Jebel are covered in lush vegetation, but in the winter the mountains are mostly barren.

From the safety of their mountain hideout, the rebels carried out raids on the lowlands, ambushing army bases and mining the main routes used by civilian vehicles. Repeated RAF airstrikes failed to dislodge the rebels and the Sultan's forces lacked the manpower to blockade all the routes up and down the Jebel. As long as they remained camped on top of the mountain, no one could lay a glove on the rebels. Moreover, any direct approach was out of the question: all the well-known tracks were heavily defended by machine-gun emplacements, snipers and mortars.

The rebels, along with many other Omanis, fervently believed that the Jebel was impossible to conquer. As I say, the last attacking force to storm the defences successfully had been the Persians, back in the tenth century. Any soldiers attempting to climb the main tracks would be exposed to the defenders on the higher ground and would be clobbered long before they could reach the summit. Two previous attempts by the local military to seize the Jebel had ended in failure.

Facing the prospect of a prolonged stalemate, the British commander of the Sultan's forces, Colonel David Smiley, turned to London for help in reclaiming the Jebel Akhdar and flushing the rebels out of their stronghold once and for all.

But there was a problem: the government needed to keep its involvement in Oman a closely guarded secret. Whitehall was still reeling from the disastrous Suez affair of 1956, when British and French forces, colluding with the Israelis, had been compelled to withdraw from the Suez Canal Zone in Egypt under intense diplomatic pressure from the US and the threat of economic sanctions. From that point on, it was clear that Britain could no longer carry out unilateral foreign interventions without coming in for heavy flak from the international community.

Any suggestion of sending in a large force of green army troops to Oman was out of the question. The manpower needed to support an infantry unit is staggering. It's impossible to deploy that kind of firepower without creating a lot of attention and noise – and it costs a lot of money as well. What they needed was a small-sized force with the skills to take back the Jebel. A unit that was highly adaptable, able to deploy covertly and at very short notice.

Which is where the SAS came in.

From Muscat, D Squadron travelled to the SAF's Headquarters at Bait al Falaj, a few miles outside the city. After setting up shop, the men were given their briefing. The British government wanted the Jebel Akhdar retaken. They wanted it done speedily and with a minimum of casualties. The SAS was tasked with finding a way up the mountain and destroying the enemy strongholds.

They had three months to get the job done.

The Regiment faced some formidable odds in Oman. The unit had been whittled down to just two squadrons, A and D, with a fighting strength of around forty men each, plus a handful of support elements. Both squadrons were broken down into four individual Troops, each numbering around a dozen soldiers, although some had less than that.

Facing them was an enemy that owned the high ground, had the advantage of numbers and had lived on the Jebel for generations. They knew the area like the backs of their hands. Whereas the Regiment would be fighting uphill, against a much larger concentrated force, in an environment that was a million miles away from Malaya. Aside from one basic sketch drawing that was lacking in detail, there were no maps of the Jebel.

The enemy forces were well-armed, with some of their fighters equipped with Lee-Enfield bolt-action .303 rifles, capable of walloping a target from six hundred metres away. The rest carried old .45 Martini-Henry rifles dating back to the Boer War. They also had a number of light machine guns (LMGs) and several .50 calibre Browning machine guns (BMGs). The rounds on the .50 cal Browning are half an inch thick and can eat through concrete, walls and sandbags. The guys in the Regiment nicknamed the weapon the 'relish', after tomato relish – because that's what your insides look like if you're unlucky enough to get hit by one. The rebels even had a few 81mm mortars, which had a longer range than the standard British Army ML 3-inch mortar used by the SAS.

Tactically, Oman was on the other side of the spectrum from the jungle. The SAS was going from an environment where visibility was measured in a matter of yards to the wide plains of the desert, where a soldier might be able to see for miles on a clear day. In Malaya, the standard tactic was moving by stealth before laying an ambush on an enemy target. In Oman, they were fighting a classical type of warfare: storming enemy defences and capturing the high ground. The only difference was that they were having to do it with stretched resources and far fewer men.

Not for the last time, the Regiment was being asked to pull a rabbit out of the hat.

The men had only a few days to acclimatise before going out on patrol. Most of the time was spent on the ranges, putting down rounds at distance. Although they had some challenges to overcome, adapting to the conditions wasn't as difficult as learning how to survive in the jungle. A number of the soldiers in D Squadron had already gained valuable experience of the desert, serving with the Parachute Regiment in Egypt, which helped them to prepare for the terrain.

Oman is a country of extreme temperatures, especially during the winter months. During the day, on the low ground, it is often scorching. At night, high up in the mountain, it gets bitterly cold, to the point where the water can freeze in a bottle. To keep the men warm they were issued with old wartime sleeping bags. These were efficient but bulky, adding to the overall weight they were having to carry on their backs.

In addition to their SLR rifles, each soldier was equipped with several hand grenades, plus a couple of white phosphorus (WP) grenades. WPs are very good for clearing trenches and gun emplacements. They have a great spread, showering the targets in thermal phosphorous that burns right through the skin. All you need is one tiny sliver of that stuff on you, and you're done. Because WP is considered an incendiary weapon under international law, its use against combatants is prohibited. To get around this, soldiers would state that the WP grenades had been used as smoke signals.

Each troop was also equipped with a 7.62mm Bren LMG. The Bren is a bipod-mounted machine gun, capable of firing single shots or fully automatic. It's a brilliant suppressive fire weapon, able to take either a twenty-round capacity using an SLR clip or a box-type thirty-round magazine. The Bren chews through rounds at a phenomenal rate of 500 rounds per minute, so every soldier on the patrol carried two spare clips for it.

In Oman, SAS soldiers went out for the first time in half-squadron formations, rather than the three- or four-man teams they had used in the jungle. Patrols were supported by mortar crews using the 3-inch mortar. These guys were worth their weight in gold: they could 'directionally fire' (DF) an area that had been marked off. If the patrol had a contact, they could push the enemy into the DF zone, at which point the mortar team would rain down shells on them, decimating the targets. Mortar shots were also effective at wiping out defensive placements and provided much-needed cover for patrols moving forward across exposed ground.

The drawback to using mortar teams is that if the ranging is off and the mortars drop short, you'll end up killing your own guys. SAS men have died on training operations due to exactly this type of accident. That's why you need a great mortar team. In Oman, they were fortunate to have one trooper, Geordie Doran, who had been an exemplary mortarman in the Parachute Regiment and was a qualified instructor. He was therefore able to train the other crews, getting them up to the required standard.

In Oman, the SAS had to patrol aggressively across open

ground, against enemy forces armed with long-range weapons. It's a risky way of soldiering, and the nearest cover might be several hundred metres away from your position. Patrols relied on the Bren and mortar teams to put down suppressive fire whenever they came under attack.

Troopers armed with the Bren LMG typically acted as the overwatch. If the patrol ran into a contact the Bren gunner would open fire, giving the enemy a pasting of 7.62mm ammunition and forcing them to get down. This allowed the soldiers to either advance and close with the targets, retreat, or break to the left or right and find cover. The Bren team would move accordingly, keeping watch over the patrol as it advanced forwards or fell back. When the lads were making their way across exposed ground in these circumstances, a Bren gun team was absolutely essential. (Today, the guys would use a GPMG, Minimi or similar weapon in place of the Bren to put down suppressive fire.)

Similarly mortar teams provided valuable cover for patrols coming under harassing enemy fire, either from machine guns or rebel mortars. One man on the team would establish an observation post (OP) ahead of the crew, getting eyes on the target. His job was to watch the target area, feeding coordinates to the rest of the lads.

If a patrol was in danger, they would fire a signal flare to indicate that they needed fire support. At that point the forward observer would contact the mortar crew using a '38' radio set. This was a basic comms set with a telephone attached to it and a telescopic aerial. The '38' had a maximum range of around a mile but, if possible, the FO would try to stay within eyesight of the mortar crew. Once they had received the coordinates from the FO, the crew would put a stonk (a concentrated mortar bombardment) down on the enemy position, adjusting for range where necessary.

Airstrikes were another new dimension of SAS warfare in the desert. The men were able to call in Venom fighter-bombers, flying out of the RAF base at Sharjah (now in the UAE), getting them to drop ordnance on targets in heavily defended positions.

The Venoms carried eight mounted rockets or a pair of thousand-pound bombs, in addition to their 20mm cannon. That kind of firepower came in very useful when trying to dislodge an enemy machine-gun emplacement in a cave or covering a patrol during a tactical withdrawal.

Calling in airstrikes was the job of a specialist Forward Air Controller (FAC). His job was to direct the pilots on to designated targets, and he couldn't afford to muck it up. If the FAC got the coordinates wrong, the pilot could end up strafing friendly troops.

In Oman the Regiment didn't have its own dedicated FACs. Instead, they relied on an officer from the RAF to accompany them into the desert. This was far from ideal, because this particular man obviously lacked the training and fighting skills of the other soldiers on the patrol. That was hardly his fault – that wasn't his job, and it was unfair to expect him to be an elite soldier – but it quickly became clear that the Regiment would be better served by training up its own soldiers to become specialist FACs, rather than relying on the RAF.

With their training complete, the SAS went out into the desert.

Movement in broad daylight was dangerous for the soldiers, even with a Bren gunner and a mortar crew to support them. To counter the threat of getting slotted by a sniper or LMG post, they began moving at night, using the cover of darkness to recce targets and carry out skirmishing attacks. Patrols had no night-vision equipment and relied on their natural night vision and moonlight to feel their way through the terrain.

Two Troops were tasked with operating along the northern side of the Jebel massif. The other half of D Squadron was based to the south. From here the SAS carried out probing patrols up the slopes of the Jebel, searching for possible routes up to the summit.

The Jebel is forbiddingly steep. Scaling it is hard work, even for an experienced climber on an established track. Humping a heavy rucksack, weapon and kit up the slopes was going to be extremely challenging, whatever route they took. And there was another problem. All the established tracks were narrow and heavily guarded. It was impossible to go up those tracks without alerting the enemy.

There was only one answer. The Regiment had to find an alternative track leading to the summit. One that the rebels had left unguarded.

It didn't take them long to find one.

After a few days on the ground, the two Troops from D Squadron patrolling the north side of the massif received a tip-off about an undefended route to the summit. That evening, they went ahead to recce the track.

Moving in light order, carrying only a pair of water bottles, belt kits and their rifles, the troops began their exploratory ascent up the Jebel. After climbing six thousand feet, the patrol hit the summit without running into any enemy sentries. That wasn't down to pure luck. At the time there was a widely held belief that the Jebel couldn't be taken by an attacking force. Not only is this sort of attitude alien to the SAS, it told them something about the mindset of the rebels: they were confident in their belief that nobody would dare try to scale the massif, and definitely not at night. The soldiers knew that if they could find a way up, the rebels probably wouldn't bother to guard the route. They would still have the element of surprise, because no one would be expecting them.

Although they were knackered after their back-breaking climb, D Squadron moved quickly to consolidate their toehold on the jebel. Patrols secured the immediate area, seizing the rebels' deserted sangars (defensive positions built from sandbags, concrete or piles of rock), and establishing a defensive perimeter. Half of the soldiers stayed up on the plateau while the rest, fighting off their exhaustion, trudged back down the slopes to retrieve their kit and supplies.

Once their position was secure, the soldiers began pushing out across the plateau. For the next fortnight the two Troops carried out a series of active patrols, setting up observation posts and mapping out the enemy's defensive perimeter. At the same time, they were gathering intelligence on the rebels' disposition and strength, gauging the quality of the forces they were up against. This was all part of the Regiment's strategy to capture the Jebel: by chipping away at the rebels' territory, taking little bits of ground each day, they would push the enemy back until they either surrendered or were driven off the mountain.

The soldiers didn't go out looking for trouble, but if they ran into a contact, they would engage the enemy, hitting them hard before tactically withdrawing under covering fire. At this point D Squadron had only around twenty men on the summit, with the nearest rebel positions only three thousand metres away. As a precaution, OPs were set up a short distance ahead of their defensive baseline, ready to put rounds down in case the rebels tried it on.

The guys had an early contact, when a group of rebels attacked one of these OPs at last light. Sergeant 'Herbie' Hawkins and his six-man patrol occupied an outcrop overlooking one of the rebel positions. An hour before dusk, they came under attack by an enemy force of between thirty and forty men, apparently mistaking the Brits for SAF soldiers. The enemy were confident of an easy victory, but they didn't who know they were really up against.

Hawkins and his men kept their cool, holding their fire until the rebels were no more than 150 metres away to give themselves the best chance of hitting their targets. Once the rebels were within range, the patrol opened fire, killing at least nine of them. As darkness settled across the Jebel the enemy retreated, having been given a bloody nose by Hawkins and his men.

That outcrop became known as 'Herbie's Hump'. Hawkins was later awarded the Distinguished Conduct Medal (DCM) for this contact; another man, 'Scouse' Cunningham, got the Military Medal (MM). Both awards were hard-earned. To hold your position in the teeth of a larger attacking force, allowing the enemy to get very close before opening up, requires nerves of steel. It's what elite soldiering is all about.

Meanwhile, over on the southern side of the mountain, the two Troops in the other half of D Squadron kept the enemy busy, probing rebel positions and clearing out caves. The Regiment also suffered its first fatality when one veteran, Corporal Douglas 'Duke' Swindells, was killed by a sniper round during a contact with a group of rebels. He was aged thirty-one. Swindells was a real character, a popular figure in the Regiment, and his death was keenly felt by all the other guys. He was later buried in a small secluded cove off the coast of Muscat.

In the space of two weeks of patrolling, the SAS made rapid gains. They established a toehold on the top of the Jebel, extended their control of the ground and destroyed several rebel positions on both sides of the massif, killing between thirty and forty rebels. The speed of their ascent and their aggressive patrolling had taken the enemy by surprise. Even the officers at Middle East Command were taken aback by what they achieved in such a short space of time.

Aside from the occasional mortar rounds and small-scale attack, the rebels made no serious attempt to retake the plateau, despite the fact that they massively outnumbered the SAS. The only reasonable explanation for this is that they assumed they were up against a much larger attacking force. The SAS reinforced this impression by patrolling aggressively and responding with heavy fire whenever they got bumped by the enemy.

By mid-December, D Squadron had firmly established itself on the mountain. Several air drops were made, delivering items including mortar shells, but the drops didn't always go according to plan. Some of the parachute canopies failed to deploy, causing the cargos to crash to the earth. On other occasions the chutes were released too early and the strong winds carried the packages away from the troops, dropping them near rebel positions or over the side of the Jebel.

By now the men in D Squadron had managed to locate the enemy's main defensive line, a twin-peaked feature called the Aqubat al-Dhufar, christened 'Sabrina' in honour of a well-known

British glamour model. A stretch of rocky ground ran like a saddle between the two summits, flanked by sheer cliffs pockmarked with caves believed to be hiding up to fifty rebels. To reach the main stronghold at Saiq, on the central plateau higher up the Jebel, the SAS would have to push through this heavily defended defile.

In late December, reinforcements from the Sultan's forces and British troops from the Life Guards (LG) were brought up to the plateau, freeing up D Squadron to mount a series of night-time attacks on the area in and around Sabrina. These skirmishes resulted in several rebel dead, but failed to dislodge the main body of fighters, confirming what the SAS had already suspected: to punch through the defences, they were going to need more manpower.

With the deadline approaching for the withdrawal of British forces, there was no time to lose. The Regiment had to get the job done fast. As a result, A Squadron was recalled from Malaya in early January to help break the deadlock and bring the operation to a swift, violent conclusion. They arrived in mid-January and after spending a few days acclimatising to the terrain, A Squadron went up to relieve the guys in D Squadron. Several days later, the two squadrons, numbering around eighty men all ranks, were briefed on the plan for the major assault on the Jebel Akhdar.

To defeat the rebels, the SAS would use a diversionary tactic. The men in A Squadron were tasked with assaulting the high ground on the position at Sabrina, leaving one Troop behind to trick the rebels into thinking that the main assault would come from that direction. Meanwhile D Squadron would carry out a second feinting manoeuvre to the south, in the area of the Tanuf plateau. To add to the deceit, false intelligence was leaked to the teams of local donkey handlers who had been transporting equipment and ammunition up the mountain; a number of these handlers were suspected of feeding information to the enemy.

Diversions are part and parcel of SAS operations, even today. They draw attention and bodies away from the target area, compelling the enemy to reinforce the point where they think the assault is going to come in from. Then they realise they're getting hit from another direction, spreading confusion and panic through their ranks. At which point the main killer group rocks up and rolls the enemy over, dropping everything in sight. It's a powerful tactic, and one the SAS used brilliantly in Oman.

Two days before the main assault, A Squadron took ground overlooking the mountain pass. The following morning the main element of the squadron moved back down the hill, leaving behind one Troop at the Aqubat, while the remaining soldiers headed south to the RV (rendezvous point) with D Squadron. (D Squadron had also left one Troop behind at its diversionary attack position on top of the Tanuf plateau.)

The men spent a few hours checking weapons and kit, resting up and having a final brew. There were no signs of nerves or apprehension among the lads. They were confident in their abilities and itching to get started. At dusk they boarded a convoy of trucks and, with their headlamps switched off, made the short drive around the foot of the Jebel to the starting point for the main ascent. The soldiers would be taking a steeply sloped, untested route up the mountain. To get to the summit they would have to climb eight thousand feet, carrying total loads in excess of 120lbs – everything they needed in the event of a heavy battle.

They were expecting trouble when they reached the top. Even if the feinting attack succeeded in deceiving the rebels, they didn't know how many defenders would be diverted to the other side of the Jebel. A large number of guerrillas might still be waiting for them at the summit.

Their targets were a pair of natural features on top of the plateau, codenamed Pyramid and Vincent. The second of those features, Vincent, would bring them to a causeway leading across open ground to the rebel strongholds at Saiq and Bani Habib. The two SAS squadrons would lead the assault, supported by the Sultan's forces and the Life Guards. It was critical that the men in the advance party reached the top of the Jebel before first light and wiped out any defensive positions overlooking the approach.

Otherwise the rest of the soldiers would be caught out at dawn on the slopes of the Jebel, at the mercy of rebel fighters on the high ground. If that happened, the assault would turn into a bloodbath.

Just before the main assault got underway, the element of A Squadron that had stayed on Sabrina launched its diversionary attack, drawing the enemy's attention to the other side of the Jebel.

At 2030 hours, on the evening of 26 January 1959, the soldiers began their ascent.

The climb was a relentless, gruelling effort. Scaling eight thousand feet in the pitch black is an epic feat, even more so with the enormous weights the men were having to carry on their backs. The ground was broken, interspersed with steep cliffs and patches of scree. One wrong foot might result in loose rocks tumbling down the mountain, alerting the rebels. The men had no torches or lights and had to remain completely silent, making no sound other than their own breathing. The slightest noise, such as two spare magazines knocking against one another, or a mess tin rattling around in a hastily packed Bergen, could compromise the entire operation.

In spite of the sub-zero temperatures, the men began sweating freely and several soldiers had to be left behind suffering from exhaustion. The others carried on, determined to make the top of the Jebel before the first hint of daylight tinged the horizon, leaving them exposed to enemy fire.

The soldiers moving forward pushed themselves to the absolute limit that night. Men started dropping like flies. But there was an advantage to taking this punishing route up the Jebel: the enemy wouldn't be expecting them to attack from that direction. Along with the diversionary assaults carried out at Sabrina and the Tanuf plateau, the Regiment could retain the element of surprise and catch the rebels cold.

That was the plan. But the squadrons almost ran into serious trouble during their ascent when they hit a sheer drop not far from the summit at around 0400 hours. While the advance party constructed sangars and waited for someone to bring up a rope to scale down the cliff, one of the soldiers discovered a rebel Browning machine-gun post nearby. There was no sign of the crew, who had apparently clocked off for the night.

A patrol swiftly located the machine-gun crew in a nearby cave and killed them both. They had paid the ultimate price for some pretty slack soldiering. One of the first rules the British Army teaches recruits is never to abandon your position, no matter what else is going on. These guys had ignored that rule, lazily thinking they could let the ground do the work for them. But if they had been doing their jobs properly, the SAS could have blundered straight into a deadly hail of fire.

By now dawn was coming up fast and the leading troopers were still short of the summit. There was no way they were going to make it in time unless they picked up the pace, so they hurriedly cached their rucksacks and rushed up the Jebel in light order, reaching the top with mere minutes to spare. Their deception attacks had worked: except for the BMG crew and a handful of rebel snipers taking pops at them, they encountered virtually no opposition.

For the first men to reach the summit, there was a sense of anti-climax, tinged with relief. Even with the feinting manoeuvres to divert the enemy's attention, they had expected to find a determined force waiting for them on top of the Jebel. Instead, the place was deserted. The rebels had seemingly given up the ground without a fight.

There was time for the soldiers to take a deep breath and thank their good fortune. Then it was time to start establishing a firm presence. They set about building defensive sangars, sending out small teams to secure the area around their position and clear out the caves. Meanwhile the mortar team prepared to put stonks down on any approaches the enemy might attack from. The Jebel was now a hive of activity. Teams of guys trekked back and forth from the plateau to the false summit, bringing up supplies from the donkeys.

Around this time a stray bullet from a rebel sniper hit the grenade in the rucksack of one of the soldiers in A Squadron. The grenade detonated, severely wounding the SAS trooper and the two soldiers nearest to him. Although they were casevaced by helicopter, two of the troopers later died of their injuries.

Despite this setback, the SAS pushed on with the job, supported by air cover in the form of Venom aircraft. Several air drops were made, delivering food, water and ammunition. The sight of hundreds of cargo loads floating down across the plateau was a real morale-crusher for the rebels, who apparently mistook the chutes for British paratroopers. Fearing that a huge invasion of the Jebel was underway, the rebellious Imam, Ghalib ibn Ali, and his loyal supporters bolted out of their headquarters and escaped across the border to Saudi Arabia. The remaining rebels followed their example, preferring to live another day rather than die fighting the men of 22 SAS.

There was still work to be done. The squadrons had to secure the ground on the central plateau, which meant clearing the surrounding villages, searching for any lingering enemy fighters or intelligence, and watching for booby traps. Patrols were sent out to clear the main strongholds, always staying within the orbit of the Bren gunners in case of a sudden enemy contact. The soldiers reached the villages without any further trouble and proceeded to carry out house-to-house clearances. Except for a handful of foot soldiers, both settlements were completely deserted. The prisoners were handed over to the Sultan's chief of intelligence, Said Tariq, and taken away for interrogation. Most were swiftly released.

With the defeat of Ghalib and his allies, the immediate threat to the Sultan's reign had ended. Three months after they had first arrived in Oman, the battle for the Jebel Akhdar was effectively over.

In the tenth century, the Persians had fought a bitter battle to capture the Jebel Akhdar, suffering heavy casualties before they finally overwhelmed the defenders. In 1959, the SAS managed to conquer the Jebel with only eighty men, at the loss of three lives. They had shown that a small group of determined men, using speed, aggression and surprise, could achieve results that would otherwise require hundreds of infantry soldiers.

Nobody believed an assault force could seize the Jebel, but to the SAS that sort of thinking is simply negativity. As far as they're concerned, nothing is impossible until it's been attempted. The harder the challenge, the more obstacles that are thrown in their way, the less chance that the enemy will be expecting an attack.

A lot of it comes down to mindset. Many of the guys in the Regiment are gamblers – and I don't mean the type who go down the bookies and slap twenty quid on the horses. They take calculated risks, often in the face of seemingly insurmountable odds. They're prepared to risk their safety in order to pull off an operation. If it goes wrong, it's going to go wrong badly. But if it goes well, they're going to win.

This ethos goes right back to the days of the Second World War, when 'L Detachment' patrols had strolled confidently through the streets of Axis-controlled Benghazi, barking orders at Italian sentries while they searched for targets. The Italians simply followed the orders, not believing for a moment that a band of British soldiers could be operating so far behind enemy lines.

That same mentality helped the Regiment to triumph in Oman.

Both A and D Squadrons stayed on the Jebel for several weeks, mapping out the area, marking locations on a map for water supplies and other features. Some of the guys resented these tasks, feeling that their skillsets were wasted doing what they saw as pointless treks up and down the mountain.

There is a golden rule that you don't use SF soldiers for gimmicky exercises. You use the Regiment to clear out an area, and then you bring the regular army in to mop things up and get the elite troopers out. As far as these men were concerned, they had done the hard stuff in Oman, risking their necks in the belief that they would be going home at the end of it. Having to stay on for several weeks, carrying out the kind of duties that were better suited to the regular infantry, was a bitterly disappointing end to what had otherwise been a successful operation.

By the end of February, the patrols had finished, and the squadrons returned to Muscat for a fortnight of downtime before heading home to Merebrook Camp in Malvern, Worcestershire. Their actions on the Jebel had guaranteed the future of 22 SAS. More importantly, the guys had demonstrated to the sceptics inside the War Office that they could go out and deploy anywhere in the world, at very short notice and on a shoestring budget, and still do the business.

Before Oman, the SAS had been seen as a specialist jungle warfare unit. Now they had proved themselves for a second time. All of a sudden, they started to gain a foothold inside Whitehall. From that point on, no one questioned the Regiment or its place in the order of battle. The SAS would still have to fight its battles against the top brass, but at least they had started to sit up and take notice.

At the close of the 1950s, 22 SAS had ten years of experience under its belt and had proved its worth in two distinctly separate theatres. With no conflicts on the horizon, and with its immediate future secure, the Regiment now had the chance to rapidly accelerate its development, refining the tactics they had developed in the jungle, breaking down old ideas and putting new ones into practice. In the process, the SAS would transform itself into the finest elite fighting force in the world.

CHAPTER 5

Hereford

Bradbury Lines, 1960–62

In 1960, the SAS moved from Malvern to its new home at Bradbury Lines on the outskirts of Hereford, a wartime camp recently vacated by an artillery unit. The camp was fairly basic: a few buildings and a scattering of wooden-hutted barracks called 'spiders', with rudimentary facilities for sleeping and ablutions. The gym was a big old shed. A series of brick buildings was later added and in 1984 the camp was renamed Stirling Lines in honour of the Regiment's founding father.

With the Malayan Emergency at an end and the Sultan's position no longer under immediate threat in Oman, there was a rare period of quiet for the Regiment. The soldiers had no intention of wasting this time by putting their feet up and for the next four years they threw themselves into a cycle of near-continuous training missions, taking part in exercises in Malaya, Oman, Germany, Corsica, Denmark and the USA. They trained in bush warfare on the slopes of Mount Kenya and practised desert driving on the low plains of Oman. Parachutists took courses in free-fall at RAF Abingdon. (The base at Abingdon has since closed; the Regiment now trains at Brize Norton's No.1 Parachute School and in Pau, near the Pyrenees.) Tactics they had used in the past were reworked or binned in favour of new approaches.

In 1962, both A and D Squadrons headed to Fort Bragg in North Carolina to take part in a series of training exercises with

US Special Forces. It was here that the SAS first experimented with HALO (High-Altitude, Low-Opening) descents. HALO is a highly skilled but effective method of entry: parachutists have the capability of leaving an airplane at around thirty-two thousand feet, deploying their chutes at just under four thousand feet. At the higher altitude a military aircraft can impersonate a commercial airliner, evading enemy detection. When the jumpers release their chutes, they will be too low for radar to pick up, allowing them to insert undetected.

The HALO method had only recently been invented when the Regiment started using it, but the guys are always keen to study new techniques, leaving no stone unturned in their pursuit of gaining an advantage. They look at what people are doing elsewhere in the world, civilian or military, and apply these principles to their own tactics. In that way, the SAS makes sure that it is consistently improving, never getting left behind.

When they weren't training abroad, the men were beasting themselves on the peaks of Snowdonia and the Lake District. They practised abseiling and mountain warfare techniques, advanced driving and navigation exercises. Soldiers took part in large-scale NATO exercises in Europe, studied languages and started specialist bodyguard (BG) training. They even trained in early close-quarter battle (CQB) tactics using nine-millimetre pistols and submachine guns.

Around this time a primitive version of the Killing House was constructed. This was a windowless sandbagged structure built next to one of the ranges in Hereford. The men spent countless hours in this first Killing House, practising room clearances and entry techniques. In the 1970s the house was dismantled, and a new building was constructed next to the Regimental chapel, near to the Paludrine Club.

The training these guys were undertaking was hard and dangerous. Accidents did happen, sometimes with fatal consequences. After the death of Corporal Keith Norry during a free-fall exercise on Salisbury Plain, when his chute failed to deploy, the SAS decided to build a three-faced clock tower at the camp, creating a permanent memorial for all those Blades who have lost their lives on training and operations. The names of men from C Squadron, the Rhodesian element, are also engraved on the tower. Years later, when the SAS moved to its new base at Credenhill, the clock tower went with them. If a soldier makes it through to the end of his career in the SAS, he can say he's beaten the clock.

Alongside the training exercises, 22 SAS underwent a radical transformation in terms of its structure. Following the Jebel Akhdar operation, the decision was taken to abandon Regiment-sized formations. From that point on the guys would deploy at Sabre Squadron level or below. That meant each squadron had to be self-sufficient, able to function entirely on its own.

Within each of the four Sabre Squadrons, Troops were organised into four-man patrols, with sixteen men to a Troop. Squadrons also had a small command element run by an OC, with a Sergeant Major and a Squadron Quartermaster Sergeant (SQMS), plus a couple of clerks for admin. The main Regimental HQ was run by a CO, a 2iC, an Adjutant, an RSM and an Ops Officer, their job being to oversee the four squadrons.

The purpose of this reorganisation was to make the Regiment more adaptable. The types of operations they envisaged undertaking in the near future – intelligence-gathering, observation, long-range patrolling – did not call for a large-scale fighting force. A small four-man patrol is much better at operating stealthily and independently for long periods of time than a regiment-level unit. This structure had the added advantage of freeing up one squadron to focus on advanced training while the other was deployed in theatre, allowing the men to continually broaden their skillsets.

To maintain this flexibility, each Troop took on a specialist method of entry, to cover all possible ways of insertion on operations. These were introduced at the beginning of the 1960s and still form the basis of Troop skills today.

Free-Fall Troop (now known as Air Troop) trained in anything to do with parachuting: HALO and HAHO (High-Altitude, High-Opening) free-fall, static-line jumps, air drops and tandem jumping.

Amphibious Troop (later called Boat Troop) specialised in insertion via boat and submarine. They trained as combat divers, were instructed in rebreathing systems and underwater weaponry and mastered the use of all types of boats: inflatables, canoes, and small raiding craft.

Rover Troop, which became Mobility Troop, became experts in infiltrating over the ground, using different vehicles. At the time, the dominant motor was the four-wheel-drive, long wheel-base Land Rover. Soldiers studied vehicle maintenance and repair and practised advanced driving techniques, learning how to drive through any type of terrain: snow, desert, or mud. They also modified vehicles, turning them into mobile weapon platforms.

Mountain Troop dealt with all aspects of climbing and mountain warfare. They scaled anything and everything and also took charge of winter training, such as movement on skis and snowshoes and navigating through arctic terrain. They would scramble over the rocks ahead of the rest of the group, putting in a fixed-line system whenever they encountered a cliff and then dropping a rope ladder down, so that any soldiers who weren't good climbers could easily ascend the cliff-face.

Within Mountain Troop there is always a dedicated Alpine Guide. That was my job when I served in the Regiment. The Alpine Guide is in charge of all aspects of mountain training, teaching other SAS men the fundamentals of climbing, how to put in fixed lines and so on. In later years, as the threat shifted to counter-terrorism operations, the Alpine Guide trained the guys in abseiling and fast-roping down from helicopters into urban environments.

To operate effectively, in near isolation, many hundreds of miles from the nearest friendly troops, each individual member of a four-man patrol also needed to be trained up in a dedicated skill. These were formalised during the 1960s: patrol commander, signaller, linguist (who usually doubled as a demolitionist), and medic.

Every man on the patrol had to be a capable signaller. That is the basic skillset of any SAS soldier. There is no point in getting eyes on the enemy if you cannot feed that intelligence back to

Squadron HQ. Invariably, one man on each patrol would be better at using the radio than the others, perhaps due to his specific army background. That guy was normally the designated signaller, although the others had to be able to handle the comms in the event that he got hit during a contact. That way, even if two or three guys were taken out, the surviving members could still send a message over the radio.

Demolitions experts had to be good at maths and physics. They practised all types of blowing: everything from cutting skills to create an LZ clearing in the jungle, to destroying radio towers or critical enemy installations.

Around the time of the move to Hereford, the SAS began experimenting with using different amounts of PE (Plastic Explosive). The running joke in the Regiment used to be that the 'P' stood for 'Plenty'. But it's a lot more complicated than that. Some of the men actually took extra classes, because you had to understand the science before progressing to the advanced dems (demolitions) course.

They were also trained in the use of shaped charges, which are designed to transmit the explosive energy of a charge in a certain direction. Getting the right shape on an explosive device can make a massive difference to its destructive power.

The best way to understand the impact of shaped charges is to imagine a two-inch-thick sheet of metal lying on the floor in front of you. If you then place a two-pound slab of military-grade explosive on top of the sheet, stick a detonator into it and ignite the fuse wire or battery, you'll generate a huge bang, but you'll hardly leave a scratch on that piece of metal.

To blow through it, the dems expert will employ a dedicated shaped charge. If he doesn't have one, he'll make one of his own using everyday objects and materials. A wine bottle, for example, can easily be turned into a makeshift charge by taking a piece of string, soaking it in petrol and wrapping it around the bottle, about midway down from the neck.

You set the string alight, wait a couple of minutes and the flames will cause the bottle to crack neatly, snapping it in half.

Any jagged edges are covered with a cloth or a length of black masking tape. Then you take a couple of ounces of explosive and place it inside the lower half of the bottle, making sure the material completely covers the inside of the indentation or 'punt' at the bottom.

Once that's done, you get a handful of lollipop-sized sticks and tape them around the base of the bottle so that it stands upright, leaving a gap of about two inches between the base of the wine bottle and the metal sheet. Then you wedge the detonator inside the charge and connect the wires to a battery or a length of fuse, depending on whether it's an electrical or fuse detonator.

When that two-ounce shaped charge kicks off, the explosion will invert downwards, channelling all the energy down against the metal sheet. That tiny amount of explosive will be many times more effective than the two-pound charge, blowing a four-inch hole through the metal. Using the same technique, a dems expert can blow through reinforced concrete or thick metal.

Over the years, the demolitionists honed their skills and became proficient at destroying all types of installations, sometimes using domestic chemicals. A good example of this is the use of OMO soap flakes by dems teams in the 1980s and 1990s. Soap flakes, nicknamed 'snowflakes' because of their appearance, were a popular choice for torching buildings.

The dems expert would tip a certain quantity of OMO soap flakes into a petrol container, put it next to a window, then place a charge directly behind the container. When it blew, the petrol-soaked soap flakes would stick to any surface, instantly spreading the flames across a wide area.

The Regiment also experimented with the idea of using shaped charges to target armoured vehicles. This involves cutting the bottom off a gas canister and packing the inside of the conical base with explosives. When the charge detonates, the metal base inverts itself in milliseconds and becomes a deadly projectile warhead that flies through the air, punching through armour.

An advanced dems course was later introduced. The guys studied homemade bombs made from fertilisers, booby traps, other types of shaped charge, IEDs (improvised explosive devices) and foreign landmines. That last one came about after a Training Wing instructor and a student were seriously injured while working on a Russian landmine that accidentally detonated. The instructor lost an arm and the guy he was teaching lost an eye. After that, the Regiment decided to school the demolitionists in foreign-manufactured landmines.

Soldiers who had a passion for languages took on the role of patrol linguist. These guys were able to speak in a variety of local dialects. A Spanish-language expert, for example, should be able to smoothly switch from European Spanish to Colombian or Mexican Spanish. In some cases, linguists will be posted overseas to reach the required standard; one guy was even sent away to Cairo University for two years to study Arabic.

The role of the medic was instrumental to Regiment operations. In the 1950s, a handful of SAS men had taught themselves rudimentary first aid and wound management. Trained medics from the Army Medical Corps also accompanied the SAS on operations, but it soon became apparent that, rather than relying on guys from another unit, the SAS should be training up its own specialists.

The patrol medic course was created by one of the AMC officers who had gone out on ops with the Regiment, a great guy and a tremendously skilled medic, who had done a lot of hands-on training. Since the 1960s, the course has followed roughly the same format. It lasts for twelve weeks, with six weeks of intense studying followed by an attachment with the A&E department of a major hospital.

The job of the medic is to keep an injured colleague alive, stabilising them until the helicopter can come in to exfiltrate them to a specialist medical facility. This critical period is known as the golden hour: if the wounded soldier arrives at the field hospital within sixty minutes of being shot, his chances of survival are drastically improved. Treating wounded men in the field requires a much higher standard of training than a standard army medic, which is why the course is so intense.

Patrol medics have to pass an initial test, learning a drugs list as long as your arm, advanced first aid, and trauma management. This knowledge is also vital for hearts-and-minds campaigns, giving them the expertise to administer penicillin, check for gunshot wounds and assist in childbirth. Once he passes this test, the medic then goes to work in a casualty department, dealing with everything from car crashes and knife wounds to less serious injuries such as broken fingers. In my time in the Regiment, we were introduced as registrars. Patients would discuss their ailment and the doctor would then ask us, 'What would you do with this?' At which point we offered up our assessment. If you were right, the doctor would tell you to go ahead and treat it. If you were barking up the wrong tree, the doctor would question you, pointing out where you'd gone wrong.

SAS medics were often attached to doctors at the John Radcliffe Infirmary in Oxford. Nowadays they go out to a hospital in Washington, D.C., to study gunshot wounds. Wherever they do it, the student is usually thrown in at the deep end. I did my second-ment at Oxford, and on my first morning on the job I was shown into the crash theatre to attend the victim of a serious RTA (road traffic accident). I can remember going in and seeing this guy lying on the operating table with compound fractures in both his arms and legs. His chest had been opened up. So had his head.

The surgeon looked up at me.

'Have you done a cutdown before?' he asked.

'Aye,' I said. 'I have.'

I was invited to do the cutdown on the patient's leg. When someone suffers a trauma, the veins in their body begin to shut down. A cutdown is an emergency procedure where the medic cuts through the layers of skin to expose a deep vein, usually in the leg. A cannula is inserted into the vein and then you can start pumping fluids into that person.

As I began doing the cutdown, the patient started screaming.

'You're hurting my leg!' he cried. 'You're hurting me!'

I started going into shock. I could feel the colour draining from my face and sensed that I was on the verge of either passing out or throwing up. The theatre sister saw my face and said to me in an undertone, 'Do you need to go to the bathroom?'

'Yes,' I said.

I hurried out of the theatre, made it to the toilet and looked in the mirror. I was pale, ghostly grey and sweating profusely. Somehow I managed to pull myself together and went back into the theatre.

Things improved after that and we worked on the patient for several hours. By the time we'd finished he was stabilised, although I later learned that he had died. When I asked the surgeon what had happened, he said, 'It's the trauma to the brain. Sometimes you can fix a person physically, but the brain just gives up.'

There are, rightly, ethical question marks about putting highly trained soldiers in a civilian hospital setting. The knowledge the medics obtain on attachment is priceless, but an SAS man doesn't always have the temperament to deal with the general public. I had one patient in particular who was a real gobby piece of work. A big bloke, he had dislocated his finger playing basketball and started running his mouth off from the moment he came into A&E. His attitude stank.

I did the examination and recommended to the doctor that we should X-ray the finger and put a ring-block in. This involves injecting lignocaine, an anaesthetic, into either side of the injured finger. Once the finger is numb, you can reset it.

'Sounds good,' the doctor said. 'Do you want to do this one?'

The previous day I'd refused to sew up a young girl who had come in after cutting her knee on broken glass. The wound had needed suturing, but given her age, I didn't want to take the risk of sewing her up and making a mistake, so I'd left it to the doc.

'No worries,' I said. 'I'll do it.'

By now the patient was giving it to me with both barrels, tearing into me, shouting abuse. 'Where have you been? Why have you taken so long? What are you gonna do about my finger?' All of that.

Gritting my teeth, I looked at him and calmly explained the ring-block procedure to him. 'Now, listen,' I added. 'When I put the lignocaine in, I'm going to have to be very quick. I'll grab your finger as soon as I've done the injection and reset it.'

Which was a lie. Lignocaine normally needs about five minutes before taking effect. But this guy had been acting like a real clown. So I injected the anaesthetic, and without waiting for the lignocaine to kick in, I grabbed his finger and yanked it. Hard. The bloke squealed his head off. Not my finest moment, but he had it coming.

Despite incidents like these, my personal opinion is that the hospital attachments are an essential part of the course: medics in the Regiment know how to perform cutdowns on guys who have been shot, they can get fluids into them and stabilise them, saving lives. You can't learn how to do all this from a book – you need hands-on experience in a theatre.

Alongside the attachments, SAS medics would sit in on postmortems, practised chest drains and tracheostomies on cadavers and went out with paramedic crews responding to emergency calls, dealing with everything from car accidents to people going into anaphylactic shock.

Each of these patrol skills has been honed and updated over the decades, to reflect new practices. Up-to-date techniques are introduced to the courses, old ones dropped. Soldiers who have already qualified are expected to keep up with the latest developments in their respective fields by going on six-week refresher courses every couple of years. This might be to learn anything from a new method for administering CPR to studying recently introduced drugs to treat an infection. Whether an SAS man qualifies as a medic, signaller, linguist or dems expert, his training is never complete.

Before a soldier chooses his individual skill, however, he first has to be accepted into the Regiment. And that means passing the most demanding Special Forces course in the world: SAS Selection.

CHAPTER 6

SAS Selection

The making of a Regiment soldier

A lot of the credit for the creation and development of Selection has to go to John Woodhouse, CO of 22 SAS in the early 1960s and one of the Malaya veterans originally recruited by Mike Calvert. A fearsomely determined soldier, who had seen action in North Africa and Italy during the Second World War, Woodhouse had a huge influence on the Regiment, setting up the original Selection course in 1952. He also pioneered many of the tactics later used on operations, such as the 'shoot-and-scoot' approach employed by the Regiment in Borneo.

All the guys who served under him had a lot of respect for John Woodhouse; he was universally admired and liked by the troopers, which is quite rare for a CO at Hereford. He did as much as anyone to make the SAS what it is today, setting the standards for others to aspire to.

The key to Selection is that it is continually growing and changing over time, reflecting the changing nature of the Regiment. The SAS has maintained its position by utilising different skillsets, and Selection has to keep up with those demands by supplying the raw material – men – who are capable of carrying out those roles. Having said that, the core principles of the course remain the same as they were in the 1960s. The individual is still tested to his limit on the hills and in the jungle, even though the details of Selection have changed over time.

Selection courses are held twice a year, once in the summer and once in winter. In the early days of the Regiment about a hundred soldiers took part in each course. Sometimes it was less than half that number. There was no centralised recruitment policy and many volunteers applied only after hearing about the SAS through friends who had passed Selection. This meant that very few guys were getting through Selection and the Regiment was constantly having to deal with a shortage in manpower. By the late 1990s, the number of students per course had swollen to about two hundred, partly as a result of the increased public exposure of the SAS after the Iranian Embassy Siege and the Gulf War.

The original Training Wing setup, or Selection Troop as it was then known, was fairly rudimentary. A handful of instructors, NCOs and admin staff worked under a Captain, who was usually a veteran of the Malaya campaign. Nowadays Training Wing has grown massively in size, in order to keep up with the increased number of students applying for Selection.

On the first Monday, candidates report to Hereford to book in. They are then given a short briefing from the officer in charge of training. He'll introduce himself and tell the lads what to expect, what the instructors will be looking for and what will get them sacked. The students are then issued with kit from the regimental stores: standard Army compass, webbed belt, poncho, Bergen, two water bottles and maps.

In the early years of Selection, students were given the A-frame canvas rucksack, which was much smaller and less comfortable to carry than the current Bergen. Soldiers are also issued with the standard British Army weapon of the time; in the early 1960s that was the Lee Enfield No.4 bolt-action rifle, later it was the L1A1 SLR. Weapons are issued without slings, forcing the soldiers to physically hold them at all times on the marches.

In John Woodhouse's day, the men were put up in the old 'spider' barracks at Hereford. As the numbers taking Selection gradually increased, however, the Regiment took over the hutted barracks at the nearby Sennybridge Training Area (SENTA). This prevented the students from choking up the base at Hereford, bunging up the junior ranks' cookhouse for weeks at a time with a couple of hundred extra mouths to feed. It also stopped the green army recruits from wandering around the camp and seeing or hearing things they shouldn't, listening in to conversations between SAS troopers.

The following morning, the Hill Phase begins.

Until recently, the first week of SAS Selection was spent breaking the students in. Soldiers would do all the basic Army tests – the Battle Fitness Test (BFT) and Combat Fitness Test (CFT). The BFT is a three-mile run, with the first mile-and-a-half as a group and the second half done individually, at best times. The CFT is a speed march, carrying a weighted rucksack, rifle belt and kit, moving at a jogging pace. Technically speaking, anyone in the armed forces should be able to pass the BFT and CFT.

There was also a swim test and a beep test. These were done for health and safety purposes, to make sure the students were capable of tackling the longer marches. Then they progressed to a ten-mile run as a group up and down steep, rolling hills, with the Directing Staff (DS) periodically stopping the students and beasting them with repetitions of push-ups or sit-ups. In the evenings, the men worked on their basic map-reading and navigation skills. This exercise used to take place up on the high point of Dinedor Hill overlooking Hereford.

The locations of each march on Selection vary. One week the guys might be in the Elan Valley. Another week they'll be training in the Black Mountains or Radnor Forest. The final week of the Hill Phase, however, is always held on the Brecon Beacons.

For many years, the first week was all about whittling the numbers down, getting rid of any dead wood that should never have attempted Selection in the first place: the ones who haven't trained properly and the Walter Mittys who think they're super-heroes but can't even pass the BFT.

Some idiots used to deliberately game the system. They'd apply for Selection and fly over from a British Army base in Germany or elsewhere, knowing that they were guaranteed two weeks' leave in the UK. All they had to do was show up at Hereford, stick their hand up at the first opportunity and they could spend the rest of their time on leave at home, going out on the town with their mates or seeing their wives or girlfriends.

That used to frustrate everyone in the Training Wing, because these clowns were taking up spaces that could otherwise have gone to a serviceman who had been eagerly waiting to take Selection.

The problem of weeding out the Walts and the dead wood from SAS Selection eventually led to the introduction of a pre-Selection phase, which candidates must take at some point before the main course begins. This cleverly gets rid of all the dross that shouldn't have applied in the first place, so that by the time Selection starts, all the unsuitable soldiers have already been cleared out, and the guys can go straight into the hard work on the hills. This meant that the Hills Phase could be shortened from four weeks to three.

One of the big early tests for the students is the Fan Dance. This is a timed march up and down the slopes of Pen y Fan in the Brecon Beacons. Soldiers are divided into two groups and set off from their respective starting points, either at the Storey Arms Outdoor Education Centre or the old Torpantau railway station. Each man carries his weapon, kit and Bergen weighing fifty-five pounds. A soldier carries three pints of water, divided equally between his two bottles. If he needs to top up, there are jerry cans at each rendezvous point (RV) filled with freshwater.

If his rucksack is found to be underweight at the start of the exercise, the DS will present him with a rock or wall brick to bring it up to the required weight. Candidates must complete the course in four hours or less. Anyone who doesn't make the time is out.

The Fan Dance is a great test for stamina. You usually lose quite a few guys during the march, either due to injury or lack of fitness. Out of a total of two hundred students, the Fan course might account for anything up to eighty men. Students who put their hand up return to camp and are given a mop and bucket to clean out their space in the barracks. Quitting Selection became known as 'getting the bucket'.

For the first two weeks, the students build up their training ahead of the challenges waiting for them at the end of the Hill Phase. The men are divided into small groups and taken out on a series of marches with an instructor. His job is to impart his knowledge and experience to the students, making sure they can read maps and navigate. From time to time, he'll stop one of the soldiers, point at the map and say, 'Right, you navigate me to this point here.'

The instructors also give the brief talks on how to get from A to B, how to find the best route across a particular feature and how to 'cross-grain', where they learn how to walk across ridges. The best way to think of this is to imagine a soldier marching up a pair of steep ridgelines. Instead of going straight up and down the second hill, it might be worth his while cutting round the first ridgeline at a forty-five-degree angle and moving around the second ridgeline. Although the student would have to walk a greater distance, he'll save himself the effort of a steep climb, and he'll be able to maintain a steadier pace during the march.

If any of the guys are unclear on anything, now is the time to ask for help. At the outset, the instructors tell them, 'Listen carefully. We are going to teach you everything you need to know.' But it's up to the individual to have the guts to put his hand up and say, 'I don't understand, Staff. Can you please explain it again?' One thing's for sure: if the soldier tries to bluff his way through, he'll get caught out.

Learning how to read a map, for example, might not sound like the most difficult test in the world, but in fact this is a crucial skill for anyone attempting Selection. In the Brecon Beacons the weather is often rainy and blustery, you're walking through areas of low cloud with visibility reduced to a few feet in front of you, and it's easy to get lost, even for an experienced SAS instructor. If a student doesn't know where he is on the map and how to orientate himself, he's in serious trouble.

In the second week, the men will set off individually on brutal marches through the hills, with increasingly heavy loads and distances. This part of Selection has essentially remained unchanged. Each morning the guys get up, get dressed, grab their rifle from the camp armoury and scoff down the grub being served up by the slop jockeys at the cookhouse.

After morning roll call, they pile aboard a series of Bedford four-ton trucks and are ferried to their individual starting points for the day's exercise. At certain points the four-tonner stops, the instructor calls out a student's name and gives him a verbal grid reference for his first RV. Then the truck roars off again and the soldier is on his own.

From that point on, he must hurry from checkpoint to checkpoint until he reaches the final RV. A member of the DS will be waiting at each RV, ready to give him the grid reference for the next checkpoint. This is not just a physical test – the instructors are also looking at the candidate's navigational abilities. If he gets helplessly lost and spots one of his mates walking across the mountain, for example, he can't simply follow him to the next RV, because there are multiple start and finish points, and everyone is taking a different route.

If the guy does follow his mate, he'll end up in the wrong location. Then the instructor will point out a grid reference and say, 'You there. You've got two hours to get to that RV.' To make it on time to the next RV, that guy is going to have to go flat-out, practically running across the hills with a heavy Bergen on his back. If he makes it, he'll be shattered, but at least he'll live to fight another day. If he doesn't, he'll get the bucket.

To increase the psychological pressure, soldiers are never told how long the march is, or how much further they have to go. It's a mental trick, designed to sow confusion in the mind of the student. If a guy sets off that morning knowing that he has to cover thirty kilometres, it gives him something to aim for when he's struggling. Then he gets to twenty-five kilometres and he starts to flag. He tells himself, 'Keep going, it's only another five kilometres.' It's easier to push through the pain when you know exactly how much further you have to go. But if the student doesn't know when the course ends, he has to tackle it with an element of uncertainty. It's that much harder to plough on.

Once the lads are out on the hills, the instructors are looking for individuals who are self-motivated. That is the key to SAS Selection, and it always has been since its inception. It's also why the students tackle these marches themselves, rather than in teams or pairs. If someone is having a bad day on Selection and he's going up the mountains with his mate or as part of a group, they will naturally help each other out, one man spurring the other on. But when the soldier is isolated, there is no one to help him when he's feeling down. In that situation, the self-motivated individual will push himself and carry on. Those are the men that the Regiment is interested in.

From time to time the instructors will put in 'sickeners'. These are extra tests at the end of a march, designed to catch the lads out and test their mental determination. A well-known trick involved the four-tonners waiting for the candidates at the final RV. As they approached the finish point, the trucks would suddenly pull away into the distance. The instructor then bluffs the students and says, 'Right, lads. We've got another leg of the march to do. Get moving.'

Hearing that, some of the students will put their hands up and tell the instructor that they've had enough. A few minutes later, the trucks then turn back around. The men who had said they couldn't continue would be taken off the course. The ones who were prepared to go on for another ten or twenty miles would survive.

Over time, students began getting wise to the sickeners. What happened was that guys who were thinking of attempting Selection would talk to their mates who had passed, pressing them for information. The friend would warn the prospective candidate about a sickener happening after a particular route. To keep the guys on their toes, the instructors started to move the sickeners around, so that nobody knew when they were coming.

By this point, the students are dropping like flies as the physical effort required to complete the marches begins to take its toll.

The ground in the Brecon Beacons is bogged and covered in big clumps of grass called 'moon grass', which are difficult to walk over and slow the pace right down. Soldiers will be struggling with various ailments such as Bergen rashes, where the straps on the rucksack rub against the back during the marches, causing painful welts and sores to open up. These wounds must be cleaned and treated upon the soldier's return to the camp, otherwise they will become infected. The undisciplined soldier will soon come down with an infection and fail.

Blisters are another problem – every candidate gets them on Selection. When I took the course, a popular way of treating blisters was a substance called Friar's Balsam. You'd put a sterilised needle in, suck the fluid out, then apply the balsam directly to the skin. It burns like hell. You'll be on the ceiling with the pain, but it sorts the blister out and allows you to walk on it the next day.

To survive Selection, you have to take care of your weapon, your kit, and yourself – in that order. Rifles need to be maintained at the end of each day's exercise. Socks and trousers need to be washed and hung out to dry. Feet need to be dried, preferably with talcum powder. Once a candidate has done that, he needs to get himself down the cookhouse and eat as much food as he possibly can, because the average soldier will burn through 10,000 calories a day during Selection. A lot of soldiers in my day would head down to Hereford town centre in the evening and load up with a second dinner: fish and chips washed down with two pints of Guinness.

Then it was back to the barracks. Crawl into bed and get your head down. Up at the crack of dawn the next day. Ready to go again.

You can't pass Selection unless you've done the prep. Anyone hoping to join the Regiment should ideally begin their training a year before they apply for the course, getting their boots and feet in good order. When I was prepping for Selection, I used to run five to eight miles every night. At the weekends, I'd hit the hills with an empty rucksack, fill it up with large rocks from a nearby river, and march up a steeply inclined hill with the weight on my back. At the top, I'd empty the rocks from my Bergen and jog down the hill again to stop my knees from blowing out under the weight. I'd do that all day, every weekend.

If you don't prep, you won't pass. It's as simple as that.

There's a lot of nonsense written about the advantages of doing Selection in the summer instead of winter, or vice versa. The reality is, both courses are equally demanding. The main drawback to winter Selection is the snow: in a severe winter, the Beacons will be thickly covered, and it can get bitterly cold up on the hills. The timings for each course have to be adjusted by the DS, allowing the students longer to complete the marches, because it's impossible to attain the normal times in heavy snow. Hypothermia is also a real threat: in winter Selection you have to keep moving, no matter how exhausted you are. If you sit down for a breather, you might not get back up again.

Winter Selection can be treacherous. In February 1979, Major Mike Kealy, a highly decorated officer and one of the heroes of the Battle of Mirbat in Oman, decided to join the candidates for an endurance march in the Beacons. On a freezing, rain-lashed morning, Kealy set off without wearing any specialist mountaineering kit and carrying only his rations and several bricks in his Bergen.

A few hours into the course, he began to struggle. A pair of students came to his aid and offered him their spare waterproof clothing. Kealy refused. The students did their best to keep him alive, but he was already in a very bad way and he died of hypothermia. The following winter another soldier was found dead after losing his way on the Fan.

Despite these risks, there are advantages to doing Selection in the winter. A lot of the time there are clear blue skies, the moon grass has receded and the ground is frozen solid, so the student won't be up to his knees in mud each day. Whereas in the summer it can rain a lot, with thick hummocks to navigate, and boggy, wet ground. If it's really hot, the vegetation will have dried out, but then the soldier has to battle against the heat, which means he'll be drinking a lot more fluid over the course of the day.

There is no encouragement or criticism from the instructors. They don't yell at the guys or anything like that. By shouting at a soldier, all you're doing is motivating him, helping him to push on. The job of the staff is to be utterly bland, dispensing advice when it is asked of them, never giving any indication of how a candidate is doing. This plays on the soldier's mind. He doesn't know if he's making good time or not, or how well he's performing. The instructor merely gives him a grid reference and tells him to go on his way.

Over the course of the Hill Phase, the marches get longer and longer, and the weights the guys have to lump around get heavier. In the 1950s, students taking SAS Selection had it even harder. They had to camp outside at night, sheltering beneath their ponchos in the wet and cold instead of sleeping in a barracks block.

At the end of the second week, less than half the candidates will be left standing. Sometimes, it's much less than that. Those soldiers who have made it this far must now tackle the hardest section of the Hill Phase: Test Week. This involves a series of increasingly tough marches from RV to RV: Point-to-Point, Pipeline, Heavy Carry, Sketch Map and, finally, Long Drag.

During Test Week each student is permitted a gypsy's warning. If you mess up with your navigation or fail to make the final RV on time, depending on the circumstances and your attitude, the instructor will have a quiet word and give you a second chance to redeem yourself.

A gypsy's warning can be the difference between a soldier passing or failing Selection. I remember getting hopelessly lost on one exercise during my own Selection course. I ended up going over the allotted time, pounding up and down valleys and over mountains, running like mad as I frantically tried to locate my position. Eventually I found myself on an open road. After a short while, a truck pulled up alongside me and one of the instructors clambered out. He came over, asked me where I'd been and when I told him, he said. 'You're over time, Geordie.'

My head dropped. I thought that was my Selection over.

Then the instructor said, 'Okay, I'm going to give you one chance.' He gave me a grid reference and said, 'You've got two hours to make the RV. Do you think you can make it?'

The RV was about sixteen kilometres from my position. I was shattered beyond belief, but I wasn't ready to give up. 'Aye,' I replied. 'I can. Thank you, sir.'

'Go on, then.'

I started running. After about two hundred metres, the instructor called out to me, 'You can stop now! Get back in the truck.'

The DS knew that I had been running up and down mountains for hours on end. I actually ended up covering more ground than anyone else on that march. That worked in my favour. He was willing to give me a second chance. But if I had baulked or put my hand up at the thought of running another sixteen kilometres, he would have failed me. Instead I'd passed the sickener test. When he saw me trotting off down that road, he knew that I was determined to keep going no matter what.

At the end of Test Week, the students must tackle the final endurance course. Long Drag is sixty-five kilometres long, across unforgivingly steep, rough ground. Soldiers carry a Bergen weighing fifty-five pounds, plus rifle, food and water bottles, and when you're carrying that kind of weight you can't rush it. To cover that distance you have to go at a steady, consistent pace. Students are dropped off at the starting point at the bottom of Pen y Fan in the darkness and are given twenty-four hours to complete the route.

The Long Drag is a test of pure stamina and endurance. After three weeks of hard marching, a lack of sleep, blisters and excruciating pain, the soldiers will be miserable and tired. Only the toughest minds can push through. The instructors aren't bothered about map-reading ability at this point. They're just looking to see how far each student is willing to go, how hard they're willing to push themselves.

Generally speaking, anyone who has made it this far and isn't carrying an injury should be able to make it through the exercise.

Anyone who has been nursing a sprain or has neglected to treat their Bergen rash will probably fail.

By the end of Test Week, out of two hundred students, perhaps twenty or thirty might be left. For those who narrowly fail to make the grade, either due to injury or because they had finished over the time, a handful used to be invited to join Holding Troop, otherwise known as Demo Troop or Goon Troop.

Instead of returning to their parent units, these guys stayed on at Hereford for the duration of the Selection process, doing all the menial tasks around the camp such as changing the bedding or various admin duties, and in their spare time they focused on getting ready for the next Selection course. This was a way of retaining those men who had the potential to pass, but had been undermined by injuries or bad luck.

The downside was that this created a situation where soldiers who had yet to earn their beret were eating in the junior ranks' cookhouse, socialising with mates who had passed Selection and were now on ops. This obviously carried a threat of sensitive information being shared with men who were not actually in the Regiment. Eventually they put a stop to the Holding Troop and by the 1980s it had been phased out.

Soldiers who fail Selection are RTU'd (Returned to Unit). Each student has two attempts at Selection. If he fails to complete the course due to injury, he must obtain a medical discharge, supervised by a trained doctor. If the doctor agrees that his injury is genuine, that attempt on Selection doesn't count.

Some guys feign or exaggerate injuries to give themselves another shot at passing, or, more often to try and save face when they return to their units. Rather than have to admit, 'I wasn't good enough,' they can turn round to their mates and say, 'I got medically discharged because I twisted my ankle.' It sounds better than admitting you weren't up to scratch.

One student approached me at the end of an exercise, claiming to have done his back in. As an instructor and patrol medic I had my doubts, but the doctor present was convinced that this guy's injury was for real and signed off his medical discharge.

A few nights later, I went out for a pint in Hereford. There was a disco event on that evening and the crowd was in full swing. As I looked over, I caught sight of a familiar face moving around on the dancefloor. It was the guy with the dodgy back. He was showing off his skills, pulling all of these fancy moves, not moving awkwardly at all. The next day, his medical discharge was cancelled. There was nothing wrong with that guy's back, that's for sure. His spine was another matter.

On Selection, everyone thinks the march they've just done is the hardest one. The students will get through the Fan Dance and think, 'Christ, that was tough.' Then they go and do another march on Test Week and think, 'That was bloody hard,' and they've still got to get through the Long Drag. Then they reach the end of Test Week and think, 'That's the Hill Phase done, it can't get more knackering than that.' Until they get out to the jungle and find that it gets even more difficult. Even if they make it through the Jungle Phase, the instructors can still just turn around and say, 'We don't want you.'

The SAS man is continually being tested. By himself, and his peers. New troopers are supposed to be on probation for a year, but the truth is that you are on probation for your entire career in the Regiment. If you screw up, you'll be RTU'd. It's that simple. That is why the guys in 22 SAS are so disciplined – because it's very easy to get sacked. One wrong move or drop in standards, and your career is over.

Following Test Week, the students have several days of pre-jungle training. Most of this time is spent working on the ranges, learning weapons-handling, basic contact and immediate action drills. The purpose of this is to familiarise the students with SAS patrol tactics and weapons skills ahead of the next phase of Selection. Students come from very different parts of the army: some are from the Parachute Regiment, others are engineers, signallers or even chefs. There might be one guy who is an extremely capable soldier and a good prospect for the SAS, but due to his background he hasn't done much in the way of contact drills in his army career. This week is an opportunity for the instructors to work with such students, bringing them up to speed to give them the best possible chance of passing. Nowadays this training is actually carried out in the jungle, but during my time this was all done at Sennybridge.

Officers must undertake a separate part of Selection known as Officers' Week. This is designed to test their grasp of military tactics and their ability to think while sleep-deprived and under pressure. As part of their training, officers must give an appreciation of a plan in front of a Sabre Squadron. Of course, the soldiers then proceed to tear the plan apart, criticising it in detail. If the officer isn't confident, he'll cave in.

In the late 1970s, Officers' Week took place during pre-jungle training. By the time I took Selection in the early 1980s, it had been moved and took place immediately after the end of the jungle phase. That was still the case when I joined the Training Wing in the 1990s.

Once pre-jungle training is complete, the students prepare to face the most difficult part of SAS Selection: the Green Hell.

CHAPTER 7

Green Hell

The original volunteers in 22 SAS cut their teeth in the jungle. The modern Regiment expects every student taking Selection to do the same.

Surviving in the jungle is of course a very different challenge to marching up and down the Beacons. The students used to call this phase of SAS Selection the 'Green Hell', and with good reason: it's by far the toughest part of the Selection process. All the Hill Phase does is prove that an individual can operate under arduous conditions for long periods of time. When he passes Test Week, the instructor knows that man is physically fit enough for SAS service and has the right mindset. But it doesn't tell them what's going on inside the guy's head. To find that out, they have to take the student into the jungle.

I haven't described fully how difficult it is to live beneath the canopy. Just moving from A to B is a constant, draining effort and even experienced SAS men have been known to crack when operating in it. The jungle is where the instructor gets to look into the soul of the student. Where he sees if the guy has really got what it takes to become part of the Regiment.

Jungle training used to last for four weeks. More recently, with the introduction of pre-Selection and the shortened Hills Phase, the jungle has been extended to six weeks (and now includes the pre-jungle phase of contact and weapons drills described at the end of the previous chapter). That is really pushing the envelope, in terms of testing the candidates. Six weeks in the jungle is a very long time to survive, even for an experienced Blade. At the end of that process, anyone who makes it through without throwing in the towel is almost guaranteed to become an SAS soldier.

In the early 1960s, training was held in the primary forest of Brunei. Ten years later, the SAS was flying guys out to Belize, which is mostly 'dirty' secondary jungle, full of ticks and worms. Because of the thick undergrowth, it's harder to navigate in Belize than in primary jungle. By the time I had joined the Regiment, they had gone back to Brunei again.

Regardless of the location, the training routine follows the same basic pattern as it did in the 1960s: several weeks of training, followed by a week-long final exercise.

The first few days are spent learning the basics of jungle survival: teaching the guys how to construct A-frame shelters, how to set up camp, first aid techniques. For many of the guys this will be their first experience of living under the canopy, so they have to be shown how to adapt to it.

In the 1980s, candidates stayed outside the jungle for the first week, doing beach runs, constructing A-frames at the sides of roadheads and practising drills while they adapted to the weather. Later, the Regiment realised that the acclimatisation process could be speeded up if the guys went straight out to the forest. From that point on, they would land at Sittang camp in Brunei and head out the very next day by helicopter to an LZ that had been cut out deep in the primary jungle by an advance party of instructors and local Iban trackers.

Each camp has a timber-built schoolhouse with a tarpaulin roof, lectern and wooden benches cut from the surrounding trees. The schoolhouse is where the students receive their lectures in the evening. There will also be a series of ranges and a dummy camp for practising camp attacks.

For the next few weeks, the soldiers learn everything they need to know in order to operate effectively in the forest. The men are divided up and put into separate patrols, each under the guidance of an SAS instructor. Each day, they are bombarded with lessons. They learn how to operate in patrols, how to navigate, RV procedures, survival skills and how to locate themselves using pacing.

The latter is a tried-and-tested method, where a soldier navigates in ten-metre increments. The instructors will take a strip of white minefield tape, normally used for cordoning off areas, mark it out at ten-metre intervals, then place it on the ground in the camp. Each soldier walks up and down the length of it, counting his steps as he goes. For some lads it'll take them eleven paces to cover the distance; for others it might be twelve. The exercise is repeated on the slope of a hill, with the students marching up and down, because people take shorter strides walking up an incline and longer ones when going downhill.

Once a soldier knows how many paces it takes him to walk ten metres, he can start to measure accurately the time and distance travelled on a map. He might walk five hundred metres in one direction, expecting to find a knoll or river junction at the next RV. If it isn't there when he arrives at that point, then he knows he must have deviated from his course. There's no point struggling on, because the soldier has been counting his strides in blocks of ten or a hundred and he knows he has covered the correct distance. So he stops and starts searching to his left and right for the feature he's looking for.

Students are also taught how to see things in layers. This is essential when moving through thick jungle, where visibility is sometimes no more than five or ten feet in front of you. The SAS man operating in the trees must learn how to look through the treeline in front of him, at the scene beyond.

The best way to think of this is to imagine standing in front of a window covered by a pair of net curtains, looking out across a busy street. To see what's going on outside, you don't look *at* the curtain. You have to see *through* it. Then you keep looking further and further, picking up certain details, seeing things that aren't there at first sight.

To master this skill, a soldier is taught to focus on something five or six feet from his position. This could be anything from a bush or tree trunk to a patch of dead leaves on the ground. He concentrates on that particular bush or tree trunk, draws an invisible line and scans through the immediate area from left to right. Then he moves his line of sight on another five feet and focuses on something else amid the foliage. Once he's cleared that area, he moves his eyes on again. Before he knows it, he's looking thirty or forty feet ahead of him. After a while, things begin to stand out from that thick green mass.

Seeing things in layers is critical when operating in the jungle. To patrol effectively, a soldier needs to subconsciously know where his next three steps are going to be. That frees him up mentally to concentrate on the ground twenty or thirty feet ahead, breaking it down into separate layers. If he fails to do that, he'll never know what's in front of him and blunder into an ambush or a trap. I've seen students on Selection who have wandered right past an enemy target without even realising it. In a real operation, that kind of mistake would be fatal.

Once he learns to how to look at things in layers, it becomes part of a soldier's everyday life. Even now I find myself constantly layering the terrain, without realising that I'm doing it. I'll be walking down a street, looking ahead twenty or thirty metres down the road, scanning across the other side of the street, looking for reflections of people behind me in the shop window. It's just automatic.

Students are also taught the importance of looking after their weapons, their kit and themselves. Maintenance of all three is critical when living in the trees. The instructors will show them all the little tricks they need in order to survive, many of them learned by previous SAS patrols operating in Malaya or Borneo. This could be something as simple as teaching them how to attach 'drip lines' to their shelters each night. These are small rags that are tied to the end of the length of paracord running between the roof of the student's shelter and the tree trunk. When it rains during the night, water flows down the tree and instead of running down the paracord and on to the sleeping soldier, it drips off the rags onto the ground.

Any soldier who forgets to fix a drip line to his poncho will end up sleeping beneath a leaky roof. He'll wake up the next day soaking wet, shattered and irritable. From then on, he'll be sleeping in wet kit each night, which will make him more susceptible to crotch rot and all kinds of sores. Eventually his skin will start peeling off and he won't be able to continue. That's Endex ('End of Exercise') for him.

There are other little tricks, too, such as wrapping the wooden handle of your parang in tape. If a soldier doesn't do this, the handle will become slippery and the blade will fly out of his grip like a boomerang when he swings it.

Throughout this process the instructors will be watching the men like hawks. They'll assess a guy's site selection for his shelter, for example. If he builds his A-frame near to a stream, and the instructor has already explained that in the rainy season the streams can overflow and rise to at least six feet, he knows that the soldier is either lazy or hasn't been listening. Either way, he won't last long.

Students must also pay attention to camp cleanliness. Each patrol will have a designated 'toilet' tree, which is located a certain distance from the sleeping area to keep it free from the various bugs and nasties attracted to urine. The switched-on candidates will learn to walk from their basha to the toilet tree in the middle of the night, so they know the route blindfolded. The slack ones won't bother. They'll just relieve themselves near their shelter, thinking they can get away with it. But they won't.

These things might sound trivial, but they're essential for any patrol operating in the jungle for long periods. You can't survive in that environment if you're not extremely self-disciplined. From the moment you go into the trees until the moment you emerge, you have to remain constantly switched on, even when you're tired. If you aren't on top of your game, or if you lose your focus even for an instant, you can end up in serious trouble.

I learned this the hard way as an instructor with the Training Wing. During one course in Brunei, I was taking a patrol through the jungle, following behind the tail-end Charlie, watching the guys in front of me to see how they were patrolling. Suddenly a deafening cry went up at the front of the patrol. A moment later, two of the lads at the front of the patrol suddenly came racing down the line, sprinting past their mates at top speed, shouting in alarm. Neither man was wearing his Bergen. I cornered one of the guys and started shouting at him, demanding to know why he'd ditched his rucksack.

'There's a hornet's nest up there, Staff,' the student replied frantically. 'We've disturbed it.'

'So what?' I growled impatiently. 'Where's your Bergen?'

The student pointed at a spot ahead of the patrol. 'Down there, Staff.'

Gritting my teeth, I went stomping up the line, marched past the rest of the patrol and found the student's Bergen dumped on the ground. Then I wheeled around and shouted back at the student, who was still keeping his distance, 'Get your arse over here and pick this up.'

To emphasise my point, I carelessly kicked his Bergen. Which must have disturbed the hornets, because one of them buzzed up from the rucksack and came right at my face.

Suddenly, my head exploded with pain. The hornet had stung me above the right eye, just below the eyebrow. It was like getting kicked in the face by a horse.

A few moments later, the same student hobbled over and said, 'I think I've broken my ankle, Staff.'

'Don't be stupid,' I snapped, assuming that he was faking it. 'Get that bloody Bergen on and get moving!'

The student clamped his mouth shut and did as he was told. He got on with it. I forced him to march on for several more hours that day. By that time my right eye had swollen up to about the size of a tennis ball. We found a site to basha up for the evening and at first light the next day, one of the other students approached me wearing a look of concern.

'Can you come over and have a look at Pete's ankle, Staff?'

'Yeah, okay.'

I went over to Pete's basha to inspect his injury for myself. When I got there, I saw that the other lads had cut this guy's boot off, because the ankle had swollen up so badly overnight. The skin around the joint was black as tar and the first thought that entered my head was, 'Christ, I've really messed up here. I've made this poor kid walk miles on a broken ankle.'

He clearly couldn't continue. There was only one thing to do. We put him on a stretcher and carried him all the way back to the base camp, plus his weapon and rucksack. When we arrived back at the camp, the officer in charge of Training Wing was there to greet us. He came over, looked at me with my badly swollen, purpled eye. Looked at the soldier with his busted ankle. Frowned heavily. Looked back to me and said, 'What the hell have you lot been up to?'

That was just a training exercise. If that had happened on an operation, we would have been in real difficulty.

There's an old saying that the jungle is neutral. Well, it isn't. But with the right training and mindset, it can be your ally. To survive this phase of Selection, you must get on the jungle's side.

When the soldier first goes into the trees, knowing he will be in there for several weeks, it can seem a real slog. Like a kid waiting for Christmas, it often feels as if the day he gets to leave will never come. Some soldiers get impatient and try to fight the jungle. But that's a mistake: you can't fight the jungle, and if you do, you will soon wear yourself out. Then suddenly you're being RTU'd. Instead, the student has to train his mind to accept his situation and look at it positively. He has to ignore the hardships and tiredness and tell himself, 'This is actually quite nice. I'm learning new skills, the weather is warm and I'm getting eight hours' sleep each night. It could be a lot worse.'

If the candidate learns to stop fighting the jungle, it will look out for him. Personally, I always felt very safe operating in the trees. You can hide in the forest, you can make all kinds of things from bamboo and, again, you're guaranteed a good rest. It can be dangerous and hard work, but I also knew that if I stepped off a track I would instantly disappear. There's never any shortage of water, the weather is usually pleasant, and at times it can be a place of striking beauty.

Once a soldier stops trying to resist the jungle, he can operate effectively in it. When the students go into the forest with their patrols, they frump around for the first couple of weeks, making loads of noise. They don't see any monkeys or snakes, scorpions or civet cats. Then, slowly, they become stealthier. They learn to move at a more deliberate pace, rather than crashing through the undergrowth and leaving signs behind for the enemy to detect.

Suddenly, they start to notice the different creatures that roam beneath the treetops. When a soldier sees and hears the wildlife, that's when he knows that he is moving correctly through that theatre.

There is no time to rest in the jungle. Students are continually tested and can never switch off. Countless hours are spent on the ranges, firing weapons, doing contact drills and ambushes using live ammunition. In the evening they take lessons in the school-house, learning how to put a weapons cache in, how to do camp attacks, using explosives to cut out an LZ for air resupply, and ambush tactics. Even at night they aren't *guaranteed* a proper rest: sometimes the instructors will bump them in the dark, just to disorientate them.

They must also do a full day of contact drills with blank-firing rounds. This is probably the hardest day of SAS Selection and takes place halfway through the jungle phase. This usually takes place on a knoll or hill near the camp. The training staff will direct the students down a track that has been previously cut into the undergrowth and initiate a sequence of contacts once the patrol approaches a pre-designated ambush position. They'll get a contact front and have to sprint backwards. Then they'll get hit from the right, so they have to fall back from that position.

All day long they'll be getting contacted. It's like doing the speed test, but with full kit on and in the heat of the jungle. By the end of it, the soldiers are hardly able to stand up. At that stage, a lot of lads put their hands up and say they've had enough.

Perhaps half the students will fail jungle selection. Many times, it will be far more than that. Some of the guys can't tolerate the conditions. They don't like being dirty and unshaven, having to move around in slimy wet clothes that stink of ammonia, knowing that they don't have a comfortable bed to crawl into at the end of the day. The students are having to live in almost complete isolation from the outside world, which can get to a few people. Some can't deal with being cut off from civilisation, not being able to have access to TV, radio or mobile phones.

Then there are the guys who can't work as part of a team. That's the whole point of taking them out into the jungle. In the Beacons, the student proves that he can operate as an individual, but when he gets out to the forest, he has to demonstrate to the instructors that he can gel as part of a small unit. In a four-man patrol you can't afford to have one guy who's a loner, because you're working in close proximity for weeks or months on end. An SAS man has to be able to get on with other people with contrasting personalities, or he won't work. Anyone who can't integrate with the group or blames others when things go wrong isn't going to last the distance.

As the days pass, more and more volunteers get RTU'd, shrinking the size of each patrol. A six-man patrol might be whittled down to only two or three soldiers by the third week of training. When a group gets too small to operate on its own, the instructors will merge it with the soldiers from another patrol. This constant chopping and changing poses another test for the men, forcing them repeatedly to adapt to a new team and a new set of faces.

Each night the instructors will have evening prayers and talk about the individuals in each group. They'll compare notes and ask one another, 'Who's going to pass? Who's going to fail?' If one of the staff has a guy on their patrol that they aren't sure about, they might ask to swap him for a student from another group, allowing another instructor to have a look at him. Putting a second pair of eyes on the student makes sure that nobody fails due to a personality clash.

A few unlucky guys will get injured during jungle training. That's the nature of the environment you're living in. We had one soldier on my Selection course who got bitten by a spider and went into anaphylactic shock. This was near last light. There's a rule in the jungle that you don't do any cutting with parangs after 1500 hours, because it's too dangerous for a helicopter to land in the dark, but this student was losing consciousness, so a decision was made to call in for an immediate medevac (medical evacuation).

In near-impenetrable darkness an Army Air Corps pilot managed to bring his chopper down directly over the LZ, a small clearing surrounded by tall trees, with nothing but a handful of students shining their torches to guide him. It was an incredibly risky manoeuvre, but to his credit the pilot pulled it off. To this day, it's the best piece of flying I have ever witnessed.

Those students who come up short in the jungle phase but show potential will be taken to one side by the instructor for a quiet word. They'll tell the guy, 'Listen, we want you to look at these skills, come back and try again next time.' The rest are told, 'Go back to your unit, utilise the skills you've learned here, and you'll be an inspiration to your fellow soldiers, but I'm advising you not to come back on Selection.'

Nobody gets told they're a failure. That's counter-productive. You tell the ones who haven't passed that they did well, and more importantly, you tell them why they have failed. It's important to give the soldier an explanation and point out where he went wrong. Hopefully he'll go back to his unit feeling less bitter, knowing exactly why he didn't make it, rather than holding a grudge against the SAS. Nobody should go home feeling like a failure. After all, it takes balls for a soldier to go on Selection. At the very least, the instructor should acknowledge that.

The jungle is where an SAS man is made or broken. The workload, allied to the crushing sense of isolation, makes it an incredibly challenging environment. That's why the Regiment still sends volunteers to train out there, even though the current intake has spent most of the past twenty years fighting in the Middle East. In that sense, very little has changed since the 1950s. The jungle is still the cornerstone of Selection. The recent expansion of the course from four to six weeks underscores the vital role it plays in identifying those men who have what it takes to join the Regiment.

It doesn't matter if the SAS never fights in the trees ever again – the training should always be part of Selection, because the conditions can never be replicated in any other theatre. Only the students possessing the toughest minds and bodies will make it through. The few candidates who do pass must then prepare for the final stage of Selection.

CHAPTER 8

Combat Survival

At the end of jungle training, the remaining students are called in for a briefing and told who has passed the jungle phase and who has failed. Those lads who have made it through must now face the final phase of SAS Selection, the All Arms Combat Survival course.

In the late 1970s the students had a long weekend off before going straight onto Combat Survival. By the mid-1980s, however, Officers' Week had been moved to the end of the jungle phase and while the officers did their separate block of training, the other students spent the week doing an introductory course, studying foreign weapons and mortars, demolitions, heavy machine guns and other bits of kit they might not have seen before in the course of their army careers.

Some of the officers fail to make it through Officers' Week. One man I knew was an excellent prospect for service with the SAS, but the Brigadier discriminated against him because of his age – he was only around twenty-three when he did Selection and had a glittering career in front of him. He gave his appreciation in front of one of the Sabre Squadrons, which was fine, and at the end of it the Brigadier asked him, 'What can you offer the Regiment, young man?'

This young officer gazed round at the sea of crusty old faces in the briefing room.

'Looking around,' he said, 'probably youth.'

That predictably went down like a lead balloon. The officer ended up getting sacked – wrongly, in my view.

The All Arms Combat Survival course lasts for a month and takes place in a wooded paddock, hidden from public view, on a plot of land several miles outside Hereford. At this point the course is opened up to the rest of the British Army, so the SAS volunteers will be joined by students from green army units looking to qualify as Combat Survival Instructors. This is partly to make sure that there are sufficient numbers to run the course: often there won't be enough guys left when they return from jungle training. But it's also a crafty way of helping to recruit men for the SAS. The Army units will send their best men to do Combat Survival: the course is extremely demanding, and soldiers must be fit and highly self-motivated in order to pass. These are exactly the kind of guys the Regiment is interested in.

During the course, the instructors will pair up the Army lads with the students doing Selection – those men who are close to getting badged. Consequently, the green army guys will hear a lot about the Selection process, what the students are doing and the skills they are being taught. That usually fires up their interest in joining the Regiment. Nine times out of ten, they'll come back for Selection.

For the first three weeks, the men are taught every aspect of combat survival training: shelter, fire, water, food, navigation. They learn how to hide and how to move. They're shown how to forage, how to find edible mushrooms and other things in the forest, how to trap, skin and cook animals. Talks are given by individuals from the Joint Services Interrogation Wing (now known as the Joint Services Intelligence Organisation, or JSIO). Lecturers explain the contrasting interrogation techniques and the common mistakes prisoners make when being questioned.

One lecturer on my Selection course, an RAF Wing Commander, entered the briefing room dressed shabbily, with the epaulettes on his jumper hanging off and his shirt tail hanging out at the back. His hair was ruffled and as he stumbled over to the lectern, he dropped his file, spilling his lecture notes across the floor. He got into a right flap, hurrying to pick up his papers while we all looked on and thought, what an idiot. When he got to the lectern he started talking to us in a rambling, mumbling voice.

Just as we were wondering how much worse this could get, there was a knock at the door. A figure stepped through the door and told the lecturer that there was an urgent telephone call for him. The lecturer left the room, while behind him the soldiers laughed and joked at his expense.

A short while later he came back in – and this time he looked completely different. His shirt was tucked in, his hair neatly combed, his body language had changed dramatically. He turned to us and said in a booming voice, 'Right, you lot! Sit up and listen here. You nearly failed, because you all assumed that I'm a bloody idiot.'

The lesson was: never take what you see as fact. Making assumptions about your interrogator is dangerous. If someone is questioning you and playing the fool, you can start to get arrogant, and you'll end up letting your guard down and potentially compromising yourself.

During the first three weeks of Combat Survival, the soldiers are kept busy at all hours. They're doing field work in the daytime, attending lectures and sleeping outside at night. This is done intentionally, to wear the guys down ahead of the final test.

At the beginning of the fourth week, they're removed from the training facility and prepped for a large field exercise. The men are strip-searched, given a pair of tattered trousers and an old Second World War greatcoat and taken to a barn at the rear of the training area.

Once inside, a team of lads from the Hunter Force, drawn mostly from the Parachute Regiment, bursts through the door and proceeds to give the students a 'field interrogation', beating the crap out of them. This is a taster, so that when they're on the run, they'll be extra-motivated to avoid being captured and getting slapped about. The instructors stand close by, monitoring the situation to make sure that nobody is going over the top and breaking any bones.

Accidents can happen. I once injured an intelligence officer we had been tasked with lifting on a training exercise. As he stepped into the room, I cracked him on the chin while another guy punched him on the back of the head. We bound him up, gagged him and dumped in the boot of a car, but later found out that he'd nearly died from bruising to the brain.

After the field interrogation is over, the guys are dumped in the countryside. Each soldier is given a small tin with their escape kit inside: two coins for the telephone in the event of an emergency, fishing line and hooks, two Oxo cubes, plasters, a button compass, a sketch map of the evasion area, a razor blade, sewing thread and a pack of salt.

Each group must pass through a designated area, reaching a sequence of RVs without being captured. The Hunter Force will be combing this area intensely, backed up by helicopters and dog teams. If a soldier is caught, he'll be subjected to another field interrogation before being reinserted into the search area.

Although students are supposed to fend for themselves in the wild, teams will often get one of the guys to swallow some money wrapped in a condom. That soldier can then excrete the money later on during his time on the run, allowing the patrol to buy some food. When I was doing my Combat Survival with another lad from Selection, Ken, we were in a group with three others taking the course. One of them was a really hungry bloke. Ken and I were having a heated debate about who was going to swallow the condom in our patrol. I certainly had no intention of doing it. Neither did Ken. Then I pointed out one of the three guys from outside Selection: the Food Monster.

'This bloke,' I said. 'He's always hungry. He should do it.'

The Food Monster wasn't keen on crapping out money either. So I had an idea. Before being dumped in the hills, each patrol had been given a live chicken to kill, skin and cook. This was to be our last meal before we were to go on the run. I stashed a five-pound note in a cheap latex condom, tied it up at the end and strolled over to the Food Monster.

'Here,' I said, handing him the rubber. 'Will you swallow this?'

'No way,' he replied, shaking his head.

'Okay,' I said. 'How about this. If you eat the condom, you can have our share of the chicken. The whole thing is yours.'

The Food Monster eyed the chicken hungrily as he weighed up the offer. 'Yeah,' he said after a beat. 'Alright. I'll do it.'

I gave him the condom. Down his gullet it went. That evening, the Food Monster tucked into a fat chicken while the rest of the patrol made do with thin soup. But it was a fair trade: we'd need the food later on during the evasion exercise.

Every day on the run, we kept asking the Food Monster if he felt a turd coming on yet. Every time he gave us the same response. 'No, not yet, lads, I don't need to go.' It got to the point where we were halfway through the exercise and he still hadn't done the business. By this point we were famished, so I stopped the guy and said, 'Right, that's enough. You're gonna have to try to have a crap.' The Food Monster trudged off into the woods, dropped his pants and bent over, straining and grunting noisily. Eventually he did the business and the note came out.

We spent hours looking for a building or village we could sneak into *en route* to the next RV, to spend our fiver. After a while we stumbled upon an isolated farmhouse. Ken and I looked at one another, wondering whether we should risk it.

Prior to the exercise, the instructors will invite all the locals to the village hall, lay on sandwiches, crisps and beer and tell them about the exercise. Photos of the students are circulated and the locals are asked to call a number if they see any of them around. The villagers nod along, but they usually take the side of the poor, hungry lads on the run and most of the time they won't comply. There was a risk that this farmer might shop us if we knocked on his door, but we had to weigh that up against our need for food. By now we were starving.

We scoped the farmhouse out for a while, searching the high ground for any sign of the Hunter Force. After a while, we decided it was safe to approach. We knocked on the door and were greeted by a farmer's wife. As soon as she laid eyes on us, in our grubby clothes, with our messy hair and unshaven faces, she said, 'I know exactly who you are. Go in the barn and hide. My husband's not home, but he'll be back soon.'

We hunkered down in the hay, gorging ourselves on the sandwiches and mugs of steaming hot tea the farmer's wife brought us. A short while later, the husband returned and came into the barn. We explained what we were doing and asked if he knew of a shop nearby where we could purchase some food.

'There is a place,' he said. 'It's not far from here. I can take you there, fellas. Wait two minutes.'

We waited. He came back armed with a twelve-bore shotgun, put two shells in his weapon and cocked it. 'This way, fellas.'

Then he led us outside to the barn to his Land Rover, covering us as we raced across the open ground. I dived inside the vehicle next to Ken, thinking, Christ, I hope there's no Hunter Force around here, because he's going to start putting rounds down.

The farmer drove us down to the local village, pulled up outside a small shop and turned in his seat to face us. 'It's clear, lads. Go inside, I'll be waiting out here.'

We piled out of the Land Rover, ran into the shop and made a beeline straight for the counter. This little old lady greeted us with a friendly smile, as I said, 'How many Mars bars can we have for five pounds?'

She worked it out, gave us a whole box of them and we handed over the five-pound note. Then we bugged out of the shop, shoving Mars bars into the pockets of our threadbare greatcoats, desperate to get away in case any Hunter Force patrols were patrolling the streets. We piled back inside the Land Rover, with the farmer covering us again. He drove away, dropped us off in a wooded area and sped off again. We found a spot in the middle of the woods, huddled round and stuffed our faces with Mars bars for the rest of the day.

Some people might consider this cheating. My response to that is: 'Of course it is.' But as I always told guys doing Combat Survival: 'If you're going to cheat, that's fine. Just make sure you don't get caught.'

A soldier on the run, if he's got his wits about him, will cheat if and when he has the opportunity. You shouldn't punish someone for being resourceful. That's part of what the SAS is all about, after all. But if he does get caught, one thing is for sure: he'll be sacked. It's up to the individual soldier to weigh up the risk.

Once the patrols reach the last RV, the students on Selection are separated from the other participants and told to go over to a patch of ground at the side of the road. They lie face down on the ground, with their hands placed over their head. Then a cattle truck comes roaring over. A bunch of big, hairy soldiers come charging out of the truck and grab hold of the students, throwing them around a bit before blindfolding them and tying them up. The students are then bundled into the back of the cattle truck and driven to a facility at Hereford for a thirty-six-hour interrogation.

Upon arrival the men are taken to a processing facility, stripped down and forced to wear overalls. Their hands and forehead are marked with numbers and they're blindfolded again and ushered into a holding area. White noise is played on a loop and the soldier is placed into a stress position, with his arms and legs spread against the wall at an angle. If he tries to get more comfortable, one of the guards will step inside the room and move him back into the original position or make him sit cross-legged on the floor, with his hands placed on top of his head.

After a while of being subjected to the white noise, your brain starts to play tricks. You imagine things and start seeing colours, faces, and landscapes. Every few hours you're blindfolded again and taken into a cold, windowless room. An interrogator sits behind a desk and a camera records everything. Two guards stand behind you, ready to restrain you if you attempt to attack your interrogator physically. At this point the beatings have stopped and it's a purely psychological test.

The interrogator starts throwing questions at you. Where have you been? What are you doing here? Where are you from? What's your unit? The only correct answer is the information you must provide under the terms of the Geneva Conventions: name, rank and number. That's all you are allowed to give. Deviate from that, and you'll be RTU'd.

To mix things up, there are several types of interrogator. There's Mr Nasty, who looks hard as nails and comes across as a vicious piece of work. There's an old guy who looks boring – the Bank Manager. He doesn't threaten or tempt you. He just asks you the same question, over and over. He comes across as a bit thick. Mr Nice Guy promises you the world and tries to get you to sign for things. He usually keeps a bar of chocolates on the bench, as an added incentive. Then you have the woman.

When you go into the interview with the woman, the first thing she says to you is, 'Take those overalls off.'

This is a psychological trick to demean the student. It's freezing cold in that room and she knows that when you strip off in front of her, your manhood will shrivel up to the size of a peanut. She'll then taunt you mercilessly, laughing and joking at the size of your pecker, mocking your ability to perform.

Whatever they say, you cannot react. You don't say anything, you don't even acknowledge what they're saying.

The interrogators will try every trick in the book to provoke you into a reaction. They're watching you on the security cameras, so they know exactly what buttons to press. At one point I had someone pull a pistol on me and threaten to take me outside and shoot me. The pistol wasn't loaded, but I didn't know that at the time.

After a while, your imagination takes over and you start doubting yourself. Another guy entered the interrogation room dressed in Russian uniform, telling me I'd been taken prisoner by the Soviets. This was in the 1980s, when the Cold War was still going on. By this moment I'd had no sleep and my brain was telling me, 'Jesus, this is for real. The Russians have got me.'

Some students will crack under this pressure. It's disorientating, you're sleep-deprived and as time goes on it becomes increasingly hard to remind yourself that this is a training exercise. I was lucky – I'd done interrogation training at eighteen and again at twenty-one, so I had more experience than any of the other guys. I knew exactly what I had to do, how I had to act, and I knew it was going to be a long, long thirty-six hours.

The key is to put a moronic look on your face and answer every question by stating your name and rank in a monosyllabic tone. It irritates the interrogator, but they can't show that. You don't laugh, you don't smile, you don't get angry and lash out at them when they insult you. You sit there looking like a gimp. That really messes with them.

After thirty-six hours, the interrogation phase is over. The student is led out and taken to a separate room. His blindfold is removed and he's greeted by the Sergeant Major of the Regiment Training Wing, wearing a white armband around his bicep.

Before a soldier goes into the interrogation phase, he will be told, 'Anybody who has a white armband is an adjudicator and will not mess with you. You are to do exactly as they say.'

The sergeant major on my Selection course was Don Wilson, an outstanding soldier, tall and very quiet, but with a dry sense of humour. As I stepped into the room, I had no idea what time of day it was and I didn't know my arse from my elbow. The blindfold came off and I squinted at the SM for a long beat, adjusting to the harsh lights.

Don nodded at me and said, 'Right, Geordie. It's over. Are you alright?'

I just stared at him blankly and repeated my name, rank and number.

'It's over,' the sergeant major replied patiently. 'This is Don Wilson. It's over, Geordie.'

I didn't say anything. I couldn't be sure that the exercise was finished. In the back of my head, I kept wondering if this was another test. After what felt like five minutes, Don picked up a file from the desk.

'Listen to me,' he said, indicating the file. 'I've got the assessment of you here.' Then he read the report out loud. 'The interrogators' assessment is that you're a thick Geordie from a low rank in an infantry unit and of no use to them psychologically, so they decided not to waste any more time with you. Got it?'

I still didn't crack, convinced this might be another bluff. Don eventually took me outside to wait with the other guys who had been released from interrogation. They had a fire going and somebody had got a brew on. Nobody was really talking to one another, everyone was quiet. All of us were thinking the same thing: 'Is this a trap?' You're too sleep-deprived and dazed to think clearly. Even sitting on the truck on the way back to the camp, no one said a word, in case the interrogators were playing one final trick on us. It was only when we got back to the camp and into our rooms that we finally realised it was over.

We had passed Combat Survival.

After the end of Selection, the students have a long week off before going on to Continuation Training. This brings the guys up to speed on whatever the current major threat is, so that when they join their Squadron, they know exactly what's going on. In the late 1970s and 1980s the focus was Northern Ireland, so the guys practised car drills, surveillance in urban and rural areas, carriage of weapons and operating in plain clothes. They would also do CQB (close-quarter battle) training with the Regiment's anti-terrorist team, wearing black kit and using nine-milli pistols and Heckler & Koch MP5s, getting trained in abseiling, fast-roping, breaching and room entry procedures. Nowadays the students will get to grips with the tactics, vehicles and weapon systems being used in the desert in the fight against ISIS.

By this point things are more relaxed among the soldiers. The pressure is off to a certain extent and as long as you absorb the information and don't do anything stupid, you'll get through it.

At the end of Continuation Training there's a live exercise, after which the students go up to the camp to get badged. There's no pomp or ceremony or anything like that. The CO comes in and says, 'Well done,' and the soldiers grab their berets from a cardboard box. The Sergeant Major reads out a list, telling them which Sabre Squadron each man is going to join. Then they head off to introduce themselves.

Those students who are not parachute-trained, meanwhile, are sent down to RAF Brize Norton to take the basic parachute course. That's their first posting. Once they have completed the course and earned their SAS wings, they are free to go to their individual squadrons.

Once he has received his beret, each soldier gives the Squadron Sergeant Major (SSM) his preferred choice for which Troop he would like to join. First choice and second choice. Most people get one or the other. If the soldier has a friend in one of the Troops, that guy might have a word with the SSM or the Staff Sergeant and ask for his mate to be put in the same Troop. After being trained in the particular Troop skill, the soldier will then go off to do his patrol skill course.

There are many other courses available to the SAS operator once he's passed Selection: fast driving, sniper course, languages. If he's going off on a team job, he'll be sent down to Beaconsfield for a twelve-week interpreter's course. He can train as a Forward Air Controller (FAC), learning how to direct fast air on to targets and coordinate attacks with jet pilots. There's Range Management, otherwise known as Field Firing, when a soldier learns how to set up a firing range, working out all the distances and safety aspects. This is useful if you're going overseas to train a foreign infantry or guerrilla force, bringing their shooting skills up to scratch.

Any SAS man needs to do these courses to make himself indispensable to the Regiment. When you pass Selection, you drop down to the rank of Trooper, and progressing up the ladder isn't easy. To get to the rank of Sergeant, you've got to do your Junior Brecon course at the Infantry Battle School, and you can't get promoted to Staff Sergeant without your Senior Brecon.

When I joined the Regiment, a pecking order existed in each Troop. There was an unwritten rule that the other guys wouldn't speak to the 'crow' for the first year. In reality, this lasted no more than a couple of months. It was a form of intimidation, a way for the veteran operators to keep the young bucks in their place.

Thankfully, that attitude no longer exists. The newly-badged SAS men of today wouldn't stand for it. They're not going into Troops and having to prove themselves all over again. They're getting straight down to business, in some cases almost from the day they receive their beret.

One young guy had to get kitted out and headed straight over to Afghanistan very soon after finishing Selection, with orders to link up with his Sabre Squadron. When he landed, he was told that he had to escort a group of forty Afghan fighters up to the camp where his Squadron was based. While *en route*, the party was caught in an ambush and the SAS soldier spent his first day in a heavy contact on the ground. A guy getting tested like that in the field has already proved himself. He isn't going to put up with a veteran sergeant trying to bully him. It just won't work.

Although the details of Selection may have changed over the years, the demands of the course and the qualities the instructors look for in volunteers have remained the same as they did in the 1960s. During those first years in Hereford, the SAS also established many of the principles that are still used today: the four-man patrol, the Troop and patrol skills, the Killing House. It was a critical time in the Regiment's history.

Four years after they conquered the Jebel Akhdar, the men of 22 SAS were experts in different types of unorthodox warfare, with experience in the desert and the jungle. They had trained around the world, were in peak physical condition and specialised in an incredible variety of skills, and they had established a supremely demanding Selection process for potential new recruits. They were ready for whatever came next.

They didn't have to wait long.

CHAPTER 9

Back in the Jungle

Borneo, 1963

The background to the conflict in Borneo was rooted in the twin threats of Chinese Communism and the grandiose ambitions of the Indonesian President, Ahmed Sukarno.

In 1962, the island of Borneo was divided between the Indonesian-controlled territory of Kalimantan to the south, and three smaller former British colonies to the north: Sabah, Sarawak and the Sultanate of Brunei. All three colonies were slated to join the new Federation of Malaysia, along with Malaya and Singapore. (Brunei later opted to remain a British protectorate.)

However, President Sukarno had other ideas. He had long dreamt of taking over those territories for himself, along with the Philippines, as part of a deluded plan to transform Indonesia into an Asian superpower – with Sukarno lording it over the whole lot. He opposed the Federation and plotted to undermine it whenever possible.

In December 1962, a rebellion broke out in Brunei against the Sultan's rule. The revolt was led by guerillas in the North Kalimantan National Army (TNKU), a pro-Sukarno force whose insurgents had been trained and equipped by Indonesia. Government facilities were attacked, Europeans were taken hostage and police officers were killed. A force of Gurkha Rifles and the Queen's Own Highlanders was brought in to sort out the trouble and quickly restored order, with the surviving rebels legging it across the border to Kalimantan.

Brunei was sitting on a lot of oil and gas, which undoubtedly influenced the UK's decision to intervene. But the presence of British troops in Northern Borneo gave Sukarno the perfect excuse to stir up trouble and he publicly declared his support for the insurgents. While this was going on, the Clandestine Communist Organisation (CCO), an ethnic Chinese movement based largely in the towns of Sarawak, was also becoming increasingly active. Sukarno was not a Communist, but the Communist Party in Indonesia was strong and there was a suspicion that he might form a strategic alliance with the CCO.

The situation posed a major problem for the top brass. They lacked the manpower to fight on two fronts and had to figure out a way of dealing with a potential internal uprising while also patrolling the 970-mile border with Kalimantan, plugging any gaps and stopping any Indonesian troops from sneaking across.

What was needed was a specialist reconnaissance unit – one that was capable of operating deep in the jungle, patrolling the border with Kalimantan and keeping an eye on any possible enemy activity. Alongside this, such a force could disrupt cross-border activity, denying the movement of support and supplies to the Communist insurgents inside Borneo and helping to keep the lid on any internal revolt.

After some hard lobbying by John Woodhouse, now the CO of the Regiment, the SAS was given an intelligence-gathering role in Borneo. Their orders were to penetrate the remote jungle and run surveillance on the border, feeding any information back to the commanders and helping them to build up a much clearer picture of Indonesian activity along the frontier. At the same time, they were also tasked with winning the hearts and minds of the tribespeople who lived there.

The men of A Squadron headed out at the beginning of 1963. Their involvement was a closely guarded secret and they flew out on a civilian aircraft from Heathrow, spending a week in transit before arriving in Brunei.

Four years after they had left Malaya, 22 SAS was back in the jungle.

The Indonesian Confrontation was one of several 'small wars' fought by the Regiment in the decades after the Malayan Emergency: low-level conflicts that took place largely in secret, with the general public kept in the dark. Everything was done off the books. If the men needed a new piece of kit or extra ammunition, they got it, no questions asked.

Borneo is a vast island, the third biggest in the world in terms of land mass, with tens of thousands of miles of primary jungle, mountains and swampland. At the time of their deployment, the SAS still had only two operational Sabre Squadrons, totalling around eighty men, plus support personnel. There was no way a unit that size could effectively patrol such a large area by themselves.

The only way to do it was to go out in patrol-sized formations, limiting their areas of operation to the most likely crossing points and making contact with the locals. The aboriginal tribes were hunter-gatherers who lived in villages scattered across both sides of the border; nothing happened on their patch without them knowing about it. By earning the trust of these people, the SAS could rely on them for intelligence on enemy movement.

At the time of the Confrontation, the Regiment had an unparalleled knowledge of the jungle. Many of the guys who had fought in the later years of the Malayan Emergency were still with the SAS and could impart their knowledge and experience to the younger lads. The soldiers had absorbed the lessons they had learned in Malaya, fine-tuning their tactics and applying some of the techniques they had learned during the years of training at Hereford and overseas.

Technology also played its part: helicopters were now widely deployed, meaning the troops no longer had to rely on parachuting into the trees in order to insert into the jungle. Wounded men could also be medevaced much more quickly, increasing their chances of survival.

Most of the soldiers still relied on the L1A1 Self-Loading Rifle as their standard primary weapon. The preferred tool for the lead scout was now the American Armalite, developed by Eugene Stoner in the 1950s. The design was licensed to Colt and went into service in the US military as the M16. The weapon was favoured for its lightweight feel and full-automatic setting, which made it perfect for sudden contacts at close range. The downside was that the stopping power on the smaller 5.56mm round wasn't great. Targets have been known to stay on their feet despite taking three or four bullets.

Upon arrival in Brunei, the SAS set themselves up at a private property owned by the Sultan of Brunei, known locally as the 'Haunted House', which had been the headquarters of the Japanese security forces, the Kempeitai, during the Second World War. Once they had established their base, the guys in A Squadron kitted up and went to work.

To begin with, SAS operations focused on patrolling the border, filling in details on the maps and befriending the locals. The Kelabits and the other tribes in the interior of the country were fearsome warriors. During the Second World War, they had collected the severed heads of Japanese soldiers they had killed, putting them on display outside their homes.

These tribespeople lived off the land, raising livestock and growing their own crops of rice, fruit and vegetables. What they could not grow, they caught by setting traps or going out on hunting expeditions, armed with spears, knives and blowpipes. Families lived and slept in longhouses: long timber-framed struc-tures built on raised stilts, with thatched roofs made from attap palm fronds. Pigs and chickens sheltered in the gaps below the longhouses, feasting on the scraps, excrement and bits of rubbish that dropped down from several holes cut into the floor.

To a large degree the tribes in Borneo had been sheltered from the worst excesses of Western civilisation and religion, and there was no corruption or greed among the villagers. In addition, they had an incredible knowledge of the jungle. They could track anything, knew all the wildlife and vegetation and the main routes through the forest.

Patrols spent three months at a time living with the tribes in their kampongs. Small-sized groups of between two and four SAS men would initiate contact by approaching the village bearing gifts and introduce themselves to the headman. Over the next few days, a degree of trust would be established between the soldiers and the tribe. Eventually they would be invited into the longhouse for a communal feast of meat and rice, washed down with jars of *tuak*, a potent drink made from rice or tapioca.

The SAS continued to work hard to earn their hosts' confidence. They shared meals together and provided basic medical aid, treating open wounds and dispensing penicillin. Some of the lads even got tribal tattoos during a ceremony with their hosts. In return, the villagers told them the secrets of the forest, telling them what to eat, what to avoid, and teaching them about the different plants.

The soldiers were generally very strict and disciplined, careful not to show any sign of disrespect towards the tribespeople or their way of life. There was one story of a headman's daughter lying down next to one of the guys in the village one night. Among the tribes, that gesture is almost equivalent to a marriage proposal in a Christian country. Nothing untoward was going on, but it was deemed that the soldier and the woman were getting too friendly. That kind of situation had to be avoided at all costs, because it would upset the menfolk and cause them to lose face.

Such incidents were rare. In most cases, the soldiers' behaviour was exemplary, and they struck up genuine, lasting friendships with the tribes they were living with. In one village a pair of SAS men, Geordie Doran, one of the heroes of the Jebel Akhdar operation, and Stan Jenks, a signaller, forged a close relationship with the locals. In his memoir, Geordie recalls: 'About a week before we were due to leave Bario the headman made Stan and me his honorary sons and planted two orange trees near the school in our honour.' The villagers also presented the two soldiers with several gifts, including 'a blowpipe with a spear attached which had been used for hunting by one of the men.'

Another tribe, the Ibans, had previously worked alongside the SAS in Malaya. They proved such good allies that they later formed a specialist unit, called the Cross-Border Scouts, to help patrol the region and gather information. The SAS continues to work closely with the Ibans today, helping to set up camps in the jungle for Selection training.

In Borneo, the Regiment proved that a policy of deep engagement with the locals could work. They understood that to win their hearts and minds, you had to live among the people, fully participating in their way of life. By endearing themselves to the tribes, they laid the foundations for an intelligence network that would play a big role in the outcome of the conflict.

In the autumn of 1963, incensed by the formation of the Malaysian Federation, the Indonesians ramped up their operations with a deadly raid across the border, hitting the military outpost at Long Jawai. The small number of defending Gurkhas, Border Scouts and Malaysian police came under attack from a force of around two hundred Indonesians. After a firefight lasting several hours, they were compelled to withdraw.

The Indonesians ransacked the village and executed ten of the Border Scouts who had surrendered, as horrified locals looked on. A counter-attack involving helicopters airlifting in Gurkha reinforcements inflicted heavy casualties on the retreating enemy, but it was now clear that things were heating up.

On 29 December, the Indonesians launched another attack on the town of Kalabakan, ambushing a unit of the Royal Malay Regiment (RMR), before they were eventually repulsed by a force of Gurkhas.

These incursions were followed by a series of deadly raids into Northern Borneo at the beginning of 1964, killing dozens of Malay soldiers. The Regiment also suffered its first losses of the campaign after a four-man patrol accidentally crossed the border and stumbled into an enemy position. During the firefight the patrol signaller, Harry 'Paddy' Condon, got hit and became separated from the other soldiers. He was captured by the

Indonesians and later tortured and killed. Two other troopers, 'Buddha' Bexton and Billy White, were also killed in separate contacts with the enemy.

With the situation worsening, the gloves finally came off.

In the autumn, Whitehall authorised a series of cross-border recces known as 'Claret' operations. The Regiment now took the war to the enemy. Operating in four-man teams, they went across the border to seek out targets to attack, including Indonesian army bases and river supply routes. Claret ops were initially permitted to a depth of 3,000 yards, although this was later relaxed. Once a target had been located and reconnoitred, the SAS patrol would guide in a strike force to finish the job. Early on, this role was carried out by the Gurkhas.

This was classic SAS work. It's something the guys are very good at. Rather than sending out an infantry unit to search for the enemy and get into a scrap, the Regiment will go in ahead of a main force to recce locations for days on end. They'll observe enemy movement, studying the guards' routines, looking at sentries and weaponry and defensive positions before pulling back. Once back on friendly soil, they'll find a clearing and build a crude replica of the target from rocks, sticks and other bits and pieces, using mounds to represent hills, rocks to indicate sentry posts, black masking tape for rivers. Then they'll walk the strike force through the target, telling them where to attack, the best routes in and out, where the weak points are.

Claret ops were top-secret. The SAS carried no ID and wore no item of clothing or piece of kit that could identify them as British soldiers. Even the tread pattern on their boots was changed to make them different from standard British Army-issue boots. Each man carried morphine syrettes – flexible tubes, each containing a single dose of morphine, with a needle attached to the end of it, allowing a medic or a soldier to inject the drug, usually in the meaty part of the thigh. Escape money was also carried in case the guys were compromised. If they were captured, they would tell the Indonesians that they had accidentally crossed the border due to a map-reading error.

Cross-border patrols operated for a maximum of fourteen days. The men were on their own the entire time, with no possibility of air resupply, so everything they needed had to be carried on their backs. In addition to their SLRs, ammunition and survival kits, they carried a sleeping bag, first aid kit, water bottles and a SARBE (Search and Rescue Beacon). Bergen weights were restricted to thirty-five pounds – any heavier and the guys would have been too weighed down to operate effectively.

The only way of making the weight was to whittle down the ration packs, keeping the bare essentials and throwing away everything else. That lightened the load, but it meant that the guys were getting only around half their daily calorie intake while in the jungle. The men consequently spent their patrols in a state of permanent hunger.

The jungle they were operating in was similar to conditions in Malaya: clean primary forest, with high canopies, wide trunks and little undergrowth. In Borneo the jungle floor is clear in most places, and it isn't until you get down to the rivers, where the light breaks through, that the undergrowth thickens. There's plenty of water, lots of high ground and lowlands, although visibility can vary. A soldier might be in an area with a lot of saplings and growth, where he can see no more than ten or fifteen feet ahead. Then he'd climb a ridgeline, away from all the vegetation, and the jungle would suddenly open up, allowing him to see a lot further – sometimes up to two hundred metres.

Much of the jungle in Borneo is relatively undisturbed by logging. There are fewer roadheads and railheads, making it harder to find an insertion point for a patrol. Once they found a way across the border into enemy territory, the soldiers went into an ultra-hard routine. The men were under strict instructions not to leave any sign of their presence behind, which meant moving at a slow and deliberate pace, replacing every disturbed leaf and picking up every scrap of waste. Tinned food containers were crushed once empty and put back in the guy's rucksack. Everything they took in was brought out again, including their own excrement.

It's difficult to imagine the strain these guys were under. They were going in with no backup or air support, with choppers only deployed across the border in an emergency. If they became sick or sustained an injury, they had to make their own way back to friendly territory. Then there was the constant stress of moving stealthily through enemy territory. If the soldiers were caught, it would have triggered a legal and political nightmare back home. The effect on the morale of the Regiment would have been devastating, not to mention the PR boost the Indonesians would have gained from parading captured British soldiers in front of the press.

The pressure proved too much for a few of the men. One of the survivors from Harry Condon's patrol had a breakdown during an incursion into enemy territory; he left the Regiment soon after, citing a pre-existing injury.

The SAS tried to avoid engaging the enemy on the early Claret operations. The Indonesians patrolled in larger numbers, sometimes in platoon-strength of between twenty and thirty men, and the four-man patrols didn't have the manpower or ammunition to take on such a large force. If the lead scout spotted a target but the enemy didn't see him, he'd stop, go down and make himself invisible. The other men, seeing the lead scout freeze, would follow him and wait for the enemy to disappear, or bug out and box round their position.

If the patrol ran into a contact by chance and they were seen, they would engage the enemy before pulling back, firing as they moved. This approach is known as shoot-and-scoot. It's all about making sure the soldiers have got one foot on the ground at all times, putting down a stream of rounds to cover their retreat.

For shoot-and-scoot tactics to work, each man has to have a clear mental picture about where everyone else is during the contact. This comes out of the soldier's training, his ability to think clearly and under pressure, and his communication skills.

When the lead scout spots an enemy, he'll put down a quick drilled burst, aiming in the general direction of the target. The first shots are intended to buy the soldiers time: the lead scout isn't going for a precision kill. He just needs the enemy to get their heads down, giving him valuable seconds to react.

As the lead man puts the initial shots down, he shouts at the three men behind him and then breaks left or right, taking himself out of the firing line of the guys behind him and sprinting back down the line towards the rest of the patrol, five or six paces to his rear.

In the same breath the other soldiers begin engaging the targets with well-aimed shots. The patrol commander drops to his knee, emptying rounds while the lead scout pulls back alongside him, to his left or right. The scout then goes to ground, turns and fires at the enemy. As soon as he starts shooting, the third man in line and the tail-end Charlie at the rear of the patrol move off, breaking to the opposite side of the track from the lead scout and patrol commander. If the scout breaks off to the left, the third and fourth guys will move to the right, take a knee and open fire. Then the scout and commander both fall back, moving side-by-side, one pair moving while the other team puts down rounds on the enemy positions.

All of this happens in a matter of seconds. It's drilled into the guys repeatedly until it's instinctive, but mastering this tactic is about more than muscle memory. The operator must be able to think clearly and act flexibly.

Communication is essential. The soldiers will be talking to one another all the time. If someone runs low on ammunition he'll shout out, 'Changing mags!' The other guy in his pair will know that he's got to keep on firing while his mucker reloads. As soon as he hears a burst, he knows the first man has reloaded. Then they can start moving.

Similarly, if the patrol commander breaks left, the second guy will move off to the right, yelling at the others, 'Breaking right!' Before the first man moves again, he must know where everyone else is during the contact. If he doesn't, he'll push off in the same direction as the guy behind him and end up getting one in the back of his head.

In that situation, it's up to the guy behind the commander to shout out, 'Push to the left!' Everyone mucks in. Nobody waits for the patrol commander to take a decision. Even the tail-end Charlie gets involved. If he sees that the formation is breaking up, he'll start screaming at the men in front of him. Handled wrongly, shoot-and-scoot can descend into chaos. But if the guys are slick and well-drilled, they'll be able to tactically withdraw from the firefight, keeping the enemy pinned down until they can move further away and disappear into the jungle. From then on, it's a straight race to the border.

CHAPTER 10

Secret Wars

Yemen and Aden, 1963–67

The SAS was stretched to breaking point in Borneo. Squadron rotations in the country lasted for periods of three months and sometimes longer. The men had only a few days off between patrols in the jungle, which they spent eating vast quantities of food and trying to regain some of the pounds they had shed before they went back under the canopy. They maintained this punishing routine for months at a time before returning to Hereford.

With only two full-time Sabre Squadrons, A and D, the workload was very heavy and there was little time for the guys to rest between rotations in Borneo and their various training commitments around the world. The theoretical strength of the SAS at the time was around 120 men in total, but it was often a lot less than that.

At the same time, the Regiment was increasingly in demand elsewhere, prized by the Foreign Office for its adaptability, its experience in fighting counter-insurgency warfare and its ability to operate on a shoestring budget. As Britain withdrew from its overseas colonies, SAS soldiers were sent to trouble spots around the world, helping Whitehall to sustain an illusion of military strength through a policy of smoke and mirrors. The first of these operations took place shortly after the Confrontation kicked off, when a small team took part in a clandestine mission to Yemen.

The previous year a group of hardline left-wingers, led by Abdullah al-Sallal, commander of the Yemeni army, had launched a *coup d'état* against the country's ruler, Imam al-Badr. The Imam and his supporters had promptly fled into the mountains and raised a ragtag army from the tribal loyalists in the surrounding villages. A bitter civil war had ensued, with both sides supported by foreign powers. The Saudis provided the royalist forces with money and arms, while the republicans were backed by Egypt's ruler, Gamal Abdel Nasser, who had posted tens of thousands of troops to Yemen in an effort to crush the royalist resistance.

Whitehall feared that if Nasser succeeded, he would soon turn his attention to British interests in Aden and the Persian Gulf. With the tacit support of the government, David Stirling, the wartime founder of the SAS, and the former CO of 21 SAS, Jim Johnson, organised a secretive mission to Yemen to assess the strength of the royalist forces.

The mission was to be led by Johnny Cooper, the wartime SAS recruit and veteran of the Malaya and Jebel Akhdar campaigns. At the time, Cooper held a position with the Sultan of Oman's armed forces. He was granted a leave of absence and given three experienced Regiment soldiers for the operation, including Geordie Doran. Four Frenchmen made up the rest of the team. Their mission was completely unofficial, with the SAS men put on leave in order to take part. If anything went wrong, they were on their own.

Armed with foreign weapons and dressed in civilian clothing, the small party flew to Beihan, part of the Federation of South Arabia, and crossed the border into Yemen with a camel train bearing supplies, ammunition and guns for the royalists. Moving only at night to avoid getting hit by enemy aircraft, they covered a distance of more than eighty miles until they reached the RV with the royalist forces bottled up in the Khowlan mountains. After swiftly assessing the situation on the ground, Cooper and his team went to work.

A plan was hatched to lure the Egyptian forces into a narrow wadi where several gun teams were hidden. As the enemy crossed into the killing ground the royalist soldiers opened up, pouring down a torrent of machine-gun fire on the Egyptians. The battered soldiers finally withdrew at last light, leaving behind more than eighty bullet-riddled corpses. Cooper and his men followed this up with a spectacular dawn assault on an enemy camp, shelling the unsuspecting soldiers with round after round of HE ammunition before melting away.

Having given Nasser's troops a bloody nose, the three serving SAS men were sent home to rejoin the Regiment. Although their involvement was short-lived, several former Hereford men were sent out over the next few years to train and assist the royalists. Their presence helped to keep the Egyptians bogged down in the country for several years, at a considerable cost in terms of manpower and morale.

A year after the Yemen op, the SAS was called out to the Middle East again, this time to assist in Aden (now part of Yemen). The port city of Aden and the immediate surrounding area had been a British colony in one form or another since the mid-nineteenth century. While the city was a key trading post with bars and restaurants and an oil refinery, the desolate, impoverished hinterland, known as the 'protectorate', was a series of backward states ruled by a gaggle of sultans and tribal chiefs. In 1959 a number of these states were cobbled together to form a federation; more states from both the western and eastern protectorates joined over the next three years, eventually becoming what was known as the Federation of South Arabia. In 1963, Aden also joined the federation.

These administrative changes failed to address the underlying troubles of Aden, however, and when General Sallal seized power in neighbouring Yemen, it didn't take long for trouble to spill over into the protectorate. The Aden Emergency officially began on 14 December 1963, when Marxist rebels carried out an assassination attempt on Sir Kennedy Trevaskis, the British High Commissioner, killing two people and leaving dozens wounded. Shortly afterwards, a state of emergency was declared.

To put down the insurgency, the government realised it had to cut off the flow of weapons, supplies and men pouring across the border. A plan was drawn up to send in a large military force of Royal Marine Commandos, men from the Parachute Regiment, artillery, engineers and armoured vehicles, plus RAF support and local soldiers from the Federal Regular Army (FRA). Their mission was to go in and put down a tribal uprising in the forbidding Radfan mountains. The SAS's role was to secure a patch of high ground and establish a Drop Zone (DZ) for the Paras. A ten-man patrol from A Squadron was given the job.

As darkness descended over the mountains, the soldiers began their trek up the slopes of the jebel towards their RV. During the march, one of the troopers, signaller Nick Warburton, fell seriously ill and a decision was made to basha up for the night rather than risk getting caught on the exposed hillside at dawn.

The next morning things went from bad to worse for the patrol when a goatherd stumbled upon their position. One of the guys shot the villager dead before he could sound the alarm, but at that point the mission was blown.

A large number of rebels quickly began to converge on the stone sangars occupied by the patrol. In a firefight lasting several hours, the soldiers managed to hold the rebels off with a combination of LMG fire and airstrikes from RAF Hunter jets, but as dusk gathered they were in serious danger of getting overrun. Knowing that they would have no more air support once it grew dark, the patrol commander took a decision to bug out, using the cover of an artillery barrage to make their escape on foot.

As night fell across the land, the patrol prepared to make a run for it. The guys decided to move out in light order in two groups, one team putting down suppressive fire while the other broke for cover. Before they could set off, however, Warburton was shot in the head by a sniper. A second soldier, patrol commander Captain Robin Edwards, was killed as he made a run for it with the rest of the group from behind one of the sangars. The other eight soldiers managed to slip away, but were forced to leave the bodies of the two dead men behind. The survivors marched on through the night, exhausted and dehydrated, pursued by the enemy. They finally reached safety the following morning.

Later on, the severed heads of Warburton and Edwards were exhibited on poles by the enemy in the town of Taiz, an act that provoked outrage among the men of 22 SAS.

The Regiment continued to operate in Aden for the next three years, carrying out a series of covert patrol operations on the Radfan. The men laid up by day in their concealed OPs, watching for signs of rebel movement, ready to call in airstrikes or warn of imminent attacks on friendly bases. At night they moved out to recce potential ambush locations. It was hard work, carried out in savagely hot conditions, with limited scope for contacts.

Alongside this, the Regiment conducted its first urban counter-terrorism operations in Aden town. Nicknamed 'Keeni-Meeni' jobs, after the Swahili word to describe a hidden snake slithering through the grass, SAS men went undercover dressed as Arabs, looking for opportune targets in the city streets. These were small-scale ops, using fewer than two dozen guys, with mixed results. But they did give the SAS a first taste of the kind of work they would later be doing in Northern Ireland.

By now the British government had publicly announced its intention to withdraw from Aden, emboldening the rebels, and the protectorate soon descended into bloody chaos as rival factions jostled for power. In the midst of all this, the Regiment continued to do its job, but many of the guys privately wondered why they were being asked to defend a place they would soon be leaving for good.

The Union Jack was lowered for the last time in Aden in November 1967 and the SAS's involvement in the Middle East was over – at least for the time being.

Borneo, 1965–66

The result of these extra commitments was that manpower became a serious problem for the Regiment. Soldiers were coming back to Hereford from a rotation in Borneo and barely had time to unwind before prepping for another tour in Aden.

By the time the men started going out on Claret operations in 1964, B Squadron had been re-formed to help ease the workload, having been originally disbanded at the end of the Malaya campaign. This brought the SAS back up to three operational Sabre Squadrons and a fighting strength of between 100 and 120 men.

Although on paper a Sabre Squadron has sixty men, in reality there are far fewer lads on active duty. During my time in the Regiment, we had four squadrons, which should have meant that we had a total of 240 soldiers to call on. In fact, our total strength never exceeded 150 men and was routinely many fewer than that, with roughly a quarter of the guys on external postings. Some of these guys would be serving as Permanent Staff Instructors (PSIs) with one of the two Territorial Army units, 21 and 23 SAS. Others were attached to the counter-terrorism team, or posted to friendly SF units. At one point, B Squadron had less than thirty Blades – half its supposed strength.

Further reinforcements would arrive in Borneo the following year in the form of a squadron from the Australian SAS and an element of the New Zealand SAS, but resources remained stretched until the formation of G Squadron in 1966, drawn from the ranks of the Guards Independent Parachute Company.

The decision to fully badge a group of guys who hadn't passed Selection and who carried over their existing ranks into the Regiment sparked anger among the other guys, which was understandable. But there's an argument that the fast-tracking of the Guards was necessary for the short-term survival of the SAS. They desperately needed the manpower to operate effectively, the Guards were better-trained than the regular infantry units, they were highly motivated and had been working alongside the Regiment in Borneo, so they already had experience of fighting in the jungle.

Once the ball was rolling and G Squadron was operational, anyone else who wanted to join would have to pass Selection.

Over time, the squadron could gradually be brought up to the standard of the others. It wasn't ideal, but it was better than the alternative.

The success of the early Claret ops in Borneo encouraged the top brass to relax the restrictions imposed on the SAS. By early 1965 the raiders were pushing deeper into Indonesian territory, up to depths of 10,000 yards, and the SAS was carrying out pinprick attacks on key targets, ambushing river routes and enemy patrols. The aim was to apply greater pressure on the Indonesians, making them feel unsafe on their own turf and disrupting the flow of supplies across the border. Letting them know that the British were prepared to risk their lives to defend the new Malaysian Federation.

One such mission took place in February of that year, when an eight-man patrol under the command of Sergeant Edward 'Geordie' Lillico was ordered to cross the border and recce a section of the Sekayan River. Intelligence had identified a force of Indonesian troops in the area and suspected the river was being used to transport supplies.

The patrol moved forward to a Gurkha Rifles base at Sain and headed out the next morning, crossing the border the next day at a place called Melancholy Mountain. Moving slowly and steadily through the vegetation, they reached a stream junction and decided to stop and set up an LUP. The men cached their rucksacks and four guys stayed behind while Lillico, signaller Iain 'Jock' Thomson and two others moved forward to do an area recce.

This is basic jungle SOP (standard operating procedure): once a team reaches an RV or LUP, they'll box round it, clearing the area immediately to the north, south, east and west of their position, so they know they've got four square kilometres of safe ground around them. Once that area is cleared, the patrol can then move forward and set up another LUP, before sending out another team to do an area recce of that site. It's all about strengthening your position on the ground, making sure you've got enough support behind you, before you take another step forward into hostile terrain.

After advancing around three hundred metres, Lillico and his men hit a patch of bamboo. Moving cautiously, Thomson, as lead scout, manoeuvred around the bamboo and stumbled upon what appeared to be an abandoned enemy camp.

The men recced the site for a while, but with the light fading they had to return to the LUP. They briefed the rest of the patrol on their discovery and a decision was made to carry out another recce of the camp the next day. At first light Lillico set off again with Thomson and two other troopers, leaving behind the rest of the patrol. Before setting off, Lillico designated the LUP as the team's Emergency RV.

Every SAS patrol has to have an Emergency RV, a Patrol RV and a War RV. The Emergency RV is a rallying point for the team. If they run into a contact and get separated, they'll fall back to that position, wait for a certain amount of time and regroup. The Patrol RV is usually picked off a map and could be anything from a stream to a river junction. If a soldier makes it back to the Emergency only to find that no one else is there, he'll head to the Patrol RV. The War RV is normally the patrol's forward mounting base, located in friendly territory.

The four-man patrol made their way back towards the abandoned camp, with Thomson as lead scout and Lillico several metres behind him as patrol commander. As Thomson moved around the clump of bamboo, everything went noisy. An enemy patrol opened up with a barrage of automatic fire. One round struck Thomson in the left thigh, severing his femoral artery. Lillico realised what was happening and shifted to the right, ready to put down rounds on the enemy. Instead he found himself stepping into the line of sight of the Indonesian lead scout, who had taken up an immediate ambush position directly ahead of him.

Before Lillico could depress the trigger on his SLR, the Indonesian nailed him through the left hip, badly wounding the SAS sergeant. In the next second Thomson snatched up his rifle, arced the muzzle across and emptied a savage burst into the Indonesian soldier standing over Lillico, stitching him with bullets.

Amid the noise and confusion, the third and fourth members of the patrol had bugged out to the Emergency RV, exactly following the SOPs they had been taught. Lillico and Thomson were now by themselves on the wrong side of the border, severely wounded and with an unknown number of hostiles ahead of them. In spite of their injuries they both returned fire, dropping two more soldiers and killing at least one of them. That sent the rest of the Indonesians scrambling for cover and the two sides settled down to exchange sporadic bursts of gunfire through the dense tangle of jungle.

During a lull in the fighting, Thomson managed to crawl over to Lillico's position to check on his sergeant. Both men were in rag order. Lillico was bleeding heavily and couldn't stand up. Thomson's left femur had been shattered, although he had stemmed the loss of blood with a makeshift tourniquet. A severed femoral artery is a life-threatening wound: in most cases, the victim will bleed out in a matter of minutes. Getting a tourniquet on the wound had saved his life, but Thomson still needed immediate medical attention.

Despite his injury, Thomson reckoned he could make it back to the Emergency RV, so Lillico sent him off up the hill, the lead scout crawling along on his elbows and knees while his patrol commander stayed behind, letting rip at anything that moved. Thomson put down a few bursts on the enemy from near the ridgeline, keeping their heads low as he edged away.

Lillico now took up a concealed position in a patch of bamboo a short distance from the enemy camp and considered his situation. It looked grim. He couldn't walk, he had lost a lot of blood, and unless he received urgent treatment there was no way he was going to survive. About the only bit of good news was that he was in possession of the patrol SARBE. In those days only one rescue beacon was issued per patrol and as the commander, Lillico had been carrying it when everything had gone noisy. Without the SARBE, there would have been no way for any search party to locate him.

Realising that he couldn't make it to the Emergency RV on foot, Lillico tended to his wound with a shell dressing, injected a syrette of morphine and settled in to wait for several hours. He was severely dehydrated but not in a great deal of pain. The effects of the morphine, combined with the large amount of blood Lillico had lost, had left him lightheaded, in a state of near bliss.

Although he was in no condition to move, Lillico knew that he couldn't remain in his present location for much longer. The Indonesians were likely to sweep through the area again and would easily discover his position. Gathering his strength, Lillico dragged himself over to a small clearing located a few hundred yards away from the camp site. As dusk fell, he found a good hiding spot in a water-filled pig-hole beneath a fallen tree trunk, crawled into it, and laid up for the night.

He awoke the next day to find an enemy patrol scouring the area. During the search, an Indonesian soldier climbed a tree overlooking Lillico's location and began scanning the ground. Luckily, he failed to spot Geordie: the SAS man had smeared his face with mud to camouflage himself. The patrol eventually moved on.

A short while later, Lillico heard the *whump-whump* of an approaching helicopter. He knew it must be a friendly, since the Indonesian Army didn't have any choppers in service at that time.

As the Westland Whirlwind drew closer, Lillico automatically reached for his SARBE and switched it on, ready to transmit his location to the crew. Then he hesitated. There was no way of knowing how far away the enemy patrol was by now. If they were still close by and he signalled the helicopter to land, the Indonesians would almost certainly shoot it down.

Lillico then made a selfless, split-second calculation. There was no way he was going to risk the lives of the crew, even if it meant bleeding to death in enemy territory. He switched the SARBE off.

He remained in his pig-hole for the rest of the afternoon, drinking water from cut sections of bamboo to stave off his thirst. Eventually, he managed to crawl to a ridgeline a few hundred yards from the clearing, putting more distance between himself and the enemy.

In the evening, thirty-six hours after the initial contact, Lillico heard the chopper making another pass. Judging that enough time had passed since he'd last seen the Indonesian patrol, Lillico activated his rescue beacon and dragged his ragged body out of the ditch to make himself visible to the crew. After some difficulty he was winched up to the cabin and escorted back across the border to the Gurkha Rifles camp before being ferried over to the hospital in Kuching. Jock Thomson was already there, lying in the hospital bed next to his.

Comparing stories, Thomson explained how he had crawled back to the Emergency RV only to find that the rest of the patrol had already bugged out to the forward operating base at Sain to bring up reinforcements from the Gurkhas before returning to search for the two men. He was too exhausted to go any further and hauled himself into a concealed position until he was eventually discovered by the Gurkhas. When they found him, Thomson was doped up to the eyeballs on meds. During the course of his escape he'd pumped himself with twelve syrettes of morphine – a ridiculously high dosage, enough to kill a man several times over. He'd only survived because of his incredible levels of fitness and determination.

For his selfless action in switching off his SARBE, Lillico was later awarded the Military Medal (MM). That helicopter circling overhead was his survival ticket: there was no guarantee that it would come looking for him a second time. If it didn't, he was as good as dead. With his SARBE turned off, there was also a risk that HQ would assume he was dead and call off the search. For his part in the operation, Jock Thomson was given a Mention in Dispatches.

Throughout 1965, the SAS continued to mount Claret operations south of the border. They were going out aggressively, looking for the enemy and striking terror into the hearts of the Indonesians. In one operation, a four-man patrol was sent across to the Koemba River to recce the traffic and, if possible, ambush the enemy. They set up an LUP near an abandoned rubber plantation and spent several days observing the passing boats and tapping out messages back to HQ in Morse code, before they received the go-ahead to set the trap.

Shortly before dusk, the patrol commander sighted a vessel coming down the river. On his signal the team opened fire, riddling the boat with a vicious stream of 7.62mm brass, killing several of the soldiers on board. As the smoke-wreathed vessel drifted down the river, the patrol withdrew from the LUP and made it back across the border the following afternoon.

Leaving an ambush was often the riskiest part of any op. Hitting a team on their way back from an ambush is a time-honoured tactic, for a number of reasons. The ambushers have been on hard routine for days or even weeks, expending a lot of nervous energy. Everyone is tired and there's a tendency for guys to switch off. They're in close proximity to their own camp, they start thinking that they're safe – and that's when they get whacked.

It's the same reason why more people are killed coming off Mount Everest than climbing up: when you're scaling the mountain the adrenaline is pumping, you're fresh and focused on reaching the summit. Then you get there, the adrenaline fades and now you've got to make your way back down again. That's when mistakes happen.

Individually, the Claret operations were disruptive. Together, they had a devastating effect on Indonesian morale. The death toll prompted widespread unrest in Jakarta and in September there was a failed attempt to remove President Sukarno from power. This was followed by a murderous purge, resulting in the deaths of hundreds of thousands or possibly millions of suspected Communists. The SAS was now going across the border in full-squadron formation, hitting the enemy hard and continuing to inflict heavy losses.

The following year Sukarno was forced to hand over much of his authority to General Suharto. The general had no intention of plunging Indonesia into all-out war and in the summer of 1966 the country finally ended the conflict with Malaysia. The SAS continued to patrol the northern side of the border for several months, but there was no real trouble to speak of.

In Borneo, the Regiment had played a small but hugely significant role in one of the most successful small wars fought by Britain. Perfecting the skills and tactics they had first learned in Malaya, they had patrolled deep into the jungle, gathering vital intelligence, recceing targets and disrupting enemy supplies and movement with covert raids.

In three years of conflict the SAS had lost three men, while the total number of Indonesian casualties numbered in the thousands. More than that, the guys had been instrumental in winning the respect and friendship of the Ibans, the Kelabits and the other tribes. Without their support and the information they supplied, patrolling the border effectively would have been an impossible job.

The hearts-and-minds experience the Regiment had gained in Borneo would become a vital component of their next major operation three years later. A campaign that would see the SAS fight one of their most famous battles, against incredible odds.

CHAPTER 11

Operation Storm

Oman, 1970–76

In the summer of 1970, Oman became the focus of a secret war, fought between the Sultanate's British allies and a Communist-led uprising in the south – and the Regiment was in the thick of the action. The prize was control of one of the most strategic pieces of real estate anywhere in the world: the Strait of Hormuz.

The Strait is a deep-water shipping channel, twenty-one miles across at its narrowest point, linking the oil-rich states of the Persian Gulf with the Gulf of Oman and the Arabian Sea. It's also one of the most critical chokepoints in the world: roughly a third of all seaborne oil passes through the waterway each year, amounting to one-fifth of the global oil trade, along with a significant portion of natural gas. Whoever controls the Strait of Hormuz controls a massive chunk of the world's energy supply.

In 1970, the security of the Strait came under serious threat.

The source of the problem was the Sultan of Oman, bin Taimur, the same guy the Regiment had helped to keep his grip on power eleven years earlier. Despite the fact that Oman was sitting on vast oil deposits, the country still looked like something ripped from the pages of the Bible. The average Omani lived a bleak existence of crushing poverty and political repression.

After surviving two assassination attempts, the Sultan had retreated to his palace in Salalah, surrounded by his coterie of African slaves and bodyguards, rarely venturing outside while maintaining a vice-like grip on power. The Sultan ruthlessly punished his enemies, blocked journalists from entering his country, and even insisted on personally approving all foreign visa applications himself.

Predictably, the Omanis grew exasperated with the Sultan's oppressive policies and started rebelling. For several years, trouble had been brewing among the tribes in the mountainous Dhofar region in the south. The Dhofaris despised the Sultan and were demanding improvements to their way of life. Supported and trained by the Soviets, the Chinese and the Communist authorities in neighbouring Yemen, the rebels, known as the Adoo, had slowly driven back the Sultan's Armed Forces (SAF) and by 1970, they had taken almost complete control of the region, putting the capital of Salalah under threat.

Suddenly, a full-scale Communist takeover of Oman was a very real possibility. If that happened, Beijing and Moscow would have de facto control of the Strait of Hormuz. This was a nightmare scenario, one that Britain couldn't allow to happen. Oman was still a British Protectorate, with British officers in command of the Sultanate's armed forces. The UK maintained RAF bases at Salalah and Masirah and British companies were heavily involved in the burgeoning oil industry. The country was of vital strategic importance to London, at a time when it was losing influence elsewhere in the Middle East.

It was time to act.

The first thing to do was get rid of the old Sultan. Aside from the mercenaries and lackeys on his payroll, bin Taimur was almost universally hated and had refused to heed calls to speed up civil development. Nothing could be done until he was out of the way. Fortunately, an ideal replacement was waiting in the wings.

Qaboos was the Sultan's only son. He had been privately educated in the UK, studying at Sandhurst and serving with a British regiment in Germany before returning to Oman after finishing his studies. His father had promptly placed him under virtual house arrest, holed up in a wing of the palace at Salalah. From London's point of view, Qaboos ticked all the boxes: he was young, charismatic and open to the idea of reform. The fact that he was seen as a good friend of the British didn't hurt his chances either.

On 23 July 1970, bin Taimur was deposed in a nearly bloodless *coup d'état* engineered by Whitehall. The Sultan initially refused to abdicate, drawing a pistol when one of his governors arrived at the palace to give him the bad news, shooting himself in the foot and accidentally killing a manservant. Once it became clear that Britain had abandoned him, however, the Sultan realised the game was up. He was whisked out of the country on a waiting aircraft and flown to England, never to return. He spent the last years of his life in a suite at the Dorchester Hotel in London, living in exile.

Getting rid of the Sultan was the easy part. Defeating his sworn enemies, the Adoo, would be much harder. They held the high ground on top of a sprawling range of mountains overlooking Salalah, rising to at least 3,000 feet above sea level. During the months of the monsoon, the jebel was wreathed in mist. The people who lived in the villages on the massif were called *Jebalis*, and the Adoo moved freely among them.

Unlike the poorly trained guerrillas in the earlier Jebel Akhdar operation (1958–9), the Adoo were well-trained and heavily armed, and they weren't going to give up without a fight. Clearly, the Sultan's forces couldn't defeat them on their own. They needed help from the Regiment, but it had to be done in secret, without the public getting wind of their involvement. Although British support in the form of officers and advisers was well known, the deployment of Special Forces teams in the Sultanate was kept out of the public eye to avoid drawing attention to a conflict that might go disastrously wrong, as had happened in Aden and elsewhere.

Once again, the SAS was going to fight in Oman.

Once again, the root cause was oil.

The first Regiment boots were on the ground within hours of the old Sultan's abdication. Their first job was to safeguard Qaboos while he was bedded into the role. A small BG (bodyguard) team was assigned to protect him while the main effort was concentrated on a counter-insurgency campaign, drawing on the lessons the Regiment had learned in Borneo and Malaya.

Their first job was actually an operation in the Musandam Peninsula, a pocket of land belonging to Oman but physically cut off from the rest of the country. A detachment of men from the SAS and the SBS had been sent in, acting on intelligence about Iraqi rebels operating in the area. After initially inserting by boat, the SAS subsequently inserted by freefall and helicopter. Tragedy struck when one of the soldiers, Paul 'Rip' Reddy, died after his parachute failed to properly deploy. Several weeks later, having befriended the local tribespeople, the guys returned to Hereford.

The approach the SAS took in Oman was very different to the one they had pursued on the Jebel Akhdar. Back then, they had stormed the rebel stronghold in a matter of months, driving the enemy off their mountain fortress. In Dhofar, the guys didn't have the manpower to go in and seize the hills straight away. At least two thousand Adoo were believed to be camped out on top of the Jebel, more than enough to defend it from one or even two squadrons of SAS men. From the beginning, it was clear that this was going to be a more protracted campaign than the lightning assault on the Green Mountain.

The Adoo were kitted out with the latest Soviet weaponry: AK-47 and AKM assault rifles, Simonov SKS semi-automatic carbines chambered for the 7.62x39mm round, 82mm mortars and Russian-manufactured RPD light machine guns. They also had an arsenal of grenades, rocket launchers, landmines and RCL (recoilless) rifles – lightweight anti-tank weapons that look like a bazooka mounted on a tripod, with a range of more than four miles. Their fighters had been trained in Beijing and Moscow and they knew how to use their tools properly. The firepower they had was more than a match for anything the Sultan's Armed Forces (SAF) could throw at them.

The Adoo were also formidable fighters. Many of them had

been trained in Yemen, China and the Soviet Union in the art of guerrilla warfare, while others were deserters from the Trucial Oman Scouts, an internal security force run by the British.

Their Communist advisers meanwhile sought to indoctrinate the local population in Marxism, banning prayers and ruthlessly executing all those who refused to reject Islam, including young children. Any tribal leaders who defied them were brutally put to death. In the long run this attempt to impose an alien ideology on the conservative tribespeople was counter-productive and simply drove more of them off the mountain and into the welcoming arms of the Sultan's forces.

Clearly, however, attacking the Adoo on day one was not an option. Even if the Regiment had wanted to, the mandarins in the Foreign Office initially refused to let the guys go out on patrols in rebel-held areas, fearing the political fallout if they started taking casualties. Common sense later prevailed, but to begin with it was the usual story of the SAS being sent out to do a job with one hand tied behind its back.

A plan was drawn up to win the hearts and minds of the Dhofaris. Codenamed Operation Storm, it utilised some of the tactics the soldiers had perfected in the forests of Borneo. SAS medics set up mobile clinics, using the expertise they had learned on their courses to treat the sick and wounded. Veterinary services, civil aid projects, intelligence-gathering missions and psychological operations (psy-ops) were also instigated, with varying degrees of success.

It wasn't long before the first rebels started coming down the hills to switch sides. Many were persuaded by the removal of the old Sultan, others by the amnesty on offer for any Adoo who chose to surrender, with the promise of a cash reward for every weapon they handed in.

In the autumn, the number of rebel defectors increased when the uneasy alliance between the traditional Dhofari rebels and the Communist guerrillas in the People's Front for the Liberation of the Occupied Arabian Gulf (PFLOAG) began to crack. The alliance had always been more of a marriage of convenience than anything else, and the PLFOAG's clumsy attempts to indoctrinate the Jebalis in Marxism prompted more and more of the Adoo to switch sides. These Surrendered Enemy Personnel (SEPs) were given a soft interrogation and then put on the government payroll, trained up into militia units known as *firqats*.

The Regiment took charge of training up the firqats, working under the cover of British Army Training Teams (BATT). The firqat were tough fighters, unquestionably brave, but they lacked the motivation and discipline of professional soldiers. There was also the risk of them switching sides again and turning their weapons on their SAS instructors. By themselves, they were not an effective fighting force, but with direction from small groups of SAS men they were able to overcome their deficiencies and play a vital dominating role in the campaign.

Training up foreign troops has become a staple of Regiment activities around the world. This can serve a variety of functions. The most obvious one is to provide a key ally with a fighting force capable of tackling potential threats to the regime. They can also act as an extension of psy-ops, bolstering the credentials of a particular leader by actively recruiting fighters from the other side and turning them against their old comrades. As word spreads about the good treatment, well-paid job and training the surrendered rebels receive, more guys cross the divide, weakening the enemy's hand as well as strengthening your own.

The firqats also played an important propaganda role in Oman, which meant that their instructors had to be careful not to disrespect the recruits, ignoring some of their more frustrating customs and quirks. When you're trying to pull guys over to your side, there's no point raking them over the coals or berating them for slack timekeeping. It doesn't work. You have to let certain things slide and focus on the big picture, making the best of what you've got, bringing the fighters up to a basic level.

Training the firqats and winning the respect of the Jebalis was vital to the mission. But to win the war, the SAS needed to do more than hand out painkillers and pamphlets. The most important goal was to drive the Adoo from their strongholds on the high ground. And that meant getting up on the Jebel massif and dominating the plateau.

The Sultan's forces had repeatedly tried to establish a toehold on top of the plateau, but each time the Adoo had driven them off. In the autumn of 1971, the Regiment decided to make its move with a massive assault on the Jebel. This time, they intended to stay.

In any situation where the enemy hold the high ground, the key is to seize a foothold on the summit and establish a permanent presence. Then you can start going out aggressively, taking chunks of enemy territory and forcing them back from their forward defensive positions. This denies the other side freedom of movement and chips away at their morale. A bunch of guys who have been used to moving freely up and down the hill to carry out attacks are suddenly having to watch their backs for contacts. They start wondering where they're going to get hit next.

The assault on the plateau was taken straight from the Jebel Akhdar playbook. A series of aggressive patrols was conducted during the build-up to the op, scoping out potential routes up the plateau. A diversionary attack was also mounted to deceive the Adoo, with a force of SAS men and two firqats moving up the jebel to the east of a point known as Eagle's Nest, drawing the rebels away from the area of the main attack to the north.

On the night of 1–2 October 1971, the men of B and G Squadron (the fourth Sabre Squadron, formed in 1967 from the Guards Independent Parachute Company) prepared to set off on their battle march up the Jebel. They were joined by five firqats of tribal fighters, plus men from the Sultan's armed forces and mercenaries from Balochistan, a mountainous area in the south-east of Pakistan. (Balochis had fought in the service of the Sultan for more than two hundred years.) The total fighting force was over eight hundred men. In terms of manpower, this was the single biggest mission the Regiment had undertaken since the Second World War.

Their objective was a slab of high ground with an old SAF airstrip next to it known as 'Lympne', a few miles east of Jibjat.

From there, the attackers could bring in resupplies by air and then fan out across the plateau in small patrols, advancing to contact with the Adoo.

The weight the guys had to carry up the Jebel was shocking, even by SAS standards. In addition to their standard kit, rations, belts and rifles, each man was loaded down with belts of ammunition for the Troop's GPMG (General-Purpose Machine Gun). The GPMG, known as the Gimpy, is a belt-fed weapon, designed to be carried by a soldier on patrol or mounted on a tripod in sustained fire mode. It fires 7.62mm belt, a slightly bigger round than the standard 7.62x51mm bullet, and has a range of 1,800 metres when mounted. The weapon can also be fired from the hip or shoulder, or from a prone position with a mounted bipod. The Gimpy packs a serious punch, but it eats through ammunition at a furious rate.

Each soldier had to carry up to a thousand rounds of belt ammo: enough rounds to keep the GPMGs topped up in a prolonged contact. Half the ammo was stashed in the soldier's rucksack. The rest was slung across his front in bandoliers for easy access. A two-hundred-round belt of 7.62mm link weighs slightly over twelve pounds, which meant that the guys had to carry a total of sixty pounds of belt ammunition, on top of all their other kit. The total weight they humped up the Jebel that night was in excess of 130lbs.

The men carried the SLR as their primary weapon, having reverted back from the M16s favoured in the jungle. The M16 of the time was a fine weapon, but the men found it far less effective for long-range desert warfare. A good shot, armed with an SLR, can nail a target at six hundred metres. The smaller 5.56mm round fired by the M16 didn't travel as far and lacked the stopping power of the SLR's 7.62mm. In the desert, if you want to put someone down, you need a tool with a bit of bump behind it.

Staggering under the weight of their Bergens, the men began their ascent on the evening of 1 October. For many of the guys who took part, the climb was one of the hardest slogs of their lives. Several men collapsed with heat exhaustion; many of the firqat were so shattered they threw away their rations. By the time the first soldiers crested the top of the plateau, the sun was coming up fast and they had been on the march for more than twelve hours.

Reaching the top, they were confronted with a deserted plateau. The two thousand Adoo were nowhere to be seen. Just as in 1959, the Regiment's feinting attack had successfully deceived the rebels, drawing them away from the Lympne airstrip. Battling severe dehydration and tiredness, the SAS moved swiftly to consolidate their position, securing the ground so that the first air resupply drops could come in, delivering much-needed food, water and ammunition. Capturing that airhead was critical to the success of the mission. Without that facility, there's no way the soldiers would have been able to carry up all the supplies and equipment they needed to conduct further patrols across the Jebel.

At dawn the next day, the men set off across the plateau to clear the surrounding area of Adoo. They went out in small patrols, tooled up to the eyeballs with 7.62mm rifles, spoiling for a fight and backed up by overwatch teams equipped with GPMGs.

When used in a support role, the Gimpy is usually operated by a two-man team. One guy to feed the belt and direct the shooter on to targets, while the number one guy puts down the rounds, firing in short bursts of three or four rounds to prevent the barrel from heating up. If there's a stoppage, the number two guy will clear it. Every fifth round in the GPMG belt is a tracer, allowing the shooter to see where he's directing his fire. The most important thing is selecting the right ground so that the support team has got eyes on the action group and vice versa. It's pointless locating the Gimpy team on dead ground in front of a hill while the rest of the patrol moves over it. They must have a visual on the team at all times.

By mid-October, the patrols had established a new base at a place called 'White City', just a few miles from the main enemy stronghold at Wadi Darbat. Buildings were erected and a permanent airstrip was constructed, allowing a regular flow of supplies to come in from RAF helicopters and Short SC-7 Skyvan transport aircraft. To disrupt the enemy's communications and supply lines, a defensive position called the Leopard Line was constructed, reinforced with barbed wire and guarded by soldiers from the Sultan's armed forces.

Throughout this time the men encountered fierce opposition from the Adoo, running into heavy contacts on a daily basis. The rebels were testing the Regiment's strength, looking to see whether they'd stand and fight, or fall back as the SAF had done in the past. Several men were clipped during these skirmishes. One soldier was shot in the stomach when on patrol as lead scout. He survived, but others weren't as fortunate. An SAS sergeant, Steve Moores, was mortally wounded after getting hit during a contact.

Despite their stiff resistance, the Adoo's grip on the plateau steadily weakened. They were stubborn, but they weren't military tacticians and had failed to grasp one of the first lessons of warfare: always hold on to the high ground. Once you let the other side establish themselves on the top, you're in serious trouble.

The Adoo made a fatal mistake in failing to properly defend the Lympne airstrip. If they had caught the SAS on the hills, it's likely that they would have been too exhausted to put up a fight. Caught cold, the guys would have had no choice but to withdraw back down the slopes. As soon as they allowed the attackers through the front door and up onto the Jebel, it was game over.

These gains gave the SAS breathing space to focus on the hearts-and-minds aspect of Operation Storm. Villagers were treated for basic ailments. Supplies were distributed and civil aid projects were undertaken. More Adoo came forward, swelling the ranks of the firqats. An attempt to drive the rebels out of their refuge at Wadi Darbat failed, but this did nothing to alter the momentum of the war, which was now firmly behind the Sultan and his British allies. By the summer of 1972, the SAS had pushed out across the plateau, winning over the local tribes and driving the rebels further back. It was now a question of when, not if, the Adoo were finally defeated.

Backed into a corner, their ranks depleted by a steady flow of defectors to the other side, the rebels desperately needed a victory. By inflicting a crushing defeat on Qaboos and his British allies, the Adoo might yet reassert their authority over Dhofar, winning back the fear and respect of the Jebalis and demonstrating their superiority over the Sultan's forces. To guarantee victory they would attack the Sultan's forces at one of their weakest points, at a small military outpost on the southern coast.

The place was called Mirbat.

The tiny fishing village of Mirbat lies on the south fringes of Dhofar, on the shores of the Arabian Sea, forty miles to the east of Salalah and a few miles due south of the Jebel massif. The SAS had set up a training area at Mirbat the previous year, basing themselves in a two-storey mud-and-brick dwelling known as the BATT House while they trained up a unit of approximately forty firqat. In July 1972, the training team from B Squadron was coming to their end of their rotation at Mirbat and they were looking forward to going home.

There were eight men on the training team: Peter 'Snapper' Warne, Roger Cole, Bob Bennett, Austin 'Fuzz' Hussey, Tommy Tobin, the patrol medic, Captain Mike Kealy, their young Troop commander, and a pair of tough, stocky Fijians, Sekonaia 'Tak' Takavesi and Talaiasi 'Laba' Labalaba.

Fijians were first enlisted into the British Army ranks during a recruitment drive in the 1960s, when Fiji was still a Crown colony. More than two hundred men and a few women came forward, joining units such as the Royal Green Jackets (now amalgamated with several other units into The Rifles regiment), The King's Own Royal Borders and the Royal Ulster Rifles. Several then applied for, and passed, SAS Selection. The Fijians were big, tough and immensely capable, with a real presence. They liked to drink and joke around when not on ops, but in the heat of battle they were world-class soldiers.

A ninth soldier was at the BATT House on that fateful day: Jeff Taylor, an Irishman from G Squadron. The lads in G Squadron had completed their build-up training and were at the HQ at

Umm al Ghawarif, near Salalah, waiting to take over at Mirbat. Taylor had gone forward to take charge of the handover, with the men in B Squadron due to leave the next day. The mood in the BATT House was relaxed, which is how it usually is at the end of a long tour.

After four months of patrolling with the firqat and dealing with frequent rebel mortar attacks, the B Squadron guys were looking forward to sampling normal life again. Nothing fancy, just the basics: the simple pleasure of being in a safe environment, sleeping in a clean bed, enjoying a cold beer and a cooked meal. Sometimes it's the simple act of being some place where you don't have to think or worry about mortars raining down on you. Everyone looks forward to getting out of the military machine, even if it's only for a short while.

The SAS compound stood to the north of the village of Mirbat, separated by a shallow wadi. To the north of the BATT House stood another structure, the Wali's fort (the *Wali* is the regional governor), occupied by around thirty hardened fighters from the north of the country called Askars. A group of Dhofar Gendarmerie (DG) policemen were based in an ancient fort to the east of the BATT House, with a gun pit outside it housing a 25-pounder artillery gun, manned by an Omani gunner. Both the compound and the village were enclosed by a barbed-wire perimeter fence, with half a dozen gendarmerie based about a mile to the north, occupying a sangar on a small feature called the Jebel Ali.

Beyond that hill rose the steep slopes of the Jebel massif.

The Askars were armed with old .303 Lee-Enfield bolt-action rifles. The Regiment's firepower amounted to a .50 Browning (the 'relish'), a GPMG, an 81mm mortar and the 25-pounder, plus the soldiers' individual SLR rifles. In total, there were just under seventy defenders at Mirbat that morning: thirty Askars, another thirty or so DG men, and the nine SAS soldiers (most of the firqat had left to go out on patrol).

Shortly before first light on 19 July 1972, the first rebel mortars started raining down. Following their SOPs, the men went to their stand-to positions at their firing points around the compound, manning the 81mm mortar, GPMG and 'relish' Browning .50. Laba hurried across to the DG fort and took up his spot in the gun pit with the 25-pounder.

At that point the guys weren't overly worried. They had been getting hit quite regularly with sporadic mortar fire in the past few months and they knew what to expect. The Adoo would lay down a few stonks, the team would respond with mortars of their own, and the rebels would flee back into the hills. There was no reason to think that today would be any different.

Except that it was.

As the bombardment increased in intensity, the defenders realised this was more than the usual early-morning mortar attack. The team responded with a barrage of 81mm mortar fire, while the guys in the BATT House banged out an urgent message over the radio.

A short while later, as the first streaks of daylight fringed the horizon, the Adoo began their advance.

Unbeknown to the garrison, a force of about 250 Adoo had gathered on the Jebel, moving into position under cover of darkness. They had already wiped out the gendarmerie officers manning the outpost on the Jebel Ali, killing four of them before the others escaped. They were the first casualties of the Battle of Mirbat. By the end of the day, they would be joined by many more.

As the defenders looked on, wave upon wave of Adoo emerged from the mist and streamed down the hill and across the plain, charging towards the perimeter wire. Any faint hopes that the rebels might retreat after letting off a few mortars instantly evaporated. The nine SAS men were now facing the most desperate fight of their lives.

They opened up with everything they had, cutting the charging rebels down with savage bursts of gunfire and mortar rounds. The Adoo kept coming. Soon they had breached the perimeter wire and although they were hitting Mirbat from different angles, they appeared to be concentrating their fire on the DG fort to the east of the BATT House. Their initial plan was apparently to overrun the DG fort and seize the 25-pounder in the nearby gun pit, turning it on to the defenders elsewhere in the compound. If that happened, the SAS were done.

As the Adoo advanced towards the gun pit, Laba and the Omani gunner frantically worked the field gun, firing horizontally, obliterating targets at almost point-blank range.

The 25-pounder is a Second World War-era artillery piece that usually requires a five- or six-man crew to operate it. One guy to traverse the weapon. A second man to work the breech. One or two men to prepare the shells. Another guy to carry the shell over, ram it into the breech and close it. Plus someone to aim and fire. It's nearly impossible for one or two men to fire such a massive weapon. But through a combination of aggression, fighting madness and strength, Laba and his gunner managed to keep the Adoo at bay.

During a lull in the firefight, Laba's voice crackled over the radio, reporting that he had been hit in the jaw. The news alarmed Tak. The two Fijians were like brothers and Tak, sensing that Laba was in trouble, now raced over to the gun pit, braving a hail of Adoo gunfire. He reached the 25-pounder unscathed and found Laba in a bad way, with his jawline shot to pieces. The Omani gunner was also seriously wounded.

Tak and Laba now fought side-by-side, the latter continuing to fight in spite of his injury. The pair of them maintained a ferocious amount of fire, pumping out shell after shell at the enemy until Tak took a bullet to the shoulder and could no longer operate the field gun.

Since he couldn't work the 25-pounder alone, Laba now decided to abandon the weapon and make for the 60mm mortar situated to the east of the gun pit. With Tak covering him, Laba crawled out of the pit and headed for the mortar.

He never made it. A rebel bullet struck Laba in the throat, killing him instantly.

Tak was now pinned down in the gun pit with the Omani gunner. Badly injured, armed with only his 7.62mm rifle and facing a horde of Adoo swarming towards him, Tak wouldn't be able to hold out for very long before their position was overrun.

Meanwhile at the BATT House, Mike Kealy was increasingly concerned about the lack of news from the team at the 25-pounder. After a brief discussion with the others, he decided to head over to the gun pit himself to see what was going on. Tommy Tobin would accompany Kealy, stabilising any injured parties before the casevac helicopter could come in.

The two figures rushed forwards from the BATT House, with the guys on the GPMG and Browning providing covering fire. They soon came under intense fire from the Adoo. Both men reached the pit safely, but as Tobin tended to the wounded gunner a bullet struck him in the face.

The situation now looked extremely bleak. Two SAS men were down, a third was seriously wounded and the Adoo were continuing to push forward. Faced with this seemingly hopeless situation, the only thing the men could do was to keep fighting. Kealy and Tak held their position at the gun pit while the guys manning the Browning, GPMG and mortar continued to fire at the enemy, cutting down more and more Adoo.

This is where the SAS man comes into his own. Where he has the ability to fall back on his training and block out the raw fear that he's feeling, doing his job in the face of impossible odds. Never once during the battle did the defenders consider waving the white flag. It didn't even enter into their minds. They were either going to win or go down fighting.

Despite their best efforts, however, the men couldn't hold out for much longer. There were simply too many Adoo and the garrison was minutes from being overrun. At this point the only way to retrieve the situation was through air power.

The BAC Strikemaster jets now came to the garrison's rescue. Flying in from Salalah in conditions of very low cloud, the pilots showed incredible skill and bravery, risking their necks to come in close to the ground. Approaching from seaward, the jets strafed the Adoo with a devastating arsenal of 7.62mm cannon fire and air-to-ground rockets.

The arrival of the Strikemasters changed the outcome of the battle. As soon as the Adoo saw those jets coming in, they started to run for cover. The demoralising effect of air power on the enemy cannot be overstated. The human instinct is to drop everything and dive behind the nearest available cover. The SAS used a similar tactic when fighting ISIS in Iraq, calling in jets to do a fly-over of enemy-held positions. More often than not, the ISIS thugs would pack up and bug out.

The Adoo temporarily regrouped, but the next attack from the jets proved devastating, destroying the enemy's machine-gun emplacements and mortars. The Strikemasters were soon joined by reinforcements from G Squadron, who had helicoptered in from Umm al Ghawarif. Appearing on the horizon in a long line instead of the usual single-file patrol formation, their weapons drawn, the defenders initially mistook their colleagues for another force of Adoo. Their apprehension turned to relief as the men of G Squadron got stuck into the fight, putting down rounds on enemy positions.

Under the combined pressure of the extra Sabre Squadron and the Strikemasters, the surviving guerrillas bolted into the hills. They left behind at least eighty dead, although their total casualties were believed to be much higher. Half a dozen members of the DG had lost their lives in the battle. Labalaba was killed at Mirbat; Tobin died several weeks later in hospital. Tak had been seriously wounded, along with the Omani gunner.

The Battle of Mirbat proved to be the turning point in the Dhofar War. The Adoo had suffered a catastrophic defeat, losing half their strength. Perhaps just as damagingly, they had lost face among the tribes of the Jebel. Anyone who had been sitting on the fence, unsure of which side to back, now knew the truth: the SAS had the measure of the Adoo.

Although the conflict dragged on for another four years, the rebels' defeat was inevitable. The Sultan's forces, backed up by the firqats, the SAS and brigades of Iranian troops, continued to push the Adoo back towards the border.

In October 1975, the Adoo's supply lines were finally cut off. A plan had been drawn up to capture a piece of high ground near the Yemeni border, with a small SAS team launching a diversionary raid from a mountaintop believed to be encircled by rebel positions. But when the guys discovered that the route had been left unguarded, the plan was ditched and reinforcements were swiftly brought forward. A heavy firefight ensued before the SAS drove the enemy back across the border.

Two months later the rebels' final remaining stronghold was seized. The Sultan was now free to concentrate on delivering a massive programme of civil development, building schools and hospitals, laying roads and improving the water supply. The last Regiment training team left Oman the following September.

The transformation of the country in the years since has been astonishing. Today Oman is a thriving modern state, unrecognisable from the Old Testament backwater of the 1960s. In 2010, a UN development report ranked Oman as the most improved country in the world over the past forty years. None of this would have been possible without the actions of the SAS at Mirbat.

Some casual observers may question why the training team didn't plant claymores on the dead ground surrounding the compound. Rigging the area with explosives would have surely inflicted a high number of casualties on the Adoo. It might even have stopped them from coming perilously close to overrunning the defenders.

It's an interesting thought, but it's possible the garrison didn't have access to claymore mines during the campaign. Even if they did, they may have been understandably reluctant to use them. They were operating in an area with civilians, and there's always the risk that someone will wander into a rigged area and blow themselves up, undermining the team's painstaking hearts-and-minds efforts. Whatever the explanation, they would have had a very good reason.

The heroism of the Storm veterans has never been fully recognised. Mike Kealy was awarded the DSO, Tak received the DCM, Bob Bennett got the MM, while Laba was only given a posthumous Mention in Dispatches – the lowest form of gallantry medal that a soldier can receive. The others were never decorated.

Ken Connor, in his excellent history of the Regiment, *Ghost Force*, makes the point that, although many of the guys who took part in Operation Storm received medals, 'none was gazetted until the campaign was over. We weren't even given the General Service Medal – the campaign medal – until well into the conflict . . . the award was then devalued when RAF base personnel were given the same medal.' This policy of devaluing medals has continued throughout the Regiment's history.

When I made it out of Iraq, I was sent down to Abu Dhabi to recover. A team of guys from the Regiment was based there at the time, training up an anti-terrorist group. The justification for this was that the Emirates had provided the SAS with a facility with a runway for the Gulf War and to pay them back, a twelve-man team had been tasked with schooling their guys in counter-terrorism tactics. These men were later awarded the same campaign medal as the guys who were out in Iraq on patrol.

That's not to say that the Abu Dhabi team didn't deserve some recognition for their efforts – I've no doubt that they were doing an important job. But to give them the same medal as the lads who were fighting behind enemy lines didn't seem right. It devalues the achievements of others.

This is further undermined by the naked enthusiasm with which a small number of officers pursue medals during their careers in the Regiment. One SAS officer attended a briefing not long after I'd escaped from Iraq. His first question was, 'Will I get the Campaign Medal because I'm down here?' This was at a time when a lot of blokes from the patrols were still missing.

Every guy in the Regiment knows someone who has been awarded a medal they didn't deserve. I personally know of one officer who was awarded a Queen's Gallantry medal for a successful operation that involved the killing of a high-value target overseas. That particular officer wasn't even in the country in question when the operation went down. He was back in Hereford at the time, enjoying a drink in a local pub.

The professional soldier has no interest in gong-hunting. That isn't why you join the Regiment, and if it is, you won't last very long. But there is a minority of individuals who have one eye on their future careers and know the weight that decorations carry. Medals open doors. They lead to promotions, and potentially well-paid jobs on Civvy Street once that person's military service comes to an end. I never once thought on the job, how can I get a medal out of this? No SAS man worth his salt thinks like that. But a clever few think differently.

In my opinion, the medals system in the British Army is broken. It is too easy for officers to scoop up gongs, in some cases even writing up their own citations, while the efforts of the other rankers often go unrecognised. Men like Talaiasi Labalaba.

There has been an active campaign to get Laba a posthumous Victoria Cross for his actions at Mirbat. To my mind, there's no question that he fully deserves the medal. To operate that 25-pounder field gun almost single-handedly, knowing that he was probably going to die, took exceptional bravery. Even more so when you consider that he continued to fire the gun even after getting his jaw blown off. The fact that he was only given a Mention in Dispatches is a travesty.

In its own small way, the SAS has tried to recognise Labalaba's actions. Some years ago, the Sergeant's Mess voted to build a statue of Laba outside the mess at Hereford, commemorating his actions at Mirbat. Several years later, a second memorial was unveiled by Prince Harry at the international airport in Nadi, western Fiji. Whether or not Laba ever receives the VC, his actions will never be forgotten by all those who have served in the Regiment.

CHAPTER 12

Rules of Engagement

Northern Ireland, 1969–82

A month after the Sultan of Oman declared the end of the rebellion in Dhofar, the Regiment was being committed to a dangerous new conflict much closer to home. At the end of 1975 and the beginning of 1976, a spate of sectarian violence had swept through the fiercely nationalist area of South Armagh in Northern Ireland. This culminated in an attack on the evening of 5 January 1976, when gunmen flagged down a minibus near the village of Kingsmill and opened fire on the passengers. Ten Protestants were killed, and another was severely wounded. The attackers spared the life of the only Catholic after telling him to run away.

In London, pressure grew on the government to take control of the deteriorating security situation. Two days after the Kingsmill massacre the Prime Minister, Harold Wilson, publicly declared that an element of 22 SAS would be deployed to the area. The decision to send in the Regiment had nothing to do with Hereford. It was politically motivated, taken by a government desperate to show that it was getting a grip on events in the province.

A few weeks later, having barely caught their breath after coming back from Operation Storm, the first soldiers from D Squadron were on the ground in Northern Ireland.

They were about to be plunged into a much murkier, more sinister conflict than the one they had successfully waged against the Adoo.

It was not the first time the SAS had operated in Northern Ireland. They had originally been sent in a few years earlier to the Mourne Mountains area, close to the Irish border, primarily on intelligence-gathering ops as part of Operation Banner, the code-name for the deployment of British Armed Forces in Northern Ireland that would continue until 2007. There wasn't anything like the same level of secrecy surrounding the Regiment back then and the guys had roamed freely through the Irish country-side, cutting around in their long-wheelbase Land Rovers and openly wearing their berets.

Now they were returning to a much more hostile environment.

When they had first been deployed, the British soldiers had been welcomed by the Catholic community they had been sent to protect. But by 1976, the province had descended into a mael-strom of violence. The parliament at Stormont had been suspended, British troops regularly came under attack and there were running gun battles, sniping attacks, bombings and riots on an almost daily basis.

During the mid-1970s, with the Regiment fully committed to the conflict in Oman, they were unable to maintain any large-scale presence in Ulster. They did send over a few small teams, however, playing an influential role in the army's intelligence-gathering efforts. This included assisting in the formation of an elite unit, variously called 14th Intelligence Company, 14 Int or the Special Reconnaissance Unit (SRU).

Until 1973, the Army's covert intelligence-gathering efforts had been carried out by the Military Reconnaissance Force (MRF), a notorious group made up of volunteers from the infantry ranks. Operating undercover, dressed in civvies and carrying pistols and submachine guns, MRF recruits were trained to go out in unmarked cars, running surveillance jobs and hunting for terrorists on the streets. MRF agents were also running a handful of Republican terrorists who had been successfully turned by the Army. Known as 'Freds', they supplied information and identified potential targets to their handlers.

Although the MRF had enjoyed some success, they were also involved in several disturbing incidents, including a shooting at a bus stop on the Falls Road in Belfast that severely wounded three innocent men. The MRF was disbanded in 1973 and succeeded the following year by a brand-new surveillance unit, which would later become known as 14th Intelligence Company. With the new unit came a shift in tactics. The focus was shifted away from aggressive patrolling towards more passive intelligence-gathering missions. Volunteers for the new unit were recruited from all branches of the Army, Royal Navy and Royal Air Force. At first only men were allowed to join, but servicewomen were later invited to apply as well.

The SAS was closely involved in the creation of 14 Int. They helped to set up the training course, provided the instructors and supplied the officers for the senior command posts. The new company had three detachments, one in Derry, another based in Armagh and a third in Belfast. Everyone knew it simply as 'the Det'.

The Det provided vital information to the SAS, the security services and Special Branch, the undercover unit within the Royal Ulster Constabulary (RUC). Dressing like locals, they operated in fiercely hostile environments and carried out surveillance on enemy targets, as well as running their own intelligence-gathering ops. By the mid-1980s the unit had its own command structure, led by officers who had previously completed the Det selection course, and in 1987 they came under the directive of Director Special Forces, who was also responsible for the SAS and the SBS.

The Det course was held at the army training base in Pontrilas, several miles outside Hereford, where the SAS has maintained a large training facility since the 1970s. Initially, a group of instructors from the Regiment's Counter-Revolutionary Warfare (CRW) Wing ran the course. The Det later supplied their own instructors, former operators who had done the business and could pass on their knowledge to the young bucks.

The men and women in the Det were tasked with carrying out some of the most dangerous work in Northern Ireland, sometimes without any backup. As a result, their course had to be made as realistic as possible. Volunteers studied surveillance techniques, how to put in urban and rural OPs and how to blend in on the streets, what kind of clothes and make-up to wear. A lot of work was done on close-quarter CQB training, unarmed combat and resistance to interrogation, along with advanced vehicle drills such as doing J-turns and driving at high speeds through built-up urban areas.

Det operators had to be highly perceptive, with razor-sharp memory recall and the ability to disappear into the background at a moment's notice. Students were subjected to a number of mind games and tests such as Kim's Game, named after a test in the Rudyard Kipling novel, *Kim*. This exercise involves taking a cluster of unusual items and placing them under a blanket. The blanket is pulled back and the individual has a limited amount of time to take in everything in front of them. Then the objects are covered over again, and the student must remember everything they have just seen.

Other skills were taught as well: students learned to memorise car number plates by observing their wing mirrors, how to remember what someone they passed in the street was wearing. They were schooled in the arts of covert photography and how to move without drawing attention to themselves, which isn't easy when you're carrying around a radio, weapons and tracking devices. By the end of the course, the student knew everything there was to know about operating as the ultimate grey man or woman.

Later on, SAS guys deploying to Northern Ireland were required to take the Det course as well. This wasn't a popular decision, mainly because the skills taught on the course were used for surveillance tasks, whereas the Regiment lads wanted to be in the thick of the action. Learning the secrets of following someone on foot wasn't what they had signed up for.

The female operators in the Det were invaluable assets to the unit. They had the ability to get into places that no one else could. One servicewoman, Charlie, was a lethal shot with a devil-may-care attitude. If someone came up to her on the streets and challenged her, she wouldn't bolt. Instead she'd front it up. 'Yeah, I'm English, so what? I'm over here to visit a friend I was at uni with,' she'd say. 'What the hell's your problem?'

Another female operator, Laura, would go around dangerous areas of Belfast pretending to be a lecturer at Cambridge, doing research for an academic book on the Troubles. The IRA always fell for it.

After two years of service in the Det, the brightest female operators were often selected to join 22 SAS, attached to a covert unit within the Regiment. Det servicewomen attached to the SAS had two roles. One or two worked with the training team for 14 Int, as instructors. The others were part of the covert unit, which provided manpower and skillsets for operations overseen by the security services.

The servicewomen in the Det were confident, they were highly trained and they had gained deep operational experience. In the field, they could be partnered up with a male operator for undercover surveillance duties. With the right training, they had the ability to blend into almost any environment. Nobody would spare them a second glance. Young couples don't attract attention in the way that, for example, three blokes in a car might. It's the perfect cover.

Following Harold Wilson's announcement, D Squadron was deployed to a secret location in South Armagh. Operations were initially restricted to foot patrols and running covert OPs in the border area. Provisional IRA operatives had been crossing the border at will, smuggling arms and explosives across to carry out attacks in the north before slipping back over to the safety of the Republic. It was the Regiment's job to stop them.

The Troubles presented a unique challenge to the SAS. Prior to their deployment, they had only limited experience of counter-terrorism operations, mainly on training exercises and on the streets of Aden with the Keeni-Meeni patrols. They had spent the past six years engaged in a classic counter-insurgency war in

Dhofar, fighting against an opponent that attacked them in open battle. Now they had to adapt to a new way of soldiering, fighting against terrorists who enjoyed the sympathy of large sections of the local community and support from overseas in the shape of weapons and funds.

They also had to deal with the political side of the conflict.

Like all other British Army forces operating in the province, the SAS was subject to the rule of law. All soldiers were issued with a carry-around document called the 'Yellow Card', which gave strict details covering the rules of engagement. Soldiers were only permitted to discharge their weapons as a last resort, where no form of arrest was possible, and in a situation where the terrorist presented an immediate danger to the life of the soldier or those they had a duty to protect. Wherever possible a soldier had to issue a challenge by shouting, 'Army!' three times, followed by, 'Stop, or I'll open fire!'

Aside from the obvious difficulties of consulting a piece of paper in the middle of a firefight, there were two major problems with the rules of engagement in Northern Ireland. First, they placed an immense burden on the shoulders of the SAS operator. The Yellow Card rules meant that every time a soldier went out to do a house clearance or to recce an arms dump, that guy was putting himself in a situation where the slightest mistake or misunderstanding might result in him being put up for murder.

Secondly, the Yellow Card conveniently ignored the fact that the IRA weren't playing by the same rules. The terrorists were able to operate freely, planting bombs and ambushing targets without having to consult a list of rules as long as their arm.

In many ways, the Regiment was engaged in two conflicts in the province. One was against the terrorists. The other was a political war, waged against the SAS by politicians and sections of the media, ready to pounce on the slightest infraction and portray the soldiers as an out-of-control band of remorseless killers.

The guys had to learn to tread very carefully, operating under the strictest controls, conforming not only to the rule of law but to public opinion. It was a world away from the battles they had fought in Dhofar.

There was also a degree of hostility, especially early on, towards the Regiment from the RUC's Special Branch. They didn't want to see British Special Forces on the streets of Northern Ireland and viewed the Regiment as a direct threat to their authority and power. This is a common attitude among police forces, one that the SAS would encounter again in 1980 during the Iranian Embassy Siege.

Not long after their arrival, the difficulties faced by the SAS in the province were brought sharply into focus by an incident that would threaten relations between London and Dublin.

On 5 May 1976, in an incident recounted by Tony Geraghty in *Who Dares Wins*, two plain-clothes SAS men driving a civilian car were apprehended by the Irish police force, at a checkpoint a few hundred yards into the Republic. The two men claimed that they had crossed the border by mistake after getting lost on the map and expected to be sent back to the north. 'The affair now escalated into political farce,' Geraghty writes.

A few hours later, half a dozen other SAS soldiers were stopped at the same checkpoint, driving in two vehicles and carrying several personal weapons. They had set out to look for their muckers after they had failed to radio in. The six men were placed under arrest and, along with the others, were taken down to Dublin for questioning. The Irish authorities now had their hands on eight Regiment operators, plus a number of weapons.

The incident soon turned into an international crisis. Amid speculation about what the men had really been up to across the border, the soldiers were released on bail and returned the next year to Ireland to stand trial. All eight men were cleared of the charge of taking weapons into the country with the intent to endanger life. The soldiers were fined £100 apiece for bringing weapons into the Republic without the proper licences.

This was an embarrassing episode for the Regiment, but it also illustrated the problems they were facing in Ulster. Operating in a complex environment where they had to deal with various elements of the police and the rule of law, their ability to engage the terrorists was severely restricted. Whitehall had sent in the SAS to get to grips with the IRA – and had promptly clipped their wings by binding them tightly to the rules of engagement. Every time they went out on operations, they were wearing a political straitjacket.

In 1977, SAS operations were expanded to cover the rest of the province. One Troop remained at the location in South Armagh, another was sent up to Londonderry, with a third section based in Belfast. The fourth Troop operated at the discretion of the Commander Land Forces (CLF). Throughout this time the Regiment continued to disrupt the IRA, carrying out active patrols and covert OPs.

Rural OPs lasted for days or even weeks. The men were on hard routine, usually working in pairs in twenty-four-hour shifts. Food was boil-in-the-bag rations, eaten cold. They urinated in plastic bags and wrapped excrement in clingfilm. All comms was done through coded voice, with locations referred to by code-names. This was to prevent the operation being compromised: the IRA was known to monitor traffic over the airwaves.

At the end of his shift, the soldier would walk back several miles to a prearranged RV at the side of a road. A car would bowl along, he'd jump in and another man would get out and take over OP duties. The fresh guy would then get briefed by the second man at the OP, telling him what had happened, what the routine was and what to look out for. In another twenty-four hours that second guy rotated out of the OP and was replaced by another bloke, who'd get briefed by the man who came in the previous day. That meant there was always someone on the ground who had been there for a length of time, so the new guy could quickly be brought up to speed.

In some cases, a job involved acting on intelligence that a local politician, reservist soldier or police officer had been targeted for assassination. The SAS would approach the individual's house at night so that they weren't spotted by any nosy neighbours or terrorists recceing the property. A routine was then established inside and around the house, with OPs positioned according to the layout, covering vantage points and the most likely approaches for the hit team. The guys would work out where to keep the family safe, take up their respective positions and wait for the enemy to attack.

Soldiers carried a variety of weapons. In the late 1970s, they were equipped with Browning 9mm pistols, Ingram MAC-10 Machine Pistols and M16 rifles. In the 1980s, the guys switched to the Heckler & Koch G3 7.62mm assault rifle. They also used the compact variant, the HK53, which has a shorter barrel. Shotguns were deployed, but only if they were doing a house bust and they needed to blow the hinges off a door.

Action was very much the exception to the rule in Northern Ireland. In many cases, the SAS might be waiting for days or weeks in a particular location, without any sign of the enemy.

This wasn't always down to bad intel. The IRA's Active Service Units (ASUs) were extremely cautious by nature, and if they had a sniff that something was amiss, they'd pull out of the job. It might be something as simple as the terrorists not liking the look of a civilian in a passing car. They would get spooked and think, not tonight.

On other occasions, the attackers might have stopped at a bar on the way to the attack for a quick pint. If it was nasty weather outside, they'd maybe decide to leave the job for another night and get drunk instead. Meanwhile, the SAS soldiers were lying in position at the OP, waiting to make an arrest, only for the terrorist to fail to show up. Naturally, this was a source of great frustration among the lads.

But the Regiment is very patient. It's ingrained into the nature of the guys. They're prepared to wait. That persistence helped them to bring down a number of high-level players, but it wasn't long before the SAS found itself in the headlines for the wrong reasons.

In July 1978, a teenage boy, John Boyle, stumbled upon an IRA arms dump in a graveyard in County Antrim. Mark Urban recounts the story in his excellent history of the SAS in Northern Ireland, *Big Boys' Rules*: 'Secreted beneath the slab [of a fallen headstone] was an Armalite rifle, a pistol and other terrorist paraphernalia. John rushed home to his father, Con Boyle, who immediately phoned the police.' An SAS team was duly sent in to stake out the cemetery. The following morning, John Boyle returned to the site, unaware that the SAS soldiers were concealed in an OP. Urban notes that the police had called the boy's parents, warning them to stay away from the cache, but it was too late. As he went to take a closer look, perhaps gripped by a teenage boy's natural inquisitiveness, he picked up one of the rifles. Two of the soldiers then opened fire, killing Boyle.

Both men were arrested and went on trial for murder. Although they were later acquitted, one of the soldiers was criticised by the judge as an unreliable witness.

Around this time, there was a strategic rethink over the SAS's role in the province. The Regiment now took a step back from offensive operations. Going forward, they would adopt a more reactive approach, geared towards gathering information.

Instead of rotating Sabre Squadrons in and out of the country, a Specialised Military Unit (SMU) would be deployed in Northern Ireland. If there was a big job on and the SMU needed more guys, they could call on reinforcements from Hereford in the shape of the counter-terrorism team (which will be discussed in more detail in Chapter 14).

In 1980, this new SMU was brought together with the Det under the Intelligence and Security Group (Northern Ireland), otherwise known as 'The Group', led by a single commanding officer. The creation of the Group ushered in a period of closer cooperation between the SAS and the Det (although the latter still ran their own ops alongside their work with the Regiment and the various security services).

This was to mark a major turning point in the way the Regiment operated in Northern Ireland. The plan was for the guys in the SMU to spend an extended period of time in the province and receive specialist training before deployment to

Northern Ireland, giving them the tools they needed to hit the ground running. This was a great opportunity to brush up on their skillsets, doing exercises involving OP tactics, surveillance drills and advanced driving.

For the next few years, the guys in the SMU were essentially restricted to intelligence-gathering duties. This involved running OPs on suspected locations, finding out who the IRA's main players were, where they lived, what cars they drove, who they associated with – and what jobs they were planning. The aim was to prosecute terrorists in the courts, through the painstaking collection of evidence.

Throughout this time, 14th Intelligence Company and the SAS worked hand-in-glove. When doing operations together, the Det would act as the forward observation team on the ground, following terrorists and running surveillance, building up a comprehensive picture of the situation before handing over to the soldiers to make a hard arrest.

The Regiment also suffered its first loss in the Troubles at this time, when an eight-man patrol was ordered to investigate a suspected weapons cache at a property on the Antrim Road in north Belfast.

The patrol arrived at the address and stormed inside, unaware that the terrorists were in fact holed up in the house next door. As they went in, one of the gunmen opened fire with an M60 7.62mm machine gun, killing the patrol's commander, Captain Herbert Westmacott, as he stepped out from behind the patrol vehicle. The shooter and the other seven members of the terrorist gang eventually surrendered to the security forces.

CHAPTER 13

The Group

Northern Ireland, 1983–97

In 1983, the Regiment finally went proactive in Ulster.

A combination of the IRA carrying out larger attacks and several controversial operations involving the police had resulted in Whitehall realising what every guy in the Regiment had known all along: the SAS was better placed to take on the Provisional IRA than any of the less highly trained green army units or police officers. Based on high-grade intelligence and working with their colleagues in the Det, the guys were now given the freedom to take on a more active role in Northern Ireland.

This did not mean that the SAS had licence to operate outside the law. Far from it. They knew that everything had to be done cleanly, with no room for error. Every time they went out on a job, they were fully aware that they were putting their necks on the line – and the reputation of the Regiment. They were under almost constant pressure from all sides: sections of the media, Special Branch investigators, and from their own government. The soldiers never felt the top brass had their backs and knew they would be hung out to dry if they found themselves in trouble.

Whenever they were involved in a shooting, no matter how justifiable, the SAS invariably took the blame. It meant that on any operation, everything had to be in perfect order. Even the number of shots fired was a matter of intense debate.

The politicians did not like to hear that a terrorist had been shot twenty or thirty times in a contact. If a fatal shooting was unavoidable, they preferred 'clean kills', with terrorists shot with one or two precisely aimed rounds. From the soldier's perspective it made no difference whether you put two rounds into a target or twenty. The end result is the same: that person is no longer an immediate threat to the safety of yourself or those you have a duty to protect. But officials were concerned about briefing the media and stating that, 'So-and-so was shot twenty-four times.' The practical difficulties of firing at a very small area of a moving target, at ranges of up to a hundred metres, often at night or in conditions of low visibility, were of no interest to Westminster.

There was never any 'shoot-to-kill' policy for the Regiment in Northern Ireland. Shoot-to-kill is a meaningless phrase. An SAS soldier will only open fire at a target if he believes that his life or the lives of his colleagues are in imminent danger, and an arrest is not possible. In that situation, you're not shooting to hurt the enemy's feelings or to wound him. Your primary aim is to neutralise the terrorist before further loss of life occurs.

Working under tight political and legal restrictions, the SMU acted upon information fed to them from the various security agencies. Usually this came from Special Branch, via a liaison officer acting as an interlink. The liaison, a Troop officer, did a two-year posting in the province, spending most of his time down at Lisburn with the RUC.

When a potential job came up, the liaison would call in the guys and brief them. Then Special Branch would come in and brief them in detail about the crime that was about to be perpetrated. This might be anything from a bomb plot to a tip-off about a member of the public who was about to get abducted or killed. Attacks that weren't imminent would be passed over to one of the surveillance or intelligence agencies, such as the Det.

For urgent jobs, the Det would be brought in to focus on the terrorists planning the attack. Once a target location had been identified, the SAS would then carry out a detailed recce of the area, moving around it in 360-degree profile, like a fox stalking a chicken coop. The guys would be looking at approaches to the target, dead ground, mounting positions and escape routes for the terrorists.

Once the recce was completed, the team would establish a static OP and wait for the terrorists to show up. Then, under the rules of engagement, they would seek to make a hard arrest, resulting in either the capture or death of the enemy.

Very rarely did the soldiers take part in unplanned contacts. It was almost always the case that they were given intelligence on, for example, a particular weapons cache or IRA target.

If a target was likely to be hit on their way to work, or as they went about their daily business, the SAS might attempt to intercept the terrorists and make a mobile arrest. Tom Read, in his memoir *Freefall*, describes an apparent mobile arrest operation in Dungannon in October 1984. An IRA hit squad had reportedly targeted a major in the Ulster Defence Regiment (UDR). The Regiment was tasked with apprehending the terrorists before they could strike, says Read. A soldier bearing a passing resemblance to the major would take the man's place in the target vehicle.

On the morning of the operation the IRA hit squad, driving a stolen van, came up behind the target vehicle. According to Read's account of the operation, as the SAS moved to intercept the terrorists, the latter opened fire on the soldiers in one of the cars. Shots were exchanged and a high-speed chase ensued before the ASU (Active Service Unit) team managed to give their pursuers the slip. The SAS later learned that an innocent man had been killed during the operation. The man had been driving out of a timber yard when he was hit by a stray round as the soldiers returned fire at the van.

Two months later, in December 1984, the SAS was alerted to an apparent IRA bomb plot. Mark Urban states that the plan involved planting a large bomb in a culvert outside a restaurant near Kesh, in County Fermanagh. The plan was to seemingly lure security forces into a deadly trap – known as a 'come-on' attack – by making a telephone call to police stating that blast incendiaries had been planted in the restaurant. 'As the security forces arrived at the scene,' Urban says, 'the bomb would be detonated.'

Reacting to information that had been passed to them, seven SAS soldiers were sent out in a pair of civilian cars on an urgent intercept mission. According to Tom Read in *Freefall*, the men were unaware of the bomb in the culvert at this point.

Spotting a van matching the description they had been given, the two civilian cars blocked off the road at both ends. Conditions were appalling: Read writes that freezing fog had 'cut visibility to only a few feet.' There are differing accounts of what happened next. In Read's version of events, he states that the soldiers at one of the roadblocks heard someone approaching them through the fog. One of the soldiers reportedly shouted at the man to halt, but when the figure 'realised his mistake, he turned to run'.

Lance-Corporal Al Slater launched a flare, says Read, but at that moment, two terrorists sprang up from behind a hedgerow and opened fire, fatally wounding the soldier.

It was Slater's terrible misfortune to have stopped the vehicle very near to where a group of IRA men were apparently preparing the detonation point for the bomb in the culvert. Harry McCallion, in his account of the operation, states that the runaway was captured but shot dead after he panicked and tried to flee. Two other men were later arrested in the Republic. The body of a fourth man was discovered several days later, having drowned in a river during his escape.

By far the most successful and widely reported operation of this time took place in May 1987, in the small village of Loughgall, North Armagh.

According to the many published accounts of this operation, British intelligence had learned of a plot by two ASUs from the IRA's East Tyrone Brigade to carry out an attack on the Loughgall police station. A force of soldiers from the SAS had moved into position at the target location some hours before, including reinforcements from Hereford.

On the evening of Friday 8 May, the terrorists made their move.

Mark Urban provides a vivid account of the operation in *Big Boys' Rules*. Eight men from two ASUs approached the station in a stolen Toyota van and a JCB excavator they had lifted from a farm several miles away. A very large fuse-bomb was stowed on the front bucket of the excavator, hidden beneath a load of debris. The IRA planned to use the JCB to smash through the security gate before detonating the bomb. The three men on the JCB would be supported by five IRA gunmen riding in the stolen Toyota.

As the SAS team looked on, the van pulled up very close to the police station while the JCB accelerated on towards the security gate. Then everything happened very quickly. The rear doors on the van flew open and three IRA gunmen piled out, putting down rounds on the station with their assault rifles while the crew on the JCB crashed through the gate.

At that moment, the soldiers opened up. 'The IRA men around the van were caught in a withering deluge of rounds,' Urban writes. At the same time, the three men riding on the JCB, having lit the fuse wire attached to the bomb, ditched the excavator and sprinted back towards the van.

Moments later, the bomb kicked off. The deafening shockwave tore apart one end of the building, reducing it to a smouldering mass of rubble and twisted metal.

In total, eight terrorists were killed. The Loughgall operation demonstrated that the Regiment was capable of giving the IRA a bloody nose. But it again highlighted the dangers of using hardware around civilians.

Two brothers had been driving home from work when the firefight erupted. As they attempted to reverse away, SAS soldiers opened fire on their vehicle, killing Anthony Hughes and severely wounding his brother Oliver.

No challenge had been issued. Neither man had anything to do with the IRA or any terrorist organisation. They were completely innocent bystanders, who had been tragically caught up in events at the police station.

It seems likely that the soldiers had wrongly identified the brothers as IRA men. They had been fixing up a lorry and were both dressed in boiler suits, like the terrorists. The shooting of the two innocent brothers cast a shadow over what was otherwise a successful operation.

For the men in the SMU, life could be stressful and frustrating at times. They could never truly relax or let their guard down. There were safe areas where soldiers were free to go out for a drink, but even then they had to exercise caution. There were rules for dating local women, for example. If a lad met someone, he'd get their details, go to Special Branch and get them to do a background check. If that person checked out, the soldier was authorised to see her again.

The cities were, in many ways, more difficult for a soldier to operate in than the countryside. In the sticks there is always plenty of cover available. Urban environments are a different story: you can't simply disappear into the ground, and there are potential traps lurking everywhere. You might be driving around, following a target, and they could lead you into a dead-end or other cars might block you in. It's a much harder place to soldier. That's where the Det men and women came into their own. They had an amazing ability to get around and track people in a densely populated area, without getting spotted.

The guys were never under any illusions about the risks they were taking. But one horrifying incident served as a grim reminder of the fate awaiting any SAS soldier or Det operative unlucky enough to be taken alive.

On 19 March 1988, Corporal Derek Wood and Corporal David Howes accidentally drove their Volkswagen Passat into a funeral cortège for a murdered IRA member making its way down the Andersonstown Road. The signallers had left Lisburn earlier that day without checking out at the ops room. Consequently, no one else knew that they were on the ground.

It is vitally important for any soldier to check out before going on an operation or a patrol. Doing this avoids unnecessary blue-on-blue incidents, and it lets everyone else know that you're on the ground. Which means that, if you run into trouble, the security forces know where you are and can send in the SAS to rescue you. It's also an opportunity for the intelligence officer to update the patrol before they head out, warning them about any no-go areas such as covert OPs.

It is a statement of fact that, if the signallers had checked out with the ops room before heading out, the intelligence officer would have told them to avoid the area around the funeral procession. All other security personnel had been ordered to stay well clear and as a result there was no backup in the vicinity.

As they strayed into the procession, Howes and Wood panicked and reversed, but quickly found themselves blocked in by black minicabs. The crowd, a mix of mourners, Sinn Fein stewards and IRA members, at first feared that the soldiers were a paramilitary hit team. Days earlier, a loyalist gunman, Michael Stone, had attacked a funeral party at Milltown Cemetery, killing three people. Tensions were running high and the men now found themselves surrounded by an angry throng.

Corporal Wood drew his Browning pistol and fired a warning shot, briefly scattering the mob. Things then got even worse for the two men as Wood suffered a stoppage. The magazine release catch on the Browning is located very close to the pistol grip. It's easy to accidentally depress it with your thumb, causing the clip to slide fractionally out of the magazine well. The clip won't fully eject, but it'll slide out far enough to result in a stoppage. In this case, it was fatal.

The figures in the crowd rushed forward again, realising that Wood couldn't fire any more rounds. The signallers were rapidly overpowered, dragged from their vehicle and thrown over a fence into a nearby park, the metal railings tearing through the calf muscle of one of the men. They were stripped, searched and beaten by their attackers before being thrown into a waiting taxi. Then they were stabbed repeatedly in the back of the cab, driven to a waste ground and murdered.

One of the corporals had been carrying an ID card in his wallet marked with 'Herford'. Their attackers mistakenly read this as 'Hereford' and thought that Howes and Wood were with the Regiment. In fact, 'Herford' is the name of a town in north-west Germany where a British Army base was located.

The IRA knew that the SAS carried tracking devices and transponders to mark their locations when going out on patrol. It's possible that they strip-searched the two signallers with this fact in mind. Although neither man had ever served with 22 SAS, it was obvious what the enemy would do if they ever got their hands on a pair of Regiment guys.

Sometimes the risks came from your own side. Army and police checkpoints were particularly hazardous. A young, inexperienced soldier manning a roadblock might see a bunch of SAS guys rolling up in an unmarked car, plain-clothed and tooled up, and reach the wrong conclusion. On one occasion a two-man team on the way back from a job was waiting in traffic at a checkpoint when the RUC sergeant up ahead made a move for his weapon, fearing that he was looking at a paramilitary hit squad. Thankfully the soldiers managed to convince the sergeant of their credentials before he caused a blue-on-blue.

On the other hand, a sentry waving through an SAS team could easily blow their cover. The guys would have to talk to the soldier in charge, show them their military ID and explain who they were. The soldiers would tell them, 'Listen, take us out of the car. Search us, do everything you've done to the other people passing through. Don't treat us any differently.'

Almost a year after Loughgall, the SAS was involved in a widely publicised and controversial operation in Gibraltar. Codenamed Operation Flavius, it quickly became one of the most talked-about incidents in the long history of the Regiment's involvement in the Troubles.

The episode has been extensively documented over the years. Anthony Kemp, among others, relates the affair in his classic history of the modern SAS, *Savage Wars of Peace*. The previous autumn, British intelligence had learned that a pair of IRA terrorists were poised to fly to Malaga. Another IRA team was known to have earlier cached weapons and explosives in the same place. The location is significant: Malaga is only a ninety-minute car journey to the crossing point to Gibraltar.

By early 1988, the experts were quite sure that the IRA plan involved detonating a car bomb during the changing of the guard ceremony that took place each week on the Rock. In addition, Kemp writes, there was 'disquiet about the fact that the IRA had perfected a remote-controlled detonating device that could be activated by pushing a button in a coat pocket'.

On 3 March, believing that an attack was imminent, a section of SAS men from the Special Projects (SP) counter-terrorism team flew out to Gibraltar. They were given orders to provide military assistance to the resident Police Commissioner, aiding in the arrest of the terrorists. The next day, 4 March, the two IRA members landed in Malaga and rendezvoused with a third operative, a woman. At this point the Spanish police managed to lose track of the three terrorists, although the Spanish authorities have consistently denied this.

Two days later, on Sunday, 6 March 1988, the IRA team crossed the border into Gibraltar.

At first the surveillance teams identified only two of the individuals as they crossed into Gibraltar. The third terrorist, Sean Savage, was spotted inside the town, after somehow slipping across the frontier without getting picked up. Savage had in fact been sighted a few hours earlier, seen tinkering with something inside a white Renault 5 parked near the assembly point for the military band, but at that point he had not been formally identified.

A bomb-disposal specialist was called forward to make a quick visual examination of the exterior of the Renault. There were no signs of the vehicle sitting lower to the ground than normal, which might be expected if it was weighed down with a large amount of explosive material, but as Ken Connor points out, 'fifty or sixty pounds of Semtex – enough to devastate a huge area – would have had little or no visible effect on a car's springs'. The presence of a rusted aerial fitted to the otherwise new Renault did arouse suspicion, however.

'On that basis,' writes Anthony Kemp, 'it was felt that the car could contain a remote control bomb.' At 1540 hours, Joseph Canepa, the Gibraltar Police Commissioner, signed an authorisation, officially handing control over to the SAS.

Four SAS soldiers now moved in to arrest the terrorists, following the three of them as they headed towards the border crossing. At that point Savage unexpectedly turned and started heading back towards town. The soldiers split up into pairs, with one team sticking with Daniel McCann and Mairead Farrell while the other two soldiers tracked Savage.

The SAS had been briefed beforehand that there was a high probability that all three suspects were armed and, in all likelihood, would use their weapons if they were confronted. They had also been told that any of the suspects might be carrying a remotely controlled detonator that would enable them to trigger the device. 'All the SAS men involved,' writes Kemp, 'stated that it was stressed to them most emphatically that it would be a push-button detonator.' These factors played a part in the split-second calculations the soldiers made in the moments that followed.

As Farrell and McCann made for the border, the latter abruptly spun around, startled by the wail of a nearby police siren, turned on by a local inspector who was unaware of the operation to apprehend the terrorists. According to a transcript of evidence later given by the soldiers at the inquest, McCann made eye contact with one of the men following him and dropped his smile. As the soldier drew his weapon and went to issue a challenge he stated in evidence that McCann moved his right arm across his body. Fearing that McCann was reaching for a remote detonator, the SAS man fired a single round from his pistol, hitting the terrorist in the back.

The same soldier described seeing Farrell reach for a bag she was carrying. He fired once, shooting Farrell in the back. He fired another three rounds at McCann, hitting him in the body and head. The second SAS man was now also firing at Farrell and McCann, the two soldiers discharging a total of twelve rounds between them.

The sound of shots being fired alerted Savage and he wheeled round. One of the two soldiers who had been shadowing him issued a challenge, but as he did so Savage moved a hand towards his pocket, prompting both SAS men to open fire. They shot the terrorist a total of fifteen times in the body and head.

To a layperson, the number of shots fired might sound excessive. But it only takes a slight hand movement to depress a remote trigger for an explosive device. In that situation, you do not stop shooting until you are certain that the target is dead and they cannot activate the bomb. How many rounds this takes is irrelevant. It was the job of those soldiers to make sure that the terrorists no longer presented a threat to themselves or to anyone else around them.

By 1600 hours the operation was over. Control was returned to the Police Commissioner a few minutes later. The SP Team soldiers were quickly removed from the scene.

Investigators subsequently discovered that all three terrorists had been unarmed. None of them had been carrying any type of remote-control detonator. An internal examination of the Renault revealed that there was no bomb inside. It had in fact been parked there as a blocking car, a terrorist tactic used to reserve a particular parking space ahead of a planned attack. The actual bomb car was located a day later, across the border in a Marbella car park.

A very public debate followed over whether the soldiers had been right to open fire on Farrell, McCann and Savage. The Regiment came in for a serious amount of flak in the press, with fresh accusations of a 'shoot-to-kill' policy. In their defence, the soldiers were in an impossible situation. They had very good reason to believe that there was a bomb nearby, that the terrorists were armed and had the capability to detonate remotely the explosive device.

If they had failed to act, and the bomb had indeed been in the Renault, innocent people would have died in the resulting blast – and the Regiment would have taken the blame for failing to prevent a terrorist atrocity. In that situation, you really can't win. All a soldier can do is act on the best intelligence available at the time.

Throughout the 1990s, the SAS continued to maintain the pressure on the IRA with reactive OPs, surveillance and intelligence-gathering, working closely with the Det.

In June 1991, three members of an IRA unit were killed during an operation in the village of Coagh. The following February, four terrorists were shot dead by the SAS after spraying a police station in Coalisland, County Tyrone with heavy machine-gun fire. Several years later, the SAS took part in its last operation in the province.

For years an IRA sniper gang had terrorised the area around South Armagh, killing several soldiers and police officers. A number of these attacks had been carried out from the rear of a specially modified Mazda that served as a mobile shooting platform. (In 2002, the infamous Washington, D.C. snipers, John Allen Muhammad and Lee Boyd Malvo, used a similar technique to kill their victims, firing shots through a small hole while lying prone in the boot of their 1990 Chevrolet Caprice.)

Many of the killings were carried out using a Barrett sniper rifle, known as the Light Fifty because it fires .50 calibre rounds. The shooter wasn't firing from any great distance, hitting his targets at a distance of a few hundred metres or less. The gang used lookouts, known as 'dickers', to go out and watch the countryside from elevated positions, looking for patrolling soldiers. Once the dickers had confirmed over the radio that the area was clear, they would bug out and the shooter would make his shot.

Arresting the dickers was an investigative dead-end. There was no way they would have given up the shooters. Lifting them would merely have signalled to the snipers that the security forces were actively looking for them. Instead, the SAS was dispatched to South Armagh to help stop the gang.

The SAS hatched a plan to go on a dummy patrol, posing as regular green army soldiers to lure the shooter out into the open. Meanwhile another team would lie in wait to catch the sniper. Once the shooter had been identified, they could then go in and make the arrest.

The first patrol ended in failure when the sniper realised that he was watching a bunch of SAS lads. The guys were all in their late twenties or early thirties, dressed in smocks (camouflage combat jackets) and carrying M16s. It didn't take a genius to work out that these blokes were not your average British infantrymen. The sniper called off the dickers and cleared out.

A second attempt to ensnare the sniper was made using some of the younger lads from Hereford. They went out on another decoy patrol dressed in normal Army kit and equipped with standard-issue SA80 rifles. As they were walking around, information was being passed to the patrol. One of the dickers caught sight of the patrol and reported it to the shooter. The sniper team then moved into position using their mobile platform and the shooter got himself set up.

Once he had eyes on the soldiers, the sniper ordered the dickers to clear out of the area. He identified his target, lined up his shot and announced that he was going to fire on a count of three.

When he reached 'one', the SAS man in his sights promptly threw himself into the nearest ditch. Again, the shooter realised that it was a trap and bolted out of the area. The sniper team evaded the Regiment on that occasion, but they eventually closed in on them with the help of the Det. The gang was finally captured in April during an SAS raid on a farmhouse close to the border.

The signing of the Good Friday Agreement in April 1998 brought a formal end to the Troubles, although Operation Banner, the British Army's campaign in Northern Ireland, would last for much longer, officially ending on 31 July 2007. It had been the longest-running operation in the history of the British Army.

There will always be a great deal of debate over whether the correct decision was made in deploying British SF soldiers in Northern Ireland. Whatever the rights and wrongs of that argument, the SAS undoubtedly demonstrated its ability to adapt relentlessly during its time in the province, working within the integrated structure of 'The Group' and working closely with the men and women of 14 Int. Even more remarkably, it achieved this in an atmosphere of intense public scrutiny and political restraint.

But while the conflict in Northern Ireland was rumbling on, the SAS was having to come to terms with another threat – one that would change the Regiment for ever.

CHAPTER 14

The SP Team

Counter-terrorism, 1972–87

On 5 September 1972, after years of burying their collective heads in the sand, Western governments had finally woken up to the menace of global terrorism.

Shortly before dawn, eight Palestinian terrorists struck at the Olympic Games in Munich, taking nine members of the Israeli Olympic team hostage and killing two others. A botched rescue attempt by West German security forces ended in a bloodbath, with the deaths of all nine Israeli hostages and a German policeman, along with five of the hostage-takers. Millions around the world had watched the drama unfold on TV. The operation had been a military and political disaster.

The British government, like other countries, had looked on in horror at events in Munich. A handful of armed individuals had inflicted carnage and humiliation on the West German government. This was a new type of terrorism, unlike anything they had seen in the past. To combat it effectively, they were going to need a dedicated counter-terrorism unit.

Once again, they turned to the SAS.

By this point the Regiment had already established the Counter-Revolutionary Warfare (CRW) Wing, a developmental and training unit, tasked with looking at different methods for fighting terrorist threats. The Wing had been created by a far-sighted ex-ranker, a sergeant major who was later commissioned

– proving, once again, that the best ideas in the SAS usually come from the men on the ground.

In its infancy, the CRW had a skeletal staff, but after Munich it was authorised to raise a new counter-terrorism team. The faucet was turned on. Money was, supposedly, no object. As a result, the Regiment formed its Special Projects (SP) counter-terrorism team. The CRW was also expanded to one officer and four instructors.

As always, the SAS had to start from scratch. To begin with, it was very much Keystone Cops stuff, with the soldiers having to make do with whatever kit, vehicles and weapons they could get their hands on. They used Browning Hi-Power pistols and Ingram MAC-10s for CQB exercises, although the latter was subsequently replaced with the Heckler & Koch MP5 submachine gun, chambered for hollow-point 9x19mm Parabellum. Both weapons were selected because the prevailing opinion at the time was that you had to keep the calibre down to 9mm rounds for close-quarter warfare. Anything bigger and the bullet might pass through a wall, potentially killing or wounding one of your mates or a civilian hostage.

More hardware was acquired over time, including Remington 870 pump-action shotguns, 7.62mm British Army sniper rifles effective up to a range of eight hundred yards, and Arwen 37 riot guns. Flashbangs were also developed for use in room clearances. These are G60 stun grenades, custom-made for the SAS, filled with a cocktail of magnesium and mercury fulminate. When the grenade kicks off, it creates a sonic boom, measured at 160 decibels, accompanied by a searing flash of light. It'll deafen anyone in the room, making them squint and giving the operators valuable seconds to deal with any hostiles. Because the flashbang doesn't fragment, it's safe to use in a confined space with civilians. The Regiment also used specialised grenades that contain hundreds of tiny rubber pellets. They won't hurt you, but the noise of the pellets whistling around the room disorientates anyone in close range. More often than not, they'll look around to see where the noise is coming from – taking their eyes away from the likeliest point of entry.

Throughout the 1970s, the SP Team and the CRW staff worked tirelessly to enhance the Regiment's terrorist-fighting capabilities. New techniques were constantly being developed. If there was a problem and they couldn't find a solution on the market, they would go ahead and invent one, road-testing new ideas with civilian researchers from the Ministry of Defence. By the end of the decade, the basic principles, equipment and structure of the SP Team had been firmly established. The setup was essentially the same when I joined the Regiment in the early 1980s, aside from some minor differences in weapons and kit.

The four Sabre Squadrons – A, B, D and G – each did a rotation lasting several months on the SP Team, with a handover period between one squadron finishing its rotation and the next one taking over. The new guys would do a refresher course with the CRW instructors, familiarising themselves with new equipment, weaponry and facilities. Then they'd take over and spend months of hard training on the SP Team. During this time the squadron was split into two teams, Red and Blue. Blue is the three-hour response team. Red is on a thirty-minute response. Which means that those guys have to be rolling through the gates at Hereford within half an hour of an incident going down.

The Red and Blue teams were broken down into three components: a command element, a sniper team and the main assault force. The snipers' job was to set up a cordon around the enemy stronghold and provide support for the assaulters. They had a secondary role in gathering intelligence, observing the X-rays (terrorists) and Yankees (hostages) and communicating movements back to the command and control unit. The assaulters were the guys in black kit who went in to resolve the situation using the military option.

The guys on the SP Team cut around in civilian clothing and had access to a number of Range Rovers and Ford Transit vans. Training took place at the various facilities in and around Hereford, including the nearby wooded area at the Garrabach. Snipers practised long-distance shooting at the range on both static and moving targets, while the assaulters practised drills using blank rounds at a white-block building called the embassy, based at the Regiment's training facility at Pontrilas. They also logged a ton of hours at the Killing House.

As we have seen, originally a crude one-room structure with a bunch of paper targets, by the end of the 1970s the Killing House had been expanded massively. The upgraded structure featured six rooms including a galleried range, a small room with a desk in it, a larger room and a mock-up of the inside of a commercial aircraft.

The SP Team used the Killing House to train for building assaults using live rounds in 360-degree arcs of fire. The walls were lined with metal, with thick rubber sheeting draped over the top. When a bullet struck the wall, it would pass through the rubber, fragment against the metal plate and as it bounced off the round would be caught by the sheeting.

Training in the Killing House was intense. Operators would put down thousands of rounds every day, practising every type of CQB scenario from firing a pistol accurately at a target across the length of a room to multi-room entries, with the guys storming the building from different entry points. Assault teams used helicopters to land on the roof and abseil down the side. Explosive framed charges were used to blow off the doors and breach the windows.

The SP Team spent a lot of time working on methods of entry, training with lock-picking tools, rams, sledgehammers, axes and crowbars. The lads became so skilled at breaking into any type of stronghold that they were used to test new kit for the government. Whitehall had a contract with a company that specialised in developing state-of-the-art locks and doors. They'd bring down the counter-terrorism guys from Hereford and invite them to try and smash through a new type of door or window, to see how long it took.

The answer was, usually, not very long.

Every aspect of assaulting a stronghold was studied in detail. Quite a few buildings in London had been fitted with armoured glass, for example, so the sniper teams would study the deflection of a bullet when striking the surface and factor that into their shots. Training was always hyper-realistic, with guys taking turns to play the role of hostages during Killing House exercises. This led to a few accidents. One man had his arse blown off with a Remington shotgun; several others were wounded during training at the House, with many more near misses.

On the weekends there was usually a training exercise, working alongside the police to respond to call-out scenarios. This was an opportunity for the team to test their rapid response skills, driving at high speeds to reach the scene of the 'terrorist incident' as quickly as possible. Nowadays the SP Team has access to 'Blue Thunder' Dauphin helicopters, but in the 1970s they had to rely on the Range Rovers and Transits to get about.

Exercises were made as close to real life as possible. The scenario usually went along the lines of a group of terrorists holding a number of hostages inside a stronghold. Snipers would disperse around the perimeter, lying prone on the backs of trucks, the rooftops of nearby buildings or concealing themselves in ghillie suits in the surrounding ditches or woods. Local police took part, along with trained ambulance crews and hostage negotiators. Once it had been established that the 'terrorists' had begun executing the 'hostages' and there was no way of resolving the situation peacefully, the police commander would hand control of the situation over to the SP Team and the assault would begin.

The SP Team also took part in demonstration jobs, putting on a show for VIPs, politicians and members of the Royal Family down at the Killing House. These jobs were seen as a way of selling the brand of the Regiment, winning friends and promoting ourselves to people with influence. More often than not you'd feel like a performing seal, but you had to grit your teeth and get on with it.

Away from the Killing House, the SP Team trained for assaults on every imaginable type of target, including buses, oil rigs, trains, tall buildings, civilian aircraft and ships. During my time on the team, we even rehearsed a potential terrorist attack on the London

Underground, running exercises at a couple of disused Tube stations closed to the public.

We also practised aircraft assault drills using aircraft borrowed from British Airways. The Regiment had a contact at BA, their chief engineer. Whenever a 747 was taken in for servicing, it would be parked inside a large hangar called a cathedral. The engineer would ring up Hereford and say, 'We've got a 747 here for eight hours, do you guys want to come down and use it?' This was ideal training because it was behind closed doors.

When we needed to make it even more realistic, we'd rehearse a hostage scenario using students from a local university. They were paid to act as passengers on a BA plane, taking off from Heathrow on a double-decked 747, with guys from the CRW team playing the role of the terrorists. At some point during the flight, the X-rays would hijack the plane and redirect the pilots to one of the RAF bases, either Brize Norton or Lyneham. (The latter has since closed.) At some point after landing, the SP Team would then initiate an assault on the aircraft.

Before the start of the exercise, the 'passengers' were divided into groups and given different coloured bibs to wear. Each group was then separated from the others and told, 'If your group is the first to leave the plane, you'll each get an extra tenner.' Which was a fair amount of money in the 1980s.

As soon as we attacked the aircraft, this wall of students would rush forward, clambering over the seats, pushing each other out of the way as they scrambled for the exits. As an SP Team operator, you were experiencing exactly the sort of widespread panic and disarray you'd be up against if you had to storm an aircraft for real.

By the time I had joined the counter-terrorism team we were training on high-rises, abseiling down lift shafts and working with engineers. We'd climb up the outside of tall buildings, using special suction cups developed by a German company, originally designed to help workmen lift thick, industrial-sized plates of glass. These weren't designed for scaling buildings and if you didn't maintain the air pressure on the cups, they'd slide down and you'd fall to your death. The trick, I discovered, is to have three suckers fixed to the glass while leaning outward, away from the building, at a forty-five-degree angle.

Of course, no one ever bothered to stop and work out what you were supposed to do once you reached the floor containing the terrorists. You can't exactly engage an X-ray while hanging on to a piece of glass, hundreds of feet above the ground.

We were also given tours of major public buildings – anywhere that might be a legitimate target for terrorists, such as Buckingham Palace, the Houses of Parliament, the High Court and Windsor Castle. Prisons were also studied in case of riots.

In 1987 this training was put into practice when the Regiment was called in to deal with a hostage crisis at HMP Peterhead. A gang of hardened cons had taken a prison officer hostage during a riot. The SAS was brought in to resolve the situation, in a secretive operation authorised by Downing Street.

Not everyone appreciates the tactics used by the SP Team. When they arrived at Peterhead to plan the operation, the prison warden told them, 'No weapons.' The SAS protested. They knew the prisoners were armed with shanks and all sorts. The warden stood his ground. They eventually brokered a deal so that every fourth man in a four-man team was armed with a pistol. The other three guys would carry nothing more than batons.

They also told the prison warden they'd use CS gas to incapacitate the hostage-takers. Which was a lie. The Regiment instead deployed CR, a specialist gas that is many times stronger than CS.

The effects of CR, or dibenzoxazepine, are immediate and extremely debilitating – to the point where you think you're going to die. You're temporarily blinded, you're in excruciating pain and your lungs begin to feel as if they've been filled with water. Being exposed to it is a truly horrifying experience. Every guy on the SP Team is exposed to both CS and CR as part of their training, to give them a better understanding of the effects of these gases. This involves a gas grenade being detonated in a room, while the soldier in question gives his name, rank and number. CS is quite bad – your nose, throat and eyes burn, but you knew that if you were spiked with adrenaline, you could still operate in a room filled with the stuff for a short period of time. Whereas with CR, you couldn't even stand up. Within moments of being exposed to it, you were on your arse. It didn't matter how tough you were, you'd end up being carried out of the room by a couple of guys.

At Peterhead, the SP team launched a multi-floor assault on the wing where the officer was being held. On the approach they were spotted by men in another wing, who promptly raised the alarm with their fellow cons. One of the teams hurried across the parapet and posted CR through an opening in the roof. Unsurprisingly, the prisoners holed up in the eaves were instantly disabled by the gas. They were quickly suppressed by the SAS men, and the hostage was thankfully unharmed and escorted to safety. The entire operation lasted about five minutes.

While the SP Team trained and honed their skills continuously, the CRW instructors conjured up every imaginable scenario for a terrorist attack, and then worked out how to defeat it. One line of thought was that we might be able to approach a hijacked aircraft by pretending to be the refuelling crew. We could drive the tanker up to the steps of the aircraft, hook it up and use that as an opportunity to storm the plane. Or at least have an interesting conversation with one of the terrorists.

They sent a bunch of us on a course, learning how to refuel a plane using a mobile tanker on a runway. The training was useful, but mind-numbingly dull. We were so bored out of our minds that we stopped paying attention during a refuelling job and ended up overfilling a private jet, dousing it in aviation fuel. That didn't go down too well.

Other guys from the SP Team were sent on courses to learn how to drive and operate fire tenders at airports, for the same reason.

The instructors also held a bodyguard course, run by a dedicated BG Team. This was a five-week course held down at Pontrilas. Students wore plain clothes and did training exercises, bodyguarding a VIP for the day in a chosen city. A lot of time was spent on advanced vehicle drills such as car blocking, handbrake turns, J-turns and shooting from a moving platform. The guys would practise driving in formation, with the VIP in a vehicle in the middle and protection cars located to the front and rear. Sometimes there would be a fourth car at the side, stopping any potential threats from getting close to the target. To drive at high speed in a densely populated environment and maintain the formation, without getting separated, takes a lot of skill.

Just as the first SAS soldiers had done in Malaya, the counter-terrorism team was ready to try out anything that might work. They were continually looking for the edge in any given situation. This extended to bringing in dogs from the Royal Army Veterinary Corps. The idea was to use the dogs to rush into buildings ahead of the main assault group and set upon figures dressed as terrorists. Results were mixed. Once let loose, they invariably started tearing into everybody in sight, including the hostages, biting arms and legs.

Today, the Regiment has its own specially trained dog handlers. Instead of Alsatians, they use more intelligent, highly trained Belgian Malinois dogs to enter buildings and suppress targets. An SAS team will send them in ahead of the assault force. They'll get in the faces of the enemy and the soldiers can then sweep in after them and mop up.

The guys also used a variety of specialist equipment developed by companies outside Hereford. This included the Thermal Lance, a cutting device that can rapidly slice through any type of surface, such as metal or concrete, Hatton rounds for blowing apart door hinges, and a wall-breaching device called the Harvey Wall Banger. The latter is a cannon loaded with a plastic projectile half-filled with water. When fired, the projectile smashes into the wall at high speed, blowing a hole straight through. The water disperses on impact, reducing the clouds of dust created by the breach.

As the cancer of international terrorism spread and the tactics they used became more sophisticated, the Regiment responded by upping its game. That's still going on today. There's a constant process of development at the CRW as the team acquires new skillsets and equipment. Everything is continually assessed, from the gloves the operators use to the calibre of weapons they fire and the modified vehicles they drive. In the fight against terrorism, you cannot afford to stand still.

By the beginning of 1980, the SP Team had been tested to destruction. It had sharpened its skills in the Killing House and trained for every possible type of terrorist attack. Its operators were equipped with a formidable variety of kit, including S6 respirators, integral microphones, body armour with ceramic plate inserts, abseiling ropes, assault ladders, a fleet of modified vehicles, night-vision goggles (NVGs) and all kinds of framed charges and breaching tools, along with their personal weapon systems. They were ready for anything the terrorists could throw at them.

But aside from a German-led hostage-rescue operation in Mogadishu, in which two SAS men had taken part, and a handful of sieges that had ended peacefully, the SP Team had largely been restricted to training exercises.* Few people outside of Hereford knew that it even existed.

At the end of April, they finally got the chance they had been waiting for.

Shortly after 1100 hours on the morning of Wednesday, 30 April 1980, a group of six armed men made their way towards a row of whitewashed townhouses in the heart of Knightsbridge. The men, ethnic Arabs from Iran, were heavily tooled up with Skorpion submachine guns, Browning 9mm pistols, a .38 revolver and a

---

* In December 1975, the counter-terrorism team had been called out to a siege at a flat in Balcombe Street, Marylebone, London. A four-man Provisional IRA team, responsible for a spate of bomb attacks, had taken a married couple hostage following a chase with police. The siege ended six days later, after information was deliberately passed to the BBC, reporting that the SAS was down at Regent's Park Barracks and preparing to go in and storm the flat. The prospect of coming face-to-face with the SAS did the trick: all four IRA members quickly surrendered, having heard the broadcast on the radio.

cluster of Soviet-manufactured hand grenades. Their target was 16 Prince's Gate: the Iranian Embassy.

The six terrorists were from a group calling for the liberation of 'Arabistan', which is another name for Khuzestan, an Iranian province in the south-west of the country with a majority Arab population – and also happens to be sitting on a lot of oil. Although they had genuine grievances over the oppression of their brothers and sisters in the province, the gunmen had in fact been recruited, trained and funded by Iraqi intelligence. Saddam Hussein had his eyes on Khuzestan's oil profits, and he saw the group as a useful means for stirring up trouble with his neighbours.

The police officer on duty at the embassy that day was Trevor Lock, a constable with the Diplomatic Protection Group (DPG). He tried to prevent the gunmen from getting inside by slamming shut the outer security door. A shot was fired by one of the terrorists through the glass panelling, and after a brief struggle PC Lock was overrun. In the terrifying minutes that followed, the gunmen rounded up twenty-six hostages, including two men from the BBC, the embassy's British chauffeur and the Iranian Chargé d'Affaires, Dr Gholam-Ali Afrouz.

The terrorists' leader, Salim, then issued their demands: they wanted the release of ninety-one Arab prisoners being held in Iran, international recognition of 'Arabistan' as a country, and safe passage out of the UK. The authorities had twenty-four hours to agree, otherwise they would kill the hostages.

Salim added that the building had been rigged with explosives. If anyone tried to storm the place, it would go up in smoke.

The Iranian Embassy siege had begun.

CHAPTER 15

The Iranian Embassy Siege

Prince's Gate, London, 30 April–5 May 1980

The SP Team first learned about the Iranian Embassy crisis through a former Blade, 'Dusty' Gray. Now attached to the Metropolitan Police Hard Dogs Unit, he happened to be in the vicinity at the time of the attack and put a call straight through to Hereford to let them know the score. A code was then pinged across to the personal bleepers worn by both Red and Blue Teams, ordering them to report in. The guys were briefed on the situation, although details were still sketchy at that point. A short while later, they headed up to London under their own steam.

This is often the way the Regiment works. We don't sit around, waiting for the phone to ring. We go out to where the action is, introduce ourselves, make sure we're part of the conversation. We did the same thing a decade later in the Gulf War. We weren't even part of the initial military planning, but we headed out there anyway, correctly guessing that at some point, we were going to get involved.

There's another advantage to getting in early. By setting themselves up nearer to the siege, the SAS could tell the police, 'We'll be there in twenty minutes.' Rather than taking three hours to drive up from Hereford.

The SP Team guys were travelling up in separate vehicles, so they arranged to RV at Beaconsfield Army Language School, where they could get something to eat and wait for the order to deploy to a secure location in central London. They moved forward a few hours later, arriving at Regent's Park Barracks in the early hours of Thursday 1 May. They went straight to work, setting up a forward holding area at the Royal College of General Practitioners, next door to the embassy at 14 Prince's Gate. The command and control element, under Major Hector Gullan, established themselves while the barracks gym was cleared out so a team from the Royal Pioneer Corps could get to work building a model of the embassy layout.

The first thing to do in any siege incident is to make preparations for an Immediate Action (IA) plan. The IA is an emergency response drill that the SAS implements if the talks break down and the situation inside the stronghold deteriorates. This is where the team looks at the location, the main entry points, the number of hostages and gunmen, and formulates a drill for immediate entry. The IA is not a very clever plan. It's the equivalent of going into a bar, looking at a big evil bloke, and going over and punching him as hard as you can. There's no messing about. It's all about getting in as fast as possible, hitting the enemy and sorting the problem with as few civilian casualties as possible.

Here's a good example of what an IA looks like. In 1988, a Kuwait Airways Boeing 747 was hijacked by Lebanese terrorists. After a brief stopover in Iran, the aircraft was flown to Cyprus and granted permission to land at Larnaca. Among the hostages were three members of the Kuwaiti Royal Family. After days of delicate negotiations, two passengers were tortured and killed, their bodies dumped on the runway. While negotiations continued, the Regiment's SP Team was called out to prepare for a possible assault.

Intelligence had established that the majority of the terrorists were occupying the upper deck of the aircraft, using it as a control room. The hostages were crowded in the lower deck, possibly because their captors assumed they would be easier to control if they were kept in a separate part of the aircraft rather than being spread across two decks. A few of the terrorists were believed to be keeping watch over the hostages on the lower level.

Based on this information, the SAS sketched out a plan for an immediate attack on the Boeing using a pair of Land Rovers with GPMGs (General-Purpose Machine Guns) mounted on top. One set of guys would drive towards the 747, spraying the upper deck with 7.62mm rounds through the windows, taking out the targets located there. The gunfire would also serve as a distraction, fixing any X-rays on the lower level in place and buying time for another assault group to storm the aircraft and neutralise any remaining threats.

Thankfully, that plan was never needed. The aircraft flew on to Algeria, where the authorities eventually cut a deal with the terrorists and the remaining thirty-one hostages were released.

At the time, the involvement of the SAS in the Larnaca hijacking was never reported. But the truth is that the guys were out there, on the ground in Cyprus, ready to go in.

At the embassy siege, the IA involved a frontal assault on the stronghold, with the SAS blasting their way inside with shotguns and sledgehammers while a second group battled their way down from the rooftop. It wasn't ideal – if it had been done, it would have undoubtedly resulted in a number of civilian fatalities – but it was better than no plan.

We have a rule in the Regiment. If the team is discussing an assault and somebody sticks their hand up and says, 'Oh, that's a crap plan,' but they don't put forward an alternative suggestion, that's frowned upon. If you think the plan is terrible, come up with something better. If you can't, then we're going ahead with it.

The soldiers now settled into a routine. One team waited on standby in their black kit, one up the spout, with their respirators on to protect their faces from debris, and to guard against smoke inhalation and gas attacks, in the event the terrorists had access to certain types of gas. They waited in the IA position, while the other team rested, checking and cleaning their kit. Every twelve hours the teams would rotate. This helped to keep the stand-by team fresh in case the gunmen started killing hostages and they needed to go in. At the same time, police negotiators continued to maintain a dialogue with the terrorists.

While all this was going on, a vast intelligence-gathering and surveillance effort was already underway. On Thursday 1 May, specialists from the security services were brought in to drill through the walls of the buildings either side of the embassy, inserting state-of-the-art listening devices through the holes. To mask the sound of the drilling, gas workers started digging up the road outside. Commercial aircraft were requested to pass low overhead, creating a near-constant racket.

SAS and police sniper teams also contributed to the overall intelligence effort, observing the stronghold from their perimeter positions and feeding everything back to the control room. Each time they spotted an X-ray or Yankee on the move, they'd report it over the radio, identifying the terrorists and helping to build up a detailed picture of what was going on inside.

Blueprints of the embassy were delivered, and the caretaker was located and brought in to brief the team. By a stroke of good fortune, he had been off work on the day the gunmen had stormed the place. It was extremely good luck for the Regiment, too: the caretaker turned out to be an intelligence goldmine, revealing crucial details about the building's layout and updating some of the information they had pulled from the architectural plans. Thanks to the caretaker, the Regiment discovered that a number of the windows had been heavily reinforced. If they had tried smashing through them with the sledgehammers, they would have run into serious problems.

The team received another boost with the release of one of the hostages on the same day. Chris Cramer, a producer with the BBC, had come down with severe stomach pains early that morning. With his condition worsening, the terrorists had agreed to release him shortly before noon. He was then questioned by detectives, providing them with several important details.

Released hostages are one of the most crucial intel sources in any siege incident. They're the closest thing the security forces have got to a mark-one eyeball. They can fill in any gaps that the planners might have, telling them what the morale of the terrorists and the hostages is like, what everyone is up to, what kind of weapons they're packing and whether they noticed any wires that might indicate a booby trap.

By now the police negotiators had opened a secure line with the terrorists. The negotiator's primary objective is always to secure the safe release of the hostages and bring a peaceful end to the siege. But they also have a secondary goal, calming the nerves of the gunmen, defusing the situation while buying time for their colleagues to build up a detailed intelligence picture. The negotiators did this brilliantly, using every trick in the book to keep Salim on the line. On Saturday 3 May, day four of the siege, tense negotiations resulted in the release of two more hostages, in return for the broadcast of a statement by the group on the BBC World Service that evening.

Despite this, the chances of a peaceful outcome to the siege appeared slim. The British government held talks with a number of Arab diplomats, in the hope that they could persuade the terrorists to surrender. The talks ended up going nowhere, with the Arab ambassadors insisting that the government should grant Salim and the others safe passage out of the country – something that Downing Street would not agree to.

Their position had been clear from the outset: they would not buckle to the terrorists' demands. Since there was no chance of the Iranians agreeing either to recognise 'Arabistan' or release the political prisoners, it soon became clear that the siege was going to end in one of two ways. Either the gunmen would come out of the building with their hands up and surrender to the police. Or they were going to come out in a load of body bags.

While the negotiators played their games of chess with Salim, stalling for time, the team started planning for the Deliberate Action (DA) plan.

The DA is a drill that is constantly developing throughout the course of a siege. This is when the guys look at how to plan the main attack. There are a number of ways of penetrating a stronghold and every aspect of the assault must be considered by the planning chiefs. To pull off a multi-floor 360 attack on a building, while causing as few civilian casualties as possible, the team first needs to look at methods of approach and entry.

They'll look for guaranteed entry points and ask themselves, how can we get close to the building without being seen? What dead ground is there, what cover? Can we get on the roof without being spotted? Are there any anchor points to allow a team to abseil down? Are the doors inside the stronghold fireproof? Are they lockable?

A deliberate option is always preferable to the Immediate Action. Once the SP Team has established the DA, they can attack the building at their leisure, and on their terms. It allows them to assert a degree of control over the situation.

While one half of the SP Team remained on standby at the forward holding area, the other guys worked on the deliberate plan at the barracks.

Once the plan had been worked out, the team began training with the hessian-and-timber mock-up in the Regent's Park Barracks gym. The purpose of the replica is to immerse the SP Team in the layout of the building, to the point where they are familiar with every nook and cranny, even before they've set foot inside the place itself.

The plan was for the team to attack in squadron strength. Both Red and Blue teams would take part in a 360-degree assault on the stronghold, with assault groups breaching their designated entry points. The guys at the front and rear would use framed charges to blow apart the reinforced windows on the ground and first floors and then work their way up. Another team would begin their assault from the rooftop, moving down as they cleared the upper levels.

The first priority in any deliberate assault is to clear the rooms. The SAS is trained to go in hard and dominate the ground inside that stronghold, neutralising any threat to life. That means breaking down the assaulters into small groups, each with a certain number of rooms to clear. Once each group's area has been swept, they'll make their way to a rally point, which is usually a stairwell. Then it's a case of evacuating the building.

By this point there may be extensive damage to the property. If it has been booby-trapped with explosives, there might be significant casualties. Others may have been wounded by shrapnel from fragmentation grenades or from the terrorists opening fire. The goal now is to get the hostages safely out, which means coordinating a reception party in a secure area on the outside. The reception party's job is to check everybody, detaining any X-rays who may have slipped through the net. Paramedic crews and doctors can then be brought forward to provide medical assistance to any injured parties.

All of these drills had been practised by the SP Team time and time again over the years, in exercises at the Killing House and in various parts of the country, working with the emergency services. When the time came for the SAS to carry out a stronghold assault in a live situation, each and every man on the team knew exactly what to do.

The deliberate drill was constantly refined as more information flowed in from the sniper teams, released hostages and through the soldiers' own careful recces. On the fourth day, the team crept across the rooftop and discovered that a glass panel of the skylight could be removed, providing the assaulters with access to the top floor of the building. The plan was revised accordingly.

Getting on that rooftop was also a good opportunity for the team to see if anyone had eyes on them. Whenever you're dealing with a hostage crisis, there's always a chance that the building is being watched by someone on the outside, ready to warn the terrorists when you make your move. Nowadays the security forces will block cell phone coverage in the immediate area and cut any telephone lines and internet access. All it takes is for the terrorists to place someone in a high-rise flat overlooking the building and they've got a ready-made early-warning system, giving them time to defend against an assault.

By Sunday 4 May, the fifth day of the siege, the mood inside the embassy was becoming increasingly fraught. The terrorists were growing frustrated with the negotiators' stalling tactics and a failed attempt to bring in three Arab ambassadors to act as mediators. Tempers were frayed. In the evening a fifth hostage was released, providing additional intelligence on the captors. Meanwhile the SP Team continued to rotate stand-by duties. When they weren't rehearsing drills at the mock-up, they passed the time by playing practical jokes and watching the World Snooker Championships.

On day six, Monday 5 May, events inside the embassy reached boiling point. At about midday, Salim, the leader of the terrorists, got on the phone and threatened to start killing the hostages unless his demand for an Arab mediator was met immediately.

A few minutes later, three shots rang out from inside the building.

The gunshots were followed by an ominous warning from Salim. The time for talking was over. There were to be no more negotiations. Unless the police agreed to his demands, one hostage would be killed every forty-five minutes. Which meant the next hostage would be executed at 1410 hours.

The terrorists had crossed a line. There was now only one way the siege was going to end.

In any hostage crisis, the Regiment is like a Rottweiler kept on a leash. During the first phase, the police and politicians try to keep a tight grip on the leash, guided by their instinct to preserve life and avoid violence if possible. Ultimately, if the terrorists come out with their hands up after a week-long siege, they consider that a win. That's fair enough. They're trained to think that way.

The SAS soldier takes a different view. As far as we are concerned, once you rush into a building with a bunch of weapons and start making threats, you've signed your own death sentence. There should be no negotiations. They should send us in straight away and let us get on with it.

But when negotiations collapse, the leash comes off.

On the afternoon of 5 May, that moment had almost arrived.

The SAS did not get the green light to go in immediately after the shots had been fired. The ministers and security chiefs meeting at COBRA (Cabinet Office Briefing Room A), the government's emergency response committee, required proof that a hostage's life had been taken before giving the go-ahead. So far all they knew was that shots had been fired. There was no body as yet, and there was a chance, however slim, that the shots may have been an accidental discharge or a bluff. Police negotiators managed to push back the latest deadline, but it was clear now that the situation inside the embassy was rapidly deteriorating.

In preparation for the assault, the SP Team operators were brought forward to their stand-by positions. The men carried out last-minute checks on their equipment: respirators, body armour, gloves, flashbangs, holstered Browning 9mm pistols and shoulder-slung MP5s. Each operator also carried three spare thirty-round clips of 9x19mm Parabellum fastened to their utility belts. Now they only had to wait for the signal to go.

It did not take long.

Soon after 1800 hours, a cleric was brought forward from the Regent's Park mosque in a last-ditch attempt to persuade the gunmen to give themselves up. His pleas fell on deaf ears.

Three more gunshots rang out from inside the embassy. Shortly afterwards, the body of one of the hostages, Abbas Lavasani, was dumped on the front steps. The corpse was placed on a stretcher and removed by police, covered by marksmen. A brief examination confirmed that Lavasani had been killed several hours earlier, when the first set of gunshots had been heard. Which meant that the most recent shots could indicate the murder of a second hostage.

It was now clear that the criteria for a military option had been met. The police requested clarification from William Whitelaw, the Home Secretary, who in turn consulted with Prime Minister Margaret Thatcher.

At exactly 1907 hours, the assistant commissioner of the Metropolitan Police, John Dellow, handed over control to the CO of 22 SAS, Lieutenant-Colonel Mike Rose. A scrap of paper, signed by Dellow and confirming the action was being passed to the Regiment, was then countersigned by Rose. With the legal formalities out of the way, it was time to send the guys in.

Once the decision had been made to invoke the military option (codenamed Operation Nimrod), the job of the police negotiator changed. His task was now to buy the operators time while they moved from the forward holding area into their assault positions. The negotiator on duty at the time did his job perfectly, keeping Salim on the line right up to the final few moments before the attack began.

On the rooftop, one of the men on the abseil team ran into trouble when his rope snagged on the figure-of-eight descender and left him swaying several metres above the second-floor balcony. Another trooper accidentally put his boot through one of the windows on the in-swing as he descended his abseil line. The sound of shattering glass alerted Salim, who was still on the phone with the negotiator.

'We are listening to some suspicious movements,' the terrorist leader said. Ignoring the negotiator's pleas to stay on the line, he added, 'I'll come back . . . I'm going to check.'

The assault commander, Major Hector Gullan, had been listening in to the conversation. He now gave the famous order for the SAS to begin their assault, grabbing the microphone and shouting, 'Go! Go! Go!'

In the next instant, a thunderous boom erupted through central London as the rooftop team triggered a distraction charge that they had lowered down the central lightwell. That charge momentarily disorientated the terrorists, giving the assaulters valuable seconds to gain entry to the front and rear of the stronghold.

As the rooftop teams entered through the embassy skylight and the upper-floor windows, the rest of the assaulters simultaneously breached their entry points on the lower levels. There was a second trembling explosion as a frame charge planted on the front balcony by one of the entry teams detonated, engulfing the balustrade in a plume of smoke and debris.

To the rear of the embassy, the rest of the abseiling team, having already dropped down to the balcony, smashed the windows and tossed in flashbangs before sweeping inside. At the same time the two assault groups tasked with clearing the ground floor and basement abandoned plans to blow the rear doors, fearing the explosion might kill the man dangling from his jammed abseil rope. Instead a sledgehammer was brought forward and one of the ground-floor windows was broken. The assaulters posted stun grenades and then stepped through the opening.

By now the curtains on one of the second-floor windows were wreathed in flames, roasting the legs of the SAS soldier hanging from his rope. His situation was doubly serious, because back then the guys didn't have access to flame-retardant clothing. They were wearing standard black Tank Regiment overalls, which meant the man had no protection against the fire raging just beneath him. Several minutes later, two men on the rooftop came to his rescue, cutting his rope before he burned alive.

Meanwhile the other groups pushed on, clearing the rooms on each floor with precision, aggression and speed.

In any assault, momentum is paramount. If anything goes wrong, you carry on regardless. Once you start attacking, it doesn't matter whether one of your mates gets winged or killed, you've got to keep up the momentum. If you stall, you're going to lose the elements of surprise and aggression.

To some people, the idea of leaving a colleague to bleed out might sound heartless. But you have to keep going. When you get that signal to go, you move through that door and you don't stop until your area is clear and the threat is over. That's the risk that every SAS soldier takes. If you go down, the rest of the team will carry on clearing the rooms. If you're still alive when the fighting is over, a medic will be brought forward to help you. If you get one in the head, that's too bad. The life of the SAS man is secondary at this point. Momentum – and the safety of the hostages – is everything.

In the confusion of the attack, Trevor Lock, the DPG constable, tackled Salim to the ground, knocking the Skorpion out of the latter's hand. As the two men wrestled on the floor, a team of assaulters crashed through the door. The terrorist leader was shot dead as he reached for his fallen weapon. Another X-ray was killed in a room off the main corridor after he attempted to open fire on a group of SAS men. Two X-rays were now down, which left four terrorists to neutralise.

Three of them had fled to the telex room on the second floor, where the SAS knew the majority of the hostages had been corralled. The gunmen guarding them trained their weapons on the defenceless figures in front of them and opened fire, killing one man and wounding several others. With the assaulters closing in fast the terrorists realised the game was up and started ditching their weapons, throwing themselves down next to the hostages they had just tried to massacre. A fourth gunman, who had been attempting to set fire to the carpets, was shot in the head as he rushed into the room armed with a fragmentation grenade. Another terrorist was identified and killed before he could reach for his hand grenade.

While the hunt continued for the remaining terrorists, the team moved on to the next phase of the plan: the safe evacuation of the hostages. A chain was formed and the men and women were manhandled down the stairs and forcefully marched outside to the reception party waiting for them in the embassy's rear garden.

At this point the assaulters were keeping a sharp eye on the hostages, looking for any X-rays hiding among them. It's a common tactic for terrorists to pass themselves off as hostages. Once the SAS starts crashing through the windows, the gunmen know that their best hope for survival is to try and get outside, using the confusion and chaos of the assault to slip away unnoticed.

A shout suddenly went up from one of the assaulters as he spotted one of the terrorists on the stairs, the primer on his Russian-made grenade clearly identifiable. The assaulter struck the man on the head with the stock of his weapon and sent him tumbling down the stairs. As the X-ray hit the ground floor the surrounding SAS troopers let rip, giving him the good news with their MP5s.

A ferocious blaze had now started to spread through the

building, choking the air with toxic fumes. The team worked fast, hustling the remaining civilians outside so they could be checked and processed. There was still no sign of the sixth and final terrorist, but he was swiftly identified by one of the hostages, Sim Harris, a BBC sound engineer, as they lay on the ground on the rear lawn. Hearing this, some of the old guard, veterans of Op Storm, stood in the shadows and began shouting at the guys on the reception party, yelling at them to bring the terrorist back inside the building.

One of the soldiers started to drag the X-ray towards the rear entrance. He was stopped by two other guys on the reception party, who had their wits about them and realised what the veterans were going to do.

The SAS did not know it at the time, but the events at the rear of the embassy were being filmed by a news crew. Media coverage of the areas around a terrorist incident is strictly controlled, and with good reason. In Munich, a force of armed German police officers had attempted to mount an assault on the Olympic Village accommodation block where the Israeli hostages were being held captive. The operation had to be called off after film crews broadcast images of the officers moving into position. The Palestinian terrorists, watching on a TV inside the apartment, saw the whole thing unfold in front of them.

If the surviving terrorist had been hauled back inside the embassy, the event would have been caught on camera. No one can be sure what the assaulters planned to do with him, but if later he had been found shot dead, that could have done untold damage to the reputation of the SAS, overshadowing what has gone down in history as one of the Regiment's finest hours. The troopers in the reception party, one of whom had only recently passed Selection, may well have saved the terrorist's life that day. But they may also have saved the reputation of the SAS. Sadly, that young trooper's career suffered afterwards. He was punished by some of the older guys for doing things by the book.

The terrorist was promptly handed over to police, arrested and charged with conspiracy to murder, false imprisonment and manslaughter. Sentenced to life imprisonment, he was released in 2008. At the time of publication, he is living under a new identity in south London. Personally, I think we should have sent him to live somewhere a lot less pleasant.

The SAS had saved nineteen out of the twenty hostages held inside the building at the time of the assault. Their only casualty was the man whose abseiling device had stuck. In spite of the burns he'd suffered, that guy had continued to take part in the assault after being cut down, demonstrating the strength of mind of the SAS soldier. Another guy had a minor injury to his finger.

At the end of the assault, control was formally returned to the police commander on the ground. The team handed over their weapons for forensics before returning to their barracks at Regent's Park to pack up their gear and celebrate. They were congratulated in person by a hugely relieved Willie Whitelaw, tears welling in his eyes, and Margaret Thatcher, who now became a lifelong convert to the skills of the SAS. Afterwards the guys returned to Hereford to continue an epic drinking session that lasted well into the early hours.

The Iranian Embassy Siege was a massive boost to the Regiment. But in many ways, it was also a curse.

For most of its existence, the SAS had been used to operating under a veil of secrecy. That arrangement had suited a bunch of guys who had never cared for publicity or medals. Now all that had changed. The operation to storm the Iranian Embassy had been captured by the assembled media. Broadcasters had interrupted their regular programming to relay live footage from the assault. Across the country, millions of people had watched in astonishment as men clad in black assault kit, hooded and tooled up, went in and did the business.

Those were powerful images. They captured the public's imagination and gave everyone something to be proud of. The effects of Operation Nimrod were felt not only in the UK, but around the world. Not even the US, the foremost military power at the time, had succeeded in carrying out such a daring hostage-rescue assault.

The previous month, US Special Forces had attempted to rescue fifty-three staff being held at the US Embassy in Iran. It had gone horribly wrong. The operation was eventually aborted after the helicopters tasked with ferrying the assaulters to an RV in the Iranian desert ran into a sandstorm, causing a number of them to develop mechanical faults. Another chopper was involved in a crash with a Hercules C-130 transport aircraft, resulting in the deaths of eight men. President Jimmy Carter held a press conference the next day to announce the failure of Operation Eagle Claw.

The success of the embassy assault, in sharp contrast to the disastrous Iranian hostage-rescue op, put the SAS on the map. Before 5 May 1980, the average Joe on the street had never heard of a unit called the Special Air Service. After that day, everyone wanted to know more about this mystical group of warriors. The Walter Mittys, inevitably, started cropping up all over the place.

It's easy to forget that the assault could easily have gone wrong. Up until the moment that the men crashed through the windows and doors, no one really knew for sure whether the embassy had been wired with explosives, as the terrorists had repeatedly claimed. If it had, the outcome would have been very different.

Similarly, if the surviving terrorist had been marched back inside the embassy in full view of the world's media, the credibility of the SAS could have been permanently damaged. The SAS would never have worked on British soil again. The politicians and media, from the Prime Minister down, would have no doubt distanced themselves from the unit. Instead of a wildly successful op, it would have turned into a public scandal.

The upside to the Regiment's newfound fame was that the lingering sceptics in Whitehall had been permanently silenced. The British government, and the general public, now understood that they had this powerful, professional asset at their disposal.

Suddenly, the SAS found themselves in demand all around the world. They were able to trade on their prestige to sell their services abroad, sending small training teams to foreign states to teach them tactics. Their budget was dramatically increased, allowing the SP Team to invest in more specialist equipment.

The bog-standard black Tank Regiment coveralls were replaced with fireproof underwear and clothing. Extra modifications were made to the team's Range Rovers, adding side rails with foot-stands and mounting roof racks with ladders attached to them for rapid entry assaults, allowing the team to drive straight up to a stronghold and breach the higher floors. Special Forces pay was also introduced, giving the troopers a much-needed increase on their modest salary.

More importantly, the success of the operation served as a warning to aspiring terrorists. It was a way of letting them know: 'If you come to the UK and try anything, this is what is going to happen.'

For many years, that message was a powerful deterrent.

More recently, as global terrorism has mutated, the security forces have had to adapt once more. Since 9/11, terrorist groups have increasingly used suicide bombers to carry out devastating attacks on Western targets. In the past few years, terrorists have also weaponised vehicles to kill civilians, as seen in the truck attacks in 2016 in Nice and Berlin.

The religiously motivated terrorists of today cannot be negotiated with. You can't establish a rapport with someone who believes God is on their side. Such individuals are generally not planning on surviving their ordeal, but instead wish to die as martyrs to their cause.

Their objective is to spread fear by killing as many people as possible. They have no interest in negotiating with police, except to buy themselves time to kill more victims or to prepare for an assault. The aim of the security services in such incidents is to bring an end to the siege or shooting as quickly as possible, averting the loss of further life, using deadly force if necessary.

But while the tactics used by terrorists have changed, one thing remains constant: the readiness of the SP Team to confront them. Wherever and whenever extremists strike against British citizens, they can be certain that the Regiment will be there, ready to take them on.

CHAPTER 16

Raiders from the Sea

The Falklands War, April–June 1982

By the start of the 1980s, in the thirty years since it had been re-formed, the SAS had fought in secret wars, mastered warfare in the desert and the jungle, and had pioneered a bold new approach to counter-terrorism. But in the last decades of the twentieth century they would take part in two more orthodox conflicts, squaring up against large-scale conventional military forces for the first time since the Second World War. The first of these was to be fought eight thousand miles from Hereford, over a wind-swept archipelago in a remote corner of the South Atlantic.

The Falkland Islands, located three hundred miles off the eastern coast of South America, have been a British colony in one form or another since 1833. The territory comprises two larger islands, East and West Falkland, along with hundreds of smaller islands, with a total land mass of 4,700 square miles. The 3,000-odd inhabitants speak English and are mainly of British descent, but that hasn't stopped successive Argentine governments from laying claim to 'Las Malvinas'.

In 1981, the ruling military dictatorship in Argentina was coming under increasing pressure at home, faced with a restless populace and a devastated economy. Thousands of citizens had been killed during the 'Dirty War', a murderous campaign waged by the junta in which suspected political dissidents and left-wing sympathisers were tortured, executed or thrown to their deaths from aircraft. Public unrest was spreading, and when a new junta came to power at the end of the year, the leader, General Leopoldo Galtieri, pressed ahead with plans to seize the Falklands, along with the island of South Georgia, eight hundred miles further to the south. (Until 1985, South Georgia and the uninhabited South Sandwich Islands were a Falkland Islands dependency. Today, SGSSI is a separate UK Overseas Territory.)

On Friday, 2 April 1982, Argentine forces invaded the Falklands. Facing them was a small garrison of Royal Marines along with a handful of sailors. The defenders put up a spirited resistance, but they were facing a much larger attacking force of several hundred men, and by 0800 hours they were completely surrounded. Ninety minutes later, the Argentinians had gained complete control of the Falklands.

They had acted on the assumption that Britain wouldn't go to war over a scattering of distant islands with little or no strategic value. But the day after the invasion, at an emergency session of Parliament, Margaret Thatcher reacted to the invasion by insisting that the government had a duty 'to do everything that we can' to liberate the islanders. A task force, including the aircraft carriers *Hermes* and *Invincible*, was hastily assembled and set sail from Portsmouth two days later. Vast crowds lined the docks to wave off the fleet before its long journey south.

By that point, the Regiment was already making its move, mobilising as soon as the head shed learned of the Falklands invasion. Not for the first time, the SAS was getting itself involved from the outset, rather than sitting around and waiting for someone to call Hereford.

On 4 April, the men of D Squadron were the first to be deployed, flying out from RAF Brize Norton on Vickers V-10 aircraft. Their destination was the forward staging-post on Ascension Island, a tiny volcanic speck in the middle of the Atlantic, four thousand miles from the Falklands. The squadron based themselves at a place called Two Boats, a small settlement located in the centre of the island.

The following day G Squadron was also on its way to Ascension, embarking upon the amphibious assault ship HMS *Fearless* at Portsmouth, along with a headquarters element and the CO of 22 SAS, Lieutenant-Colonel Mike Rose. The guys settled into their new home while they made their way south on a journey that would take several weeks, training on the deck as they prepared for whatever task was put in front of them.

Meanwhile, after a few days on Ascension Island, D Squadron embarked upon the Royal Fleet Auxiliary vessel *Fort Austin* and set off to rendezvous with ships from the South Georgia Task Group (SGTG). Their mission was to recapture the territory of South Georgia. A rugged, rocky island situated to the south of the Antarctic convergence, much of its expanse is permanently covered in snow and ice. The island is mostly uninhabited except for a handful of scientists from the British Antarctic Survey (BAS) team, based at a research station on the north-eastern coast.

South Georgia was very much on the periphery of the war. The island had no real strategic value, but having been caught off-guard by the Argentine invasion, the British government was desperate for a morale-boosting win and made the recapture of the island a priority. D Squadron's job was to carry out reconnaissance on South Georgia and gather intelligence on the enemy forces.

It was a mission that very nearly ended in disaster.

On 21 April, the guys from Mountain Troop inserted on to South Georgia by three Westland Wessex helicopters, landing on Fortuna Glacier.

The patrol soon ran into trouble. The conditions were atrocious, with the men having to struggle through snowstorms, high winds and sub-zero temperatures. By last light, the patrol had covered less than a kilometre. The next morning, with their weapons rendered useless in the freezing cold and a number of guys showing signs of hypothermia, they finally admitted defeat. It was clear that they would not last another night, and after requesting evacuation the helicopters were sent out again during a patch of clearer weather to pick them up.

As the helicopters took off, a fierce blizzard suddenly swept over the glacier, causing one of the pilots to lose his horizons after suffering a whiteout. His helicopter crashed into the glacier, thankfully without any loss of life or major injuries to the men on board. The survivors were distributed between the other two choppers, but at this point the pilot of another Wessex also crashed, with only minor injuries to the passengers and crew.

There was now only one remaining helicopter. The pilot returned to the task force with his passengers before heading back out to collect the stranded patrol. In rapidly worsening conditions, he showed immense bravery and skill to rescue the rest of the Troop and ferry them safely back to HMS *Antrim*. If it hadn't been for that pilot, those soldiers would have had to spend another night on the glacier, and they would almost certainly have frozen to death.

The second attempt to insert a recce team, using Boat Troop, also ran into problems when three of the five outboard engines on their Gemini inflatable boats failed. Three of the boats eventually made it to the shore and set up their OPs, while a fourth crew was rescued by helicopter. The remaining boat crew was reported missing and was only located a few days later when they were spotted by a friendly vessel. They had decided against switching on their SARBEs in case the beacon signals were intercepted by the enemy.

The mission to retake South Georgia came to a low-key end on 25 April. That morning, an Argentinian *Balao*-class submarine had been detected off the coast of the island. Royal Navy helicopters engaged the submarine with depth charges, torpedoes and air-to-surface missiles, and the crippled sub fled to the former whaling station at Grytviken. The task force proceeded to attack the garrison, pummelling the enemy defences with naval gunfire before landing a force of men from D Squadron, supported by elements from the Royal Marines and the Special Boat Service (SBS). Shortly after they came ashore, the Argentines surrendered. The following day, the defenders at the remaining garrison at Leith, another whaling station located several miles further up the coast from Grytviken, also threw in the towel.

The victory in South Georgia undoubtedly provided a boost to the morale of the wider task force. Just as crucially, it delivered a message to the enemy, letting them know that the government was serious about reclaiming its territory by whatever means necessary. The Argentinians now knew that they could be beaten. But D Squadron had very nearly come unstuck on its very first mission.

Two days after the recapture of South Georgia, the squadron headed north on HMS *Brilliant* to link up with the main task force, joining G Squadron aboard the flagship, HMS *Hermes*. The Regiment could now turn its attention to the main target: the Falklands themselves.

The SAS would take on two drastically different roles in the campaign to retake the Falklands. The first was an intelligence-gathering function, using the experience the soldiers had gained in Northern Ireland to run covert OPs on the ground, operating in areas far ahead of the green army. The SBS would support this effort, maintaining OPs on selected targets.

Alongside this, the Regiment would carry out a raiding role in the tradition of the wartime SAS. Roaming deep behind enemy lines, they would seek out and destroy strategic targets before melting away into the darkness.

Both types of operation met with varying degrees of success. When the SAS was employed properly, to achieve clear strategic goals based on sound intelligence, it proved effective at supporting the wider war effort. But there were other occasions where the soldiers were asked to do jobs that perhaps would have been better suited to the infantry units engaged in the Falklands at the time.

G Squadron was given the reconnaissance job. Beginning on 1 May, four-man patrols were inserted by Sea King helicopters, landing at last light on the barren grasslands of East Falkland. Moving through the night, they reached their LUPs and then set up forward OPs, going into an ultra-hard routine. No hot brews, no cigarettes, rations eaten cold. They maintained a watch on the enemy for periods of up to four weeks at a time, observing troop numbers, dispositions, weapons, movements and air support, while also looking out for possible Argentine patrols.

Conditions on the ground were miserable. The land was boggy and damp, strewn with rocks and coursed with inlets. The men were always wet, their clothes and skin chilled by the cold weather and the constant wind. Trench foot was a common problem. So was hypothermia. The standard of equipment the guys had in the Falklands was poor: the standard-issue British Army boots and clothing weren't up to scratch. The fact that the Argentines were suffering as well was scant consolation. Whatever side you're on, it's much harder to soldier when you're shivering cold and soaked through.

The guys also had to deal with the stress of being compromised at any moment. The almost total lack of ground cover meant that the patrols had to be extremely careful to avoid being detected. They were operating on an island crawling with Argentinian troops and with the nearest reinforcements several thousand miles away. If they were discovered, they were on their own.

While the G Squadron patrols were getting set up on East Falkland, the guys in D Squadron were preparing to launch a mission of their own. One that would deliver a serious blow to the enemy's defensive capabilities, recalling the classic SAS raids of the Second World War.

On the night of 11 May, an eight-man recce team from Boat Troop inserted into a secluded bay on the shores of West Falkland. A few days earlier, British fighter jets on patrol had picked up emissions that suggested the presence of an enemy radar installation on a small land mass off the north coast of the mainland, called Pebble Island.

Information on the island was thin on the ground. The intelligence cell knew that there was a garrison there, numbering about a hundred men, plus an airstrip, and possibly some type of radar equipment, but not much more than that.

The men in Boat Troop had been tasked with taking a closer look.

Moving stealthily, they rowed across the calm water using foldable Klepper canoes. Once they reached the southern shore, four of the men waited with the kayaks while the others advanced across the island towards their objective. Leaving their Bergens in a shallow LUP so they wouldn't be visible to the enemy, the four men moved into their OP and scanned the airfield. They couldn't find any sign of a radar site, which was disappointing. But they did find something else very interesting.

Scattered across the airfield were eleven aircraft, including one Shorts Skyvan, four Beechcraft T-34 Mentors and half a dozen FMA IA-58 Pucarás.

The Pucará was one of the most feared aircraft in the Argentinian fleet. A counter-insurgency (COIN) jet fighter, it was designed to attack ground forces. With four FN Browning 7.62mm machine guns mounted on the wings, a pair of 20mm cannons and a variety of rocket pods and bombs, the Pucará packed a devastating punch. It was quick and manoeuvrable, with armour plating to protect it from small arms fire. It had the capacity to make mincemeat out of the guys on the ground.

The main landings were scheduled to place towards the end of May at San Carlos Water, on the western side of East Falkland. The Pucarás posed a serious threat to the planned invasion. Flying out of Pebble Island, the jets could easily hammer the ground troops as they moved forward from the bridgehead towards Port Stanley, potentially inflicting heavy casualties. They needed to be destroyed. As a result, D Squadron was authorised to launch a precision raid on Pebble Island.

Going in under cover of darkness, the raiders would RV with the recce patrol and stealthily approach the airfield in a squadron-sized formation. Mobility Troop would launch the attack on the airfield, hitting the planes with a mixture of explosives, rockets and small-arms fire. Another troop would concentrate on the nearby garrison, slotting the pilots and the rest of the Argentine forces.

The attack would be preceded by a stonking from an SAS mortar crew, forcing the enemy to hug the ground while the assault group went forward. A naval officer would accompany the raiding party, ready to direct supporting gunfire from HMS *Glamorgan*.

The men were heavily tooled up. As well as their personal M16 rifles and Browning pistols, they were equipped with a number of 66mm LAW (Light Anti-tank Weapon) rocket launchers and 7.62mm GPMGs. Some of the guys had M203 40mm grenade launchers fitted to the underside of their M16s. Others carried demolition charges. Between them, the raiders had enough firepower to reduce the aircraft at Pebble Island to scrap metal.

It was intended to be a lightning raid. The Regiment would hit the Argentines hard, destroy everything and then bug out before the enemy knew what had hit them.

On the evening of 14 May, Operation Prelim began.

The mission didn't get off to the smoothest of starts. Foul, windy weather meant that the warship had to move to a new position, further to the west, to compensate for the extra fuel the helicopters would have to carry. By the time the three remaining Troops from D Squadron – Mobility, Air and Mountain Troop – finally boarded the Sea Kings, they were running behind schedule. This was a big problem, because the raiders needed to be back on the deck of *Hermes* before daybreak left the ships dangerously exposed to enemy aircraft. They decided to ditch the plan to eliminate the garrison, concentrating their efforts on the attack on the airfield.

In bright moonlit conditions, the raiding party inserted at a pre-arranged LZ several miles from the target. The three Troops met up with the recce patrol from Boat Troop, unloaded their kit from the helicopter and the reunited squadron, numbering some fifty-odd men, then set off for their target. A while later they arrived at their forward mounting position, at the firing site for the 81mm mortar.

The guys now had to deal with a second problem when they realised that Mobility Troop, which had been tasked with leading the attack on the airfield, was missing. That troop had no one to guide them and in trying to navigate on their own at night they had fallen behind the rest of the column before getting lost. There was no time to wait for them to catch up. The attack would have to go ahead with three troops instead of four. Mountain Troop, under the command of Captain John Hamilton, now took on the job of wrecking the planes.

Once the men were in position, the attack began. Under covering fire and illuminant rounds from the warship and the mortar crew, Hamilton's assault group fanned out across the open ground. They met minimal resistance and quickly set about planting their charges on the parked aircraft. Simultaneously the 4.5-inch guns on HMS *Glamorgan* pounded targets in and around the airfield, smashing into the garrison's communications tower and fuel stores. For almost half an hour the assaulters continued to let rip, pulverising the remaining aircraft with a furious stream of rockets and machine-gun fire. The other soldiers covered the garrison, but no Argentines attempted to counter-attack the assault force.

As the sky was lit up by the flickering glow of burning airplanes, Hamilton and his men pulled back from the airfield and RV'd with the rest of the squadron. (Mobility Troop, by now having caught up with the others, had taken up a reserve role during the assault.) The men made their way to the pick-up point, where they were picked up by the Sea Kings and returned to a heroes' welcome on *Hermes*.

All eleven Argentine aircraft had been destroyed in the raid. The SAS had devastated their main target with no loss of life on their own side and with only two light casualties. One man was hit in the leg by shrapnel during the attack. Another was slightly injured when a mine was remotely detonated by the garrison as the raiders were bugging out.

The Pebble Island raid was a huge success, severely reducing the enemy's air attack threat. There was also the damage to the morale of the Argentine forces, knowing that the SAS had the means and ability to operate ahead of the frontline, hitting targets almost at will. It demonstrated exactly what the soldiers were capable of when they were used as strategic assets, launching precision strikes, acting on the solid intelligence gathered by the recce patrol.

But not every operation in the Falklands was as well planned, and executed, as Pebble Island.

On 4 May, ten days before D Squadron's attack on Pebble Island, HMS *Sheffield*, a Royal Navy destroyer, came under attack from a pair of Super Étendard strike fighters. Flying out of Rio Grande airbase, the aircraft waited until they were thirty miles from their target before launching two AM39 Exocet sea-skimming missiles.

One missile missed. The second struck *Sheffield* a few feet above the waterline.

The warhead failed to detonate but punched through the hull as far as the galley, killing eight cooks and causing several fires to break out. Within seconds the vessel was engulfed in thick smoke and flames. In total, twenty sailors died and another twenty-six were injured, many with serious burns. The destroyer was abandoned and later sunk.

The attack on HMS *Sheffield* was a massive wake-up call for the task force commanders. It was obvious to everyone concerned that the Exocet posed a major threat to the main landings at San Carlos Water. The British task force in the Falklands had two aircraft carriers, *Hermes* and *Invincible*. Both ships were vital to the planned landings. If one of them was sunk by an Exocet missile, it would make the task of retaking the islands much harder – and perhaps endanger the whole operation.

Back in Hereford, the guys in B Squadron had already started training for a possible clandestine mission on Argentine soil. Now the sinking of *Sheffield* had given the mission extra impetus. B Squadron's mission, approved at the very highest level, was to locate and destroy the Super Étendards. The strike fighters were the delivery system for the missiles. The thinking was, if the Regiment could take out the aircraft, they could stop the Exocets at source. Problem solved.

The plan involved the bulk of the men from B Squadron

heading out to Ascension Island, before transferring to a pair of Hercules C-130 transport aircraft. The C-130s would then fly to the military airbase at Rio Grande on the island of Tierra del Fuego, at the southernmost point of Latin America. Coming in low at night, the two aircraft would land on the runway in a surprise assault. Twelve guys would deplane from the rear of each aircraft on three Land Rovers equipped with mounted 7.62mm GPMGs and smoke canisters on the front and rear bumpers. The rest of the lads would be on foot.

While the main attack group moved up and down the runway, blasting away at the aircraft, a separate attack team would kill the pilots in their accommodation blocks, along with any other personnel. Once their handiwork was finished, they'd hop back on the C-130s if they were still serviceable and make for a nearby Chilean airbase. If the aircraft were knackered, the plan was to go into escape-and-evasion mode, splitting up into small teams, stealing any vehicles they could get their hands on and racing for the border with neutral Chile, fifty miles away.

The codename for this operation was Mikado.

Operation Mikado

It was a bold plan, but there was plenty of scope for it to go wrong. From the outset, there was a worrying lack of detailed information on the airbase at Rio Grande. The men had no idea where the missiles or fighter planes were actually kept. They didn't know which building housed the aircrews and personnel. They didn't even know whether the Super Étendards would be at the airfield on the day of the assault. That's a basic requirement for a mission like this. You make sure that when you're sending the guys in, the target is where it's supposed to be. Otherwise you're needlessly throwing away lives.

Realising that they needed more intelligence on the target, the head shed authorised an eight-man team from B Squadron to go in and recce the airbase. With the information gleaned from an 'eyes-on' patrol, the planners would have a much clearer picture of the layout at the airfield, the locations of the targets and the enemy's defences.

The advance party headed out to Ascension Island on 15 May. From there they flew south to RV with the main task force, parachuting into the sea with their equipment. Once they were safely aboard one of the aircraft carriers, the team flew out to Tierra del Fuego aboard a stripped-down Sea King.

The plan involved inserting the patrol at night near to the Rio Grande airfield. The crew would fly on and abandon the Sea King on the Chilean coast, rigging it with explosive charges. The helicopter couldn't carry enough fuel for the return journey to *Invincible*: deliberately wrecking it was the only realistic alternative.

Approaching the coast at a low level, the Sea King successfully touched down on Argentine soil. As the patrol disembarked, they spotted the luminous glow of a signal flare rising into the sky. Realising that they had been compromised, the captain decided to abandon the landing. The soldiers climbed back into the chopper and flew on across the border to Chile, where they were dropped off in the early hours. The pilot then took off again and dumped the Sea King on the coast in accordance with the original plan. When the wreckage was later discovered, the government claimed that the helicopter had crash-landed after getting into difficulty.

After marching for several hours in treacherous conditions, the patrol laid up before first light. They spent a few days attempting to continue with their mission, but with their supplies running low they were finally forced to admit defeat.

They contacted Hereford and were told to make for an emergency RV in Chile. When they arrived at what they believed was the location, however, there was no sign of any friendlies. The team now attempted to contact local British diplomats, but the only advice they were given was that they should surrender themselves to the police. They were eventually rescued while strolling through the streets of the remote town of Porvenir. One of the soldiers happened to glance through the window of a local restaurant and was stunned to see an SAS support team seated at a table inside. The patrol spent the next several days cooped up in a private house before returning to Hereford.

Meanwhile the rest of B Squadron continued to train hard for Mikado, unaware of the failed recce patrol. But already questions were being asked about the mission.

For a start, it was almost certain that enemy radar would pick up the C-130s before they reached Rio Grande. The airfield boasted a number of surface-to-air missiles (SAMs) and anti-aircraft guns. If the Argentines detected the incoming C-130s, as seemed very likely, they'd tear the aircraft to pieces long before the guys had a chance to land.

Even if they managed to somehow make it through the anti-aircraft defences unscathed and the assault teams destroyed the Super Étendards, they still had to get out. Which wasn't going to be easy. If the Hercules C-130s sustained any kind of damage, the squadron would have to leg it to the Chilean border. By this point the defenders would surely have sounded the alarm. Every Argentine soldier on the island would be out in strength, hunting for the SAS raiders.

Alarmingly, there were reports of a garrison of 1,800 marines just down the road from Rio Grande. If the alarm was raised, these marines would surely converge on the airbase to stop the attack. In that situation, the lightly armed men of B Squadron would be totally outgunned and outnumbered. It would have taken a miracle for anyone to get out of there alive.

As the date for the squadron's departure to Ascension Island drew nearer, many of the soldiers began openly to express doubts about the operation. Some felt that they were being asked to go on a suicide mission.

Matters came to a head at a briefing led by the Director SAS, hours before the squadron was due to fly out. A lot of the guys, hardened veterans who had taken part in numerous campaigns, simply could not believe that the operation was still going ahead in the face of a potentially high casualty rate and the lack of solid intelligence. The Squadron OC was promptly sacked after voicing his concerns to the Director. One of the Troop staff sergeants also RTU'd himself in protest at the decision to go ahead with the proposed mission. The relieved OC was replaced by the 2iC, Ian 'Crooky' Crooke, a popular individual among the soldiers.

The news filtered through to the squadron as they were preparing to leave Bradbury Lines for the RAF base at Lyneham. A heated debate took place, with one or two suggesting they should all show their support for the two relieved men. Others were more pragmatic. They didn't like the odds, and they knew there was a good chance that they wouldn't be coming home, but they were Special Forces and they had a job to do.

Talk of a mutiny quickly fizzled out. The squadron got on with the job, loaded up their kit and headed out on the buses. That's a testament to the character of those men. No one can question their commitment. The fact that they chose to get on that plane, despite knowing that they were probably going to their deaths, tells you everything you need to know.

SAS soldiers are prepared to gamble with their lives, if the circumstances call for it. And in its favour, the plan was certainly ballsy. The Argentines would never have expected the Regiment to pull off something as daring as a direct assault on Rio Grande. On the other hand, all it would have taken is for some switched-on radar operator to spot the C-130s, and the whole of B Squadron would have been annihilated.

There's being brave, and then there's being reckless. You have to respect the bravery of the two men who had left the Regiment. It takes a lot of courage to stand up and say, 'Sod this, I'm not going to lead my men to their deaths, I've got to take a stand here.' Especially when you know that doing so is probably going to end your career. Both those men paid a high price for their honesty.

B Squadron continued their training after landing on Ascension Island, constantly reworking and updating the plan. Several ideas were put forward. One option involved using a diesel submarine to bring a section of troops close to the island. The soldiers would then launch from small boats and make for the shore before heading to Rio Grande, hitting the airfield from another direction.

They also considered putting in an advance party by air, freefalling onto Tierra del Fuego and setting up a makeshift runway for the C-130s on a length of a main road.

Over the next several days, the operation was repeatedly postponed. By now, even the aircrews were having reservations about the mission. Strangely, none of them fancied the idea of getting blown out of the sky or taking their chances on foot on a mad dash to the border. All of a sudden, the two Hercules C-130 transport aircraft tasked with landing the guys on the airfield at Rio Grande started breaking down. Faults were being found with the planes on a daily basis. The mission kept getting pushed back.

While B Squadron waited for the go-ahead for their ill-fated mission, disaster struck elsewhere in the Regiment.

Late in the evening on 19 May, a group of men from D and G Squadrons, along with a few attached personnel, boarded a Sea King helicopter for the brief journey from *Hermes* to HMS *Intrepid*. The troops were cross-decking to the assault ship ahead of a planned mission on East Falkland. The other soldiers had already transferred to *Intrepid* and the group on the deck of *Hermes* was the last to make the trip. The chopper was crammed full of equipment and men and had difficulty climbing under all the extra weight.

Shortly after lift-off there was a sharp, deafening clang as a seabird was sucked into the engine intake, triggering a sudden loss of power. The Sea King lurched sideways and plunged helplessly into the freezing sea. Water surged through the shattered windows, flooding the cabin. At first, there was shock and confusion. Then panic set in. Soldiers began clambering towards the hatches, fighting to get out.

By now the helicopter had capsized and was beginning to submerge. The passengers, packed in like sardines, wrestled with one another in their desperation to escape the sinking aircraft, clawing at thrashing arms and legs. A handful of men pulled themselves free and kicked their way to the surface, but most of the guys went down with the water-filled Sea King.

A good friend of mine, Chris, was the last man to make it out of the chopper alive. He very nearly didn't survive. As the Sea King was dragged down, he tried to swim free but found that his leg was trapped. There was a guy below Chris who managed to pull him loose. The soldier gave him a tap on the ankle, letting him know that he was able to escape. Whoever that guy was, he drowned, while Chris swam to safety.

It was the third helicopter crash he had been involved in during the Falklands. Chris also had the misfortune of being on board both helicopters that had come down on the glacier in South Georgia. The third crash had very nearly ended his life. If it hadn't been for that selfless soldier freeing his leg, he would never have made it out of the Sea King. The image of that soldier sacrificing his own life to save Chris haunted him for many years afterward.

The few survivors spent thirty minutes in the icy water before they were rescued. Without their immersion suits to keep them warm, it is a miracle they didn't freeze to death. Twenty men lost their lives in that crash, eighteen of them from the SAS and two who had been attached to the Regiment. It was the single biggest loss of life the unit had suffered since the end of the Second World War.

Mistakes had been made in that cross-decking procedure. None of the men had been wearing dry suits. The helicopter was so overloaded with Bergens and soldiers that the passengers stood almost no chance of escape once it started to flood. Moreover, there had been no second helicopter on standby with rescue divers on board, overseeing the transfer in case anything went wrong. Had they been following procedure, lives may have been saved.

The Sea King crash was a human tragedy, but it was also devastating to the SAS. The Regiment is a small unit, permanently short of manpower. It cannot afford to lose so many men in one blow. Among the dead were veteran NCOs, including two squadron sergeant majors and half a dozen staff sergeants. These were soldiers with ten or fifteen years of experience, a lifetime of expertise and skills. It would take many years for the Regiment to fully recover.

A few days later, the Rio Grande mission was called off at the eleventh hour. There were conflicting reports about the reason for the head shed's sudden change of mind. One possible explanation is that, in the wake of the Sea King tragedy, the top brass realised that they could not absorb the sort of high casualty rate they were facing with Mikado. The Regiment had already lost a lot of good men to the sea. The loss of many more on a runway attack would have surely crippled the SAS.

CHAPTER 17

Victory in the Falklands

There was no time for the SAS soldiers to grieve for their dead friends. The following evening, 20 May, the surviving elements of D Squadron were back on East Falkland.

Their mission was to create a diversion ahead of the main landings that took place at San Carlos Water. A small force of men would move into position near the enemy garrison at Darwin and Goose Green and put down rounds at long range, convincing the defenders that they were coming under attack from a massive British force. It was crucial to keep the Argentinians pinned down for long enough for 3 Commando Brigade to come ashore.

The men marched through the night, lugging an energy-sapping amount of weaponry and supplies. Their hardware included FIM-92 Stinger portable surface-to-air missiles, a brand-new system not available to regular ground troops in the Falklands. The Regiment, however, has many friends in the world of Special Forces. They had managed to acquire a consignment of Stingers privately, through their contacts in the US.

The fact that the SAS, the world's finest elite fighting force, has spent much of its history having to beg and borrow pieces of kit from the Americans should be a point of shame for our defence chiefs.

Once the soldiers had reached their targets, they took up their positions and put down a fearsome amount of firepower on the enemy, tearing it up with 81mm mortars, Milan anti-tank missiles and machine-gun fire, supported by a bombardment from

HMS *Ardent*. The troopers moved constantly to give the impression that the Argentines were facing a battalion-sized line of defensive positions. While the defenders were being fixed in place, the main landing force quickly secured a foothold at San Carlos. During this time D Squadron also had the opportunity to use the Stingers for the first time, shooting down a Pucará as it came in low to attack the advancing troops.

The momentum of the invasion stalled while the ground forces waited for reinforcements to be brought forward. Meanwhile Argentinian aircraft mounted raids on the task force, sinking three warships in the space of four days, along with the container ship *Atlantic Conveyer*. A number of helicopters went down with the *Conveyer*, delaying efforts to bring supplies ashore. Under pressure from the government and with winter about to set in, the task force went on the offensive on 28 May. They chose to attack at Goose Green.

Two Para's assault at Goose Green, against a determined enemy occupying well-defended positions, was one of the most impressive actions in the long history of the Parachute Regiment. The Paras, numbering 450 men, were up against a substantially larger Argentine force supported by air cover. Despite these formidable odds, they secured a famous victory, accepting the surrender of the Argentinian troops the next day. Approximately fifty enemy soldiers had been killed and more than a thousand prisoners were taken. Eighteen men lost their lives on the British side, including Lieutenant-Colonel 'H' Jones, who was later awarded a posthumous VC.

Meanwhile D Squadron had pushed ahead to occupy Mount Kent, a key feature overlooking Port Stanley. The Argentines had neglected to put a force on the hill, ignoring the first rule of warfare: always occupy the high ground. Following a close recce, the soldiers moved forward and set up OPs around the hill, watching enemy positions while they waited to be reinforced by 42 Commando. Several Argentinian patrols then went up Mount Kent to claim it. The SAS repulsed all of them, killing a number of the enemy, and directed artillery fire on to targets in and around Stanley.

In addition to the Regiment, the SBS also had guys out on

patrol ahead of the frontline. The dangers of different units operating in the same confined area were illustrated by a blue-on-blue incident, when an SBS patrol accidentally wandered into an SAS position near Mount Kent.

The tail-end Charlie in the Regiment patrol saw that a group of armed individuals were coming up behind them and, having been told that there were no friendly forces in the area, assumed that they must be Argentines. It was dark, and the lead SBS man sported a long, drooping moustache of the type that was popular among Latin American men. The Regiment went into a snap ambush and the lead SBS operator was shot dead. It was only later that they realised the man they had killed was a signaller with the SBS.

This is what happens when patrols don't check out before going on operations. Critical information doesn't get posted to the ops board. Then you end up with patrols bumping into one another in the same area, sometimes with catastrophic results.

Another tragedy occurred around this time, when a patrol on West Falkland was compromised. On 5 June Captain John Hamilton, who had led the assault team on Pebble Island, had gone in with three guys from Mountain Troop, D Squadron, to set up an OP in the area, following reports of a build-up of enemy forces. On the morning of 10 June, Hamilton and his radio signaller were mounting the forward OP when they found themselves surrounded by enemy forces.

Cut off from the two other soldiers at the LUP (who managed to escape), Hamilton and his signaller, a dark-complexioned soldier, engaged the enemy despite being heavily outnumbered. Hamilton was wounded in the ensuing firefight, but continued to put down rounds on the Argentines while ordering the signaller to escape. Seconds later, Hamilton was shot dead. He had paid the ultimate price for attempting to save the life of his signaller.

The latter was captured after running out of bullets. He was taken prisoner but managed to persuade the Argentines that he was Hamilton's batman, cooking and cleaning and doing all the menial duties. The Argentines apparently believed him and kept him in a hole, until he was eventually freed at the end of the conflict.

The war was reaching its closing stages – and B Squadron looked like they would now play a part in the final assault after all. Back on Ascension Island, they had been frustrated onlookers. Now their luck appeared to change when they were given orders for an attack on the airfield at Port Stanley.

The plan involved flying south on a pair of C-130s to link up with the task force, deploying by static-line parachute into the sea. The squadron would then insert onto East Falkland by helicopter and seize Stanley airport, stopping the Argentines from bringing in any more forces to continue the fight.

On 11 June, the Squadron set off for the Falklands. The operation immediately ran into difficulties. In order to make the round trip to the task force, the C-130s needed to refuel in mid-air with a Victor tanker. One of the Hercules successfully refuelled, but a technical problem meant the second C-130 was unable to continue the journey south and had to turn around, flying back to Ascension Island.

After a flight lasting most of the day, the remaining aircraft reached the task force and dropped to jump height before making a first pass over the drop zone. A thousand feet below, Gemini inflatable boats bobbed up and down amid clouds of spindrift, waiting to pick up the men from the sea.

Dressed in their dry suits, the soldiers jumped out of the tailgate in 'sticks' of six or seven, along with the cargo boxes containing their weapons and kit. As the heavy pallets tumbled out of the Hercules, the lightweight fittings snapped apart and the containers became separated from their parachutes. The boxes tumbled to the ocean, breaking up on the white-capped waves. The men could do nothing except look on in bitter frustration as most of their weapons, kit and personal possessions were lost to the ocean.

Most of the parachutists were rescued within minutes of hitting the water, although one man spent thirty minutes in the sea before he was finally pulled out. When the last soldier had been rescued, they learned that many of the containers had sunk beneath the waves.

As it turned out, B Squadron's efforts to RV with the task force had been in vain. The war was practically finished. On the night of 11–12 June, 3 Para seized Mount Longdon, storming the hill with fixed bayonets. On the same night, the Commandos secured further victories at Two Sisters and Mount Harriet.

There was time for D Squadron to attempt one final mission, another diversionary raid, this time in support of 2 Para's assault on Wireless Ridge. Several lads from G Squadron and a force of SBS and Royal Marines would also take part in the attack. An assault team would use four rigid raider craft to approach their target, an oil refinery, while they were covered by the rest of the force. The attack was called off after the boats came under fire from enemy defences on the far shore. The raiders managed to withdraw without any loss of life, covered by their colleagues on the opposite shore.

The following day, Monday 14 June, a white flag was raised above Stanley.

The SAS's final contribution had been to help negotiate an end to hostilities. For several days, the CO and an officer who spoke Latin American Spanish had been patiently communicating with the Argentinian commanders, in a bid to convince them to lay down their arms and avoid further bloodshed. Their efforts came to fruition when General Menendez indicated that he was prepared to discuss terms. He formally surrendered that evening.

A few days later, the three SAS squadrons flew back to Ascension Island. The next day, they were on their way back to Hereford. On 17 June, General Galtieri resigned. The ruling military junta in Argentina finally gave up power the following year.

The SAS helped to achieve victory in the Falklands, but they were never the decisive piece on the chessboard. In a conventional war, operating in a crowded theatre involving every branch of the armed forces on both sides, the outcome was always going to be decided by the Parachute Regiment and the Royal Marines.

Those were the guys out there doing the hard soldiering, carrying out frontal assaults and storming enemy positions. The Royal Navy and the RAF played their parts too, but without the Paras, the Falklands would never have been taken.

It was the Paras who charged up Mount Longdon into a hail of enemy gunfire, fixing bayonets and sticking the Argentinians. Plenty of brave young lads lost their lives on that hill, at Goose Green and other key battles. Those men are the ones who should be given the credit for the victory.

The SAS did enjoy some successes in the Falklands. D Squadron's assault on Pebble Island was a classic raid. The OPs run by G Squadron were vital in gathering information on the enemy and sending it back to the task force. In those operations, the guys generally performed well.

In other areas they were hampered by a lack of quality intelligence or deployed on missions that were perhaps not the best way of utilising the soldiers.

The ethos of the Regiment, going back to the days of Stirling and Mayne, has always been that you only use the men for strategic operations. SAS soldiers aren't supermen, and they should never be used at the point of battle.

The reality is, an infantry unit can sustain a number of casualties. Beyond a certain point, the SAS cannot. Even if the destruction of the aircraft at Rio Grande had been absolutely critical to the success of the invasion, the Regiment simply could not have absorbed casualties of fifty per cent or more, on top of the losses that the squadrons had already suffered with the Sea King disaster. It would have been a senseless loss of life and a hammer blow to the Regiment's ability to operate.

It's the military equivalent of exposing your Queen on the board. You're taking an unnecessary risk with a prized asset.

In fairness to the head shed, they're under their own pressures in a war setting. The senior officers have to be seen to be getting their boys involved. Unfortunately, this means they sometimes rush in and pick targets to justify themselves. SAS soldiers end up getting thrust into operations based on little or no information, working to plans that have not been properly thought out. Whereas it might be best to pause and take a deep breath and think, okay, where are we best placed to help out? Where can we do the most damage, strategically?

Overall, the Regiment experience in the Falklands was bittersweet. The Sea King disaster cast a long shadow over the campaign and impacted on the SAS's operational capabilities for years to come. The chronic manpower shortage led to some individuals being promoted to key positions in the squadron, simply because there was no one else around to fill the vacancies. Some of those promoted men were good soldiers. A few were not. They would have been very unlikely to reach the ranks they achieved, had it not been for the soldiers who went down with the Sea King.

The SAS ultimately emerged from the Falklands with its reputation enhanced, as a small part of a successful military endeavour, but it could have ended very differently. Mistakes were made, in everything from the standard of equipment and weaponry available to the soldiers, to the quality of mapping and the breaking of SOPs. Many of these errors would be repeated nine years later, in the Iraqi desert.

The Falklands conflict was the last major engagement the SAS was involved in during the 1980s. For the rest of the decade, the focus switched back to counter-terrorism training and the continuing operations against the IRA in Northern Ireland. The Regiment also underwent a number of changes, the biggest of which was the creation in the early 1980s of a covert unit within the SAS. This unit worked closely with the security services. Only experienced SAS soldiers were chosen, with each man thoroughly vetted beforehand. They took on jobs such as escorting ambassadors through foreign countries or accompanying agents on missions overseas. Other tasks might include training up foreign security forces or a group of freedom fighters, the type of arrangement the government might want to keep quiet about. While the guys in the CRW wing were going after terrorists, the men in this covert unit were more likely to train them.

This creation of this unit ushered in a period of closer cooperation between the Regiment and the security services. The ad hoc operations of the 1960s were replaced by something much more formalised. In the 1980s, men from the newly-formed covert unit were part of a team sent out to Afghanistan to train up the mujahideen rebels in their guerrilla war against the Russians.

Afghanistan, 1980s

In 1979, Soviet forces had swept into Kabul, killing the Afghan President, Hafizullah Amin, and installing a pro-Moscow puppet. The fiercely conservative tribespeople reacted to the arrival of foreign troops by launching an insurgency that would ultimately hasten the downfall of the Soviet Union.

The Russians had expected the poorly equipped Afghans to roll over in the face of their formidable war machine. But by adopting Viet Cong-style guerrilla tactics, the mujahideen scored some notable victories against their bitter enemies, and the invading forces soon found themselves bogged down in a costly quagmire.

Washington and London spied an opportunity to undermine the Kremlin by supplying weapons and cash to the tribal insurgents, potentially turning the tide of the war in their favour. Defeat in Afghanistan would humiliate the Russians on the international stage, at a time when they were trying to reassert their strength.

Neither Britain nor the US could risk direct intervention, however. Action needed to be covert in order to avoid the possibility of escalating the situation and triggering a confrontation with Moscow. The solution was to recruit SF operators, including ex-SAS NCOs, to train up mujahideen fighters loyal to an influential guerrilla commander, Ahmed Shah Massoud, teaching them contact drills, sabotage and demolitions. These clandestine operations were overseen by the security services and bankrolled by the CIA. Emboldened by the success of these early endeavours, the US and UK began funnelling weapons through to the mujahideen, including consignments of Stinger missiles.

These were critical in terms of levelling the playing field: until the Stingers were thrown into the mix, the Afghans had been getting hammered by the Mil Mi-24 Hind attack helicopters. Ex-Regiment men supplied the guerrillas with the deadly Stingers, teaching them how to shoot down the Russian Hinds. Armed with the latest kit and educated in battlefield tactics, the insurgents began inflicting heavy casualties on the Russians. By the late 1980s, with the body count mounting, the Kremlin was looking for a way out of the conflict. The last troops finally withdrew in 1989.

The above-mentioned covert unit within the SAS has continued to expand its role in recent years. It still works closely with the British security services, although such operations are not without risk.

In 2011, an eight-man team from the unit was captured after landing in rebel-held territory in eastern Libya. The lads had been accompanying an agent from the security services, operating under diplomatic cover, who was there to broker a deal with rebels fighting against Muammar Gaddafi. They chose not to open fire on their captors for fear of escalating the problem. Instead they were detained and subsequently released after some behind-the-scenes political manoeuvres.

Gambia, Botswana, Thailand

SAS men took part in other overseas ops during the 1980s, not all of them at the bidding of the intelligence agencies. In 1981, Ian 'Crooky' Crooke and two other Regiment guys were sent into Gambia after rebels staged a coup, taking hostages including one of the President's wives and several of his children. Troops from Senegal had moved in to restore order, but encountered fierce resistance from the rebels in the capital, Banjul.

Dressed in civvies and armed with nothing more than Browning 9mm pistols, Crooke and his colleagues overpowered the guards at the hospital where the hostages were being held and escorted them to safety. They then led an assault on the main rebel positions. Within a few days the rebels were in disarray, the ringleaders had been rounded up and the President was returned to power.

At the same time, private military companies (PMCs) were also beginning to get in on the action. Ex-Regiment guys, working alongside former members of the SBS, were hired to train up elite forces in the Middle East. That promptly came to an end when retired American Special Forces personnel muscled in and started taking over a lot of the contracts. Other ex-SAS men took up jobs at the 'Goat Farm', a military camp near Salalah in Oman, where they trained up the Sultan's Special Forces unit.

PMCs would come further to the forefront in the wars of the twenty-first century, when they took on a leading role in Afghanistan and Iraq. Over the years many ex-SAS operators have gone on to work with PMCs in some of the world's deadliest conflict zones, including Sierra Leone.

The second major change for the SAS in the 1980s was the expansion of team jobs. These were overseas training missions, instructing foreign troops around the world in Regiment knowhow. Team jobs were big earners for the SAS. They were also a political tool, used by the Foreign Office and security services to gain influence and curry favour with foreign powers.

In 1986, we were sent out on one such mission to help train up a new elite unit within the Botswana Defence Force (BDF). For years the South African Defence Force (SADF), the military wing of the apartheid regime, had been doing cross-border raids into Botswanan territory, targeting guerrilla forces fighting for the African National Congress (ANC). The Botswanans realised that in order to stop the SADF raids, they needed a specialist unit capable of effectively policing the border. B Squadron had been requested to provide the training for the new force.

Training foreign troops requires a lot of patience and hard work. A group of guys from the squadron had gone out to Botswana the year before to set up a training package, running a basic Selection course, doing range work and teaching the soldiers how to navigate and patrol. By the time we arrived, all the lessons the BDF had been taught had been forgotten. The scene that confronted us was a shambles. The recruits had reverted to a low level of soldiering. Weapons had rusted up, their kit was in bad order, everything had been neglected. We had to go back to square one and start over again.

Sometimes we would go out with the BDF on border patrol operations, setting up ambushes for South African forces attempting to infiltrate into the country. We were under strict instructions not to engage with the enemy on these missions. The SAS was there in a strictly advisory role, helping them to navigate and making sure they were doing everything correctly.

We lost one soldier on this operation during a climb in the Tsodilo Hills. Our troop, Mountain, had been running a training exercise when a veteran operator, Joe Farragher, fell the full length of his climbing rope. When we reached his body, I tried to give Joe the kiss of life, but he was already dead. It took us several hours to get him off that mountain. When the helicopter came in to lift him off, the engine caught fire and it had to return to base. Air Troop eventually brought up a vehicle to collect Joe's body and he was later flown back to the UK. Joe was a fantastic soldier, quiet and unassuming, but strong as an ox. His loss was keenly felt by the rest of the squadron.

At the same time, the SAS had been running a long-term job in Thailand, helping to train up exiled Cambodian guerrillas opposed to the Communist regime in Phnom Penh. Some of these fighters included former members of the Khmer Rouge. Under the leadership of Pol Pot, they had been responsible for the deaths of millions of Cambodians in one of the worst genocides of the twentieth century. The British government was willing to train these men because, at the time, they were more worried about the threat of Communism in south-east Asia.

In the mid-1980s, I was part of a team from B Squadron ordered out to Thailand to bolster the training group. We didn't make it very far, however. The operation was called off after John Pilger, the investigative journalist, exposed our activities. I ended up having to return the money I had been given and the Regiment pulled out of Thailand overnight, although a small team was later sent back out once the fuss had died down. Operations to train the rebels continued until late 1988.

Colombia

Several months later, we were sent out to Colombia to train a new elite unit called the Junglas. These guys were specially formed to go after Pablo Escobar and the Cali cartel, who dominated the cocaine trade in the late 1980s and early 1990s. The cartels had a lot of power and influence back then. They were better armed than the military, and corruption in the government and security forces was rife, with establishment figures being bought off and army and police officers shopping their mates. It was felt that a new, dedicated unit was needed to combat the drug threat. The Americans paid for it; we went over there to take charge of the training. It was a squadron-sized job, with B and A Squadrons doing rotations in Colombia.

The Junglas' main task was to destroy the HCl (cocaine hydro-chloride) processing labs located in the remote jungle. This is where the coca paste is converted into pure cocaine through a process involving hydrochloric acid, acetone and other solvents. The chemicals used create a vile, pungent odour. You can always smell the HCl labs before you see them.

We taught the Junglas the skills they needed to locate, recce and destroy the cocaine labs and their adjacent landing strips. They also went up against armed paramilitary groups running amok in the country. The rebel Marxist guerrillas, FARC, were at the height of their power in the 1980s and had become deeply involved in the cocaine trade, slapping a 'tax' on the producers in exchange for protecting their turf. The Junglas really had their hands full, dealing with narco gangs one minute and terrorist militias the next.

Despite these challenges, they achieved some notable successes in the war against the drug traffickers. Sadly, nobody had the foresight to see that bringing down Escobar and the Cali cartel wouldn't end the production or consumption of cocaine. Instead the business simply shifted north to Mexico.

With their traditional trafficking network closed off, the Colombians became increasingly reliant on the Mexican cartels to smuggle their products across the US border. Within a few years, the Mexicans had established themselves as the new masters of the drug trade. Between 2006 and 2019, the drug war in Mexico claimed more than two hundred thousand lives. Whatever the rationale for sending us out to Colombia, all we ended up doing was triggering chaos further north.

We soon realised that stopping the flow of drugs to the West was a thankless task, no matter how many HCl labs and airfields the Junglas destroyed. I remember speaking with a group of farmers living in grinding poverty in a rural part of the country. They told me that the only crop they could grow on their land was plantain, which didn't provide them with enough income to feed their families. But if they grew the coca leaf, they could make a living and their wives and kids wouldn't starve. They weren't concerned about some wealthy politician snorting lines at a party in Kensington. All they cared about was putting food on the table.

Until we have a solution for that farmer, the drugs problem is never going to go away. There's too much money in it.

The 1980s had been a period of relative independence for the Regiment. In the Falklands, the SAS had been a cog in a much bigger military machine. But for the next nine years, we had been the machine itself. Whether it was on training jobs abroad, serving in Northern Ireland or on the counter-terrorism team, we were the ones running the show on the ground.

All that changed in 1990, when Saddam Hussein invaded Iraq.

CHAPTER 18

Return to the Desert

The Gulf War, Iraq, 1990–91

In 1988, at the end of a brutal eight-year war with Iran, Iraq was financially crippled and owed billions of dollars in loans to Kuwait and the other Gulf states. The country's ruler, Saddam Hussein, had no intention of paying and called on his creditors to cancel the debts. When they refused, Saddam started threatening Kuwait. He had long had his eyes on the tiny oil-rich sheikhdom, arguing that it was a fundamental part of Iraqi territory.

Saddam now claimed that the Kuwaitis had been stealing oil from fields on the Iraqi side of the border. To make matters worse, he also accused Kuwait of deliberately increasing its oil production, driving down the price per barrel and further destabilising the Iraqi economy.

Attempts to mediate the dispute failed and in the early hours of 2 August 1990, Saddam ordered his troops, numbering 100,000 men, to cross the border. The Kuwaiti forces were taken by surprise and completely overrun. Within a matter of hours, Kuwait City had fallen to the Iraqis and the ruling Emir and his family had escaped to Saudi Arabia.

Saddam had invaded in the belief that the liberal democracies of the West would not risk a military confrontation, especially in what he perceived was a strictly Arab affair. 'Yours is a society which cannot accept ten thousand dead in one battle,' he told the

US ambassador before the invasion. As far as he was concerned, Kuwait was rich and ripe for the plucking.

His gamble backfired catastrophically. Between them, Kuwait and Saudi Arabia were sitting on around half of the world's oil reserves. Saddam's actions threatened the global oil supply and sparked widespread condemnation. In a matter of days, a massive US-led international coalition was being formed, demanding the withdrawal of Iraqi forces from Kuwait. Sanctions were imposed and in November, a UN resolution was passed authorising the use of force to drive Iraqi troops out of Kuwait if necessary. The deadline for the withdrawal was set for 15 January 1991.

Throughout the autumn, the Coalition began building up their forces in Saudi Arabia. At first, this was to defend Riyadh from possible Iraqi aggression. As the days and weeks progressed, however, it became clear that Saddam had no intention of pulling out of Kuwait and the focus shifted to removing the Iraqi troops by force. A massive military machine was being assembled in the desert, bringing together countries from around the world, including the US, UK, Australia, France, Poland, South Korea and a number of Arab partners.

The Regiment's early involvement was low-key. A handful of advisers had been sent out to the Gulf, operating in a strictly passive role, bodyguarding various diplomatic staff and assessing the situation on the ground. Meanwhile at Hereford, everybody was wondering who would get the chance to go out. On paper, there was only one answer.

Soon after Iraqi forces rolled into Kuwait, G Squadron had been sent out to the Middle East to do build-up training. In mid-September, the guys in D Squadron flew out to replace G Squadron and continued their preparations, practising their vehicle and contact drills. Both squadrons were the obvious choice for any deployment in the Gulf.

Throughout this time, A Squadron had been overseas doing team jobs. Some were in Colombia. Others were dispersed on various top-secret operations. As for B Squadron, we had spent months on the SP Team. Neither ourselves nor the guys in A Squadron had done any desert training. Our rotation on the SP Team was due to end at Christmas, with G Squadron taking over from us. We would then take over the team tasks and squadron training.

The logical decision should have been to postpone the rotations, let B Squadron do another tour on the counter-terrorism team and allow G Squadron to fill the standby role in the Middle East, supporting D Squadron. The guys from A Squadron could stay out in Colombia running the team task. That arrangement made total sense, because D and G were both up to speed on their desert warfare training and were ready to go in immediately.

None of this was of much concern to me at the time. I wasn't really interested in what was going on in the Gulf. As far as I was concerned, I would soon be off to climb Mount Everest with Harry Taylor, an ex-Blade, and another guy, Russell Bryce. The head shed had already given me authorisation to join the others once B Squadron's rotation on the SP Team came to an end. Right up until the end of November, I was told that I wouldn't be getting involved in any action in the Middle East. The Everest expedition would go ahead as planned. That was fine by me.

Then in December, everything changed. We were told, 'B Squadron will come off the SP Team. G Squadron will take over, A and D will go out to the UAE.' B Squadron was to be split into two groups. Half the squadron would go out on the team training jobs, as originally planned. The other half would deploy to the Gulf, to support A and D Squadrons as battlefield casualty replacements (BCRs).

The concept of BCRs is to replenish any casualties the other squadrons sustain while on operations. If we were needed, we would head out to RV with the two squadrons during resupply and replace their wounded or missing colleagues. Within twenty-four hours of linking up with the patrol, the BCRs would be brought up to speed on how the team was operating, their procedures for basha'ing up, and the formations they were using.

The news was a bolt out of the blue. None of us in B Squadron had a sniff that we were about to be sent out. We hadn't done any work in the desert, none of our kit had been sorted out and we had hardly any time to make our preparations.

There was a mass panic as we raced to get our stuff ready, securing all the equipment, weapons and clothing that we might need, sorting out life insurance policies and other admin. Meanwhile the remaining half of B Squadron – the ones who weren't going to the Middle East – had to get briefed on the team tasks they were going to do. Some went to Colombia, others were sent off to parts of Africa.

Everyone knew that G Squadron should have been part of any deployment to the Gulf. Those guys had done the training. They had been out in the Emirates for months before it all kicked off, acclimatising to the environment and getting themselves updated. Sticking them on the counter-terrorism team while we shipped out as BCRs defied logic.

It was to be the first of a series of cock-ups that ultimately cost three men their lives.

The squadrons flew out to Abu Dhabi in late December and early January. The men in A Squadron were first to leave, shortly after Christmas. They joined the elements of D Squadron who were already in-country, with the rest of the guys in D joining up very soon after that. We were the last to leave Hereford, flying out of Brize Norton on 5 January and arriving in Abu Dhabi the following day.

The main SAS camp had been loaned to us as a result of a deal the Regiment had cut with the ruler of Abu Dhabi, Sheikh Zayed bin Sultan Al Nahyan. At the time the SAS hadn't yet been invited to the party and they were looking around for a well-placed camp they could take over at short notice. They agreed to supply the Sheikh with a ten-man team from B Squadron to train up an Emirates counter-terrorism unit, teaching them CT tactics. In return, we were given the use of a disused military camp with a runway at a place called Swaihan. We designated it as Victor.

To begin with, nobody seemed quite sure what sort of role the Regiment would have in the war. It seemed likely that A and D

Squadrons would be used as mobile fighting patrols, raiding behind enemy lines, and they focused their training with that in mind. There had also been some talk early on of using the SAS alongside American Special Forces to rescue the hundreds of Western hostages being held inside Iraq. Saddam had been using them as human shields, scattering them across the country to protect key installations. That plan was scrapped in early December, when he ordered their release under intense diplomatic pressure.

Behind the scenes, the Allied Commander-in-Chief, Norman Schwarzkopf, was blocking any attempt by the British commander to deploy the Regiment across the border in Iraq. He didn't see the value in risking the lives of SF soldiers on the ground, preferring to conduct the war from the air. His two-stage plan involved sending in massive air attack formations to pound the living daylights out of Iraqi positions, and then following up with a large-scale ground offensive using conventional forces. SF teams operating ahead of the frontline weren't part of the plan.

While this argument went back and forth between the commanders, we were getting briefed daily on operations. In the absence of any grand strategy, the OCs and officers were asked to put together plans for how the Regiment might be used. Many of these ideas were badly thought out, ill-conceived or simply not appropriate for a Special Forces unit. By now the head shed was keen to get B Squadron involved as well and they started looking at tasks for us other than standing by as battlefield replacements. At one point someone suggested that we should be sent into a block of flats in Iraqi-occupied Kuwait City. From there, we would direct Coalition aircraft on to Iraqi positions in and around the streets.

I couldn't believe what I was hearing. Once the B-52s started dropping bombs all over the place, it would have taken the Iraqis about five minutes to work out where the pilots were getting their information from. They would have turned their big guns on that apartment block and demolished it, killing us and everyone else inside. Thankfully, that one never got approved.

One bad idea followed another. People were coming in,

saying, 'We'll be doing this or that.' The next day, we were told, 'No, that's not happening anymore.' The plans changed with every cup of tea we were drinking.

This is how mistakes get made in a war. Everyone is running around like headless chickens, wanting to get involved. Decisions are rushed, plans are put forward without being subjected to rigorous analysis. No one stops to take a breath and think things through. And it's the soldiers who suffer as a result.

Our role shouldn't have changed. We had been sent out as BCRs, which was acceptable given our lack of desert preparation. If we had been called upon individually to join the other patrols, we could have been brought up to speed without affecting the operational ability of the rest of the group.

The problems for B Squadron began when the head shed decided to look for another role for us, without giving us time to properly train or plan for it. The logical decision should have been to stick to our initial directive and hold us in reserve until we were needed. This wasn't the fault of our OC, though. He was a good guy and a highly capable soldier and officer, in my opinion. But he wasn't well supported by the upper echelons of the SAS.

In the meantime, we got on with our desert training. The other two squadrons were well into their build-up training by the time we had arrived. Although they didn't know what specific targets they would be going after, the guys had clarity over the general scope of their operations and they could plan accordingly. They were doing range work and running night-time assault exercises, shaking out in half-squadron formations.

B Squadron wasn't so fortunate. As the reserve team, we were lucky to get one day a week on the ranges, which is nowhere near good enough. Much of the equipment we were given was either unsuitable for the desert or almost completely useless.

A and D squadrons were given Land Rover 110s, known as 'Pinkies' because of the colour they had been painted in Oman in the 1970s. (The Omani desert is mostly a light reddish-pink. Vehicles were painted the same tint to help them blend in.) The name stuck, even though our vehicles had been coated in a sandy paint to match the landscape of western Iraq.

The Pinkies are formidable mobile fighting platforms. They can carry a lot of spare fuel – sixteen jerry cans in total – and you can load them up with enough kit, ammunition and supplies to operate for a fortnight. They also have weapon mounts for GPMGs, Browning .50 calibre 'relish' heavy machine guns, M19 grenade launchers and Milan anti-tank missiles.

We didn't have any 110s. All we had were a few Land Rover 90s, the short-wheelbase, two-door version of the Pinkies. They didn't have any mounts so we couldn't fix any weapons to them, and they couldn't carry anywhere near as much of a load. We worked day and night on these vehicles, stripping them down to try and adapt them so we could use them in the desert. Then we took them out and did NavExes (navigation exercises). It didn't take us long to realise that the 90s were not fit for purpose. If we tried taking them into Iraq, it was obvious that we'd soon get compromised.

The work was non-stop. Between the training, trying to adapt our shoddy equipment and the endless briefings, we were getting really worn down. It was like being on a sleep-deprivation exercise. We were knackered before we'd even set foot inside Iraq.

Then we were given anthrax jabs, which put everyone on their arses for a few days. It was like coming down with the worst flu you've ever had. We were coughing up huge lumps of phlegm and some of the lads had to have the injection sites opened up because the tissue had gone septic. The jabs were supposed to protect us against the effects of the chemical weapons that Saddam was known to possess. He had the capability, and he was certainly willing to use them, as he'd demonstrated in the Iran–Iraq War. How effective the vaccine would have been against anthrax, I have no idea. But it certainly had an effect on us.

On 15 January, the deadline for the Iraqi withdrawal from Kuwait passed. The war was about to kick off, and we still had no idea what role we were going to play in it. The other squadrons were also waiting to be clued up on their precise targets. The following day, the Deputy Director Special Forces gathered A and D Squadrons, plus our half of B Squadron, in the camp hangar and stood up on one of the tables to address us.

'Gentlemen,' he began. 'When this military machine starts moving, you will be the lead cog. You'll go directly to where the action is.'

He laid it on thick. We were to be the first into action. We were going to be kept fully informed, we'd be briefed on our missions any day now and then inserted into the theatre. The SAS was going to be the tip of the Coalition spear, thrusting at the heart of the Iraqi military.

We woke up early the next morning, 17 January. Somebody turned on the radio. The airwaves were filled with reports of the first airstrikes that had gone in overnight. Apache helicopters had destroyed Iraq's radar sites, paving the way for Coalition aircraft to swoop in, obliterating airfields, communications lines, factories and military bases across the country.

'So much for being Special Forces and the tip of this particular spear,' somebody said. We all started laughing. It was a complete joke.

The day after the airstrikes, the first Scud missiles rained down on Israel.

Saddam Hussein had already vowed to attack Israel if the Coalition forces tried to kick him out of Kuwait. In the early hours of 18 January, he proved as good as his word, lobbing eight Scuds in the direction of Tel Aviv and Haifa. Many more would follow, threatening to drag Israel into the war.

For the military commanders, this was a nightmare scenario. The Coalition's Arab partners had only agreed to join forces on condition that the Israelis stayed out of the fight. If Israel retaliated, it would shatter the fragile alliance and possibly unite the Arab nations against Israel, plunging the Middle East into an even deadlier conflict. There were also concerns that Saddam might use the Scuds to deliver biological or chemical weapons. There was no telling how the Israelis might respond if that happened.

Patriot guided missiles were able to shoot down some of the Scuds, but others were still able to get through as Saddam targeted cities in both Israel and Saudi Arabia. The big problem was the mobile Scud launchers, known as transporter erector launcher (TEL) vehicles. These could be easily concealed in the desert, beneath road bridges, or hidden under cam nets. Coalition aircraft had great difficulty in locating and destroying the TELs and it was obvious that air power alone wasn't going to get the job done. To get at the Scuds, they needed men on the ground.

They turned to the Regiment.

By the time the Scuds started falling, Schwarzkopf had finally agreed to deploy the SAS behind enemy lines. D Squadron would target the enemy's lines of communication and vehicle compounds. A Squadron's brief was more generalised – they were given free rein to roam through the desert, hitting any opportune targets they encountered. By disrupting Iraqi supply bases and communication facilities, they would compel Saddam to divert resources away from the front. This would reduce the threat the Coalition ground forces faced when they finally moved in to liberate Kuwait.

B Squadron's directive was to gather intelligence on the ground. We would move in ahead of the other groups and carry out static OPs, feeding information back to HQ so the other lads could act on it, performing broadly the same tasks as G Squadron had done in the Falklands. This would strengthen our hand in terms of expanding operations behind enemy lines.

The Regiment is very good at this. Once we've established a toehold somewhere, putting soldiers on the ground, things tend to start happening. We find ways of making ourselves useful. Generals begin to look at us and think, 'How can we use this asset?' The vital thing is to get the guys in to where the action is. Then we can start causing mayhem.

The Scud threat changed the tactical focus of our mission. Getting rid of the Scuds became the number-one priority for the allied commanders. We were now given two main objectives.

The first task was to locate the TELs. Three eight-man patrols from B Squadron would insert into Iraq and set up covert OPs along the main supply routes (MSRs) believed to be used by the mobile Scud launchers. We would then start watching for possible targets. Whenever a Scud came past, we'd get on the satellite communications unit and put in a real-time report. Fast air would then fly in to the coordinates and blow up the mobile launcher before it could get into position and fire.

A subsidiary mission involved sabotaging the network of fibre-optic cables rigged up across the Iraqi desert. These cables were believed to allow Baghdad to communicate directly with the TELs, sending information and coordinates to guide them on to targets. They were buried deep under the surface, so knocking them out with fighter-bombers wasn't an option.

According to the Regiment intelligence cell, the cables ran along the side of the MSRs we had been tasked with observing. We were given cutting equipment to take out sections of the line, but there was a problem. Iraqi engineers could rapidly identify exactly where the cable had been cut by bouncing a light up and down the length of it. To stop them from repairing the damaged sections, we would rig the area with anti-personnel mines, taking out any engineers who showed up. That would hopefully dissuade their mates from coming out and taking a closer look. Both A and D Squadrons were also tasked with disrupting the fibre-optic cables, either by pulling out sections of the cable using chains attached to their Pinkies, or blowing up the service shafts placed at regular intervals along the line.

We began getting our kit sorted ahead of our deployment from Swaihan to the forward operating base at Al Jouf, in Saudi Arabia. From there we would insert across the border into Iraq. We would be operating in the northern part of the Anbar province, which was fiercely loyal to Saddam Hussein. If we were compromised, we could expect no help from the locals. They'd simply hand us straight over to the authorities. That, we had been told, was a fate worse than death.

There was a lot of hype about the Iraqis, the Republican Guard and their proclivity for torturing and executing captured soldiers.

241

At an initial briefing, the CO of 22 SAS had said, 'If it looks like you're going to get caught, save the last bullet for yourself.' As it turned out, that was a load of cobblers.

If we did find ourselves in trouble, we were reassured that RAF helicopters would come in to airlift us out. There was a forty-eight-hour lost comms procedure, which meant that if we had been out of radio contact for two days after our insertion, the helicopters would fly in and either extract us or relocate the patrol and supply us with a new radio. Casevacs would come in within twenty-four hours of a message being sent. It all sounded fine on paper.

But as we began sorting out our kit, it became clear that there was a massive difference between what we were being told, and what was really happening.

During the years leading up to the Gulf War, whenever we had expressed our concerns about outdated or missing equipment, we had repeatedly been fed the same line. 'If there's a major conflict, you'll get the war stocks. You'll get all this brand-new kit. You'll have everything you need.'

After our briefing, we quickly realised that the equipment situation at Victor was dire. Ammunition was in short supply. All of B Squadron's claymore anti-personnel mines had been lost in transit, which was a complete disaster. When you're being pursued by the enemy, it is standard procedure to stick down a claymore and detonate it. That is guaranteed to stop the enemy in their tracks, firstly to deal with their wounded, and also to slow them down as they scan the ground looking for more explosive devices. Claymores are also ideal for securing defensive positions, in case you get bumped. Inserting without them left us at a serious operational disadvantage.

When we complained, one sergeant major suggested we should go to the camp cookhouse, grab some empty ice cream cartons, fill them with C4 plastic explosive and shove a detonator in it. That sort of makeshift claymore isn't fit for purpose.

Then we discovered that our Browning pistols had also been mislaid. This meant that we'd have to rely on our M16 rifles when operating across the border. The M16 is a fine battlefield weapon, but it's long and unwieldy and totally ill-suited to contacts in a confined area. Pistols are easily concealed, and they weigh a lot less. If you suffer a stoppage, you can instantly reach for your Browning and continue to return fire. In a firefight, that could mean the difference between dropping an Iraqi soldier and getting cut down.

Other equipment was either missing or substandard. Our rifles had M203 grenade launcher attachments fixed to the underside of the barrel, but we were told there were no grenades available for them. We ended up having to scrounge a few from here and there.

Our desert camouflage trousers were made from such cheap materials that they began falling apart within a day or two. Our smocks dated back to the 1940s, and so did the maps we had been issued. The mapping was all aviation maps on a 1:250,000 scale. That's fine for a pilot who is hurtling along at 300 mph. But for a soldier on the ground, there is nowhere near enough detail to navigate. Our silk escape maps were even worse. They had been drawn on a scale of 1:1,000,000.

Better quality maps were readily available. The Americans were using satellite imaging technology to prepare their own maps of Iraq and Kuwait. They had the ability to take an image of a location and ping it over to Washington, D.C. for expert analysis. From that image, they could tell if there had been any recent vehicle movement or activity on foot in the area.

All we needed to do was drive fifteen miles up the road and ask the Americans for their help. The powers-that-be refused to do this, on the grounds of operational security (opsec). They were paranoid about anyone finding out that we were in Iraq.

Strangely, this didn't seem to apply to the security at our own camp. The opsec at Swaihan was disgraceful. We had local Arab workers strolling freely around the base, doing the cleaning jobs. They could easily have seen all of our mapping with the location of each patrol marked on it. Nobody did anything about this, but apparently we couldn't go and ask our American mates for a few up-to-date maps. If it wasn't so serious, it would have been comical.

At this point, I understood the old saying about lions being led by donkeys.

Despite the mounting problems, we flew up to our forward base at Al Jouf late on 18 January and waited for the green light to insert. We were sharing the base with a unit of US Special Forces, but while they enjoyed first-class tented facilities, we were living in an area away from the main terminal, sleeping under vehicle cam nets in bitingly cold weather. There was dust everywhere. It got into our food, our sleeping bags, under our clothes. We had to eat on the floor and use a hole in the ground as a toilet. We were living like tramps.

On the same day, A and D squadrons had also been airlifted forward to Al Jouf, flying out in half-squadron convoys aboard RAF Hercules C-130s with all their vehicles and kit. Because they were going in by vehicle, it would take them a few days to reach their areas of operation. The eight-man patrols from B Squadron would be the first boots on the ground in Iraq.

Two of the patrols – Bravo One Zero and Bravo Three Zero – had opted to take the Land Rover 90s with them. Our group held a Chinese Parliament and decided against taking them in. (A Chinese Parliament is where the guys sit down and discuss a problem. It doesn't matter what your rank is, everybody chips in.) There were arguments for both sides, but we felt that the negatives outweighed any advantages. Although the 90s would have offered us some extra mobility, they couldn't transport as much equipment as the 110s, which meant that we would have had to take two of them with us. With the profile of two Land Rovers in a flat desert landscape, we would have been much more visible against the horizon.

As soon as we got the go-ahead, we would insert via Chinook into Iraq, disembarking at our drop-off points and setting up LUPs before moving into our OPs along the supply routes. The information we had suggested that the Iraqis were driving the

Scuds along the MSRs and taking them right up to the Syrian border before launching them, to ensure that they would reach Israeli soil.

We had the northernmost MSR, running between Haditha and a string of airfields. The other two patrols were tasked with watching roads further to the south, designated Central and South MSRs. We would run two separate OPs at each supply route. One half of the patrol would have eyes on the route. The other lads would face out in the opposite direction, looking at the ground to the rear of the main OP.

At the same time, D and A Squadrons would penetrate the area to the south of us, ripping it up in the deserts of western Iraq. They would operate in half-squadron formations, with the Land Rover 110s in A Squadron's columns supported by motorbike outriders on the flanks. The bikers were the recce group. If the Pinkies ran into some rough ground or hit an impassable tank berm (a type of raised sand wall), the outriders would speed off to look for a route through. Each fighting column was supported by a Unimog all-terrain truck, which carried all the spare fuel, water, ammunition, rations and other supplies.

Roll bars can be fitted to the frame of the Pinkies to protect the guys on the back in case the vehicle overturns. There was some debate among the guys in A and D Squadrons about whether to keep them. D Squadron ended up removing them: they reckoned that without the roll bars the Pinkies would be less visible when they were laid up during the day. The drawback is that driving through rough terrain is much more dangerous without the roll bars attached, especially at night. A friend of mine in D Squadron was nearly killed when the 110 he was riding on flipped over. He was only saved because the mounted Browning .50 calibre stopped him from being crushed.

In addition to their fighting columns, both squadrons were supported by eight A-10 Thunderbolt 'Warthogs', fighter-bombers armed with Maverick air-to-ground missiles, GAU-8 rotary cannons, cluster bombs and Hydra rocket pods. They would provide top cover for the columns whenever the guys requested it.

Our patrols had no such support. Except for the emergency helicopter support, we were basically on our own. That meant having to hump everything on our backs. Our Bergens weighed between 120–140lbs, depending on which radio we were carrying. Our belt kits added another 35–45lbs. Then we had a jerrycan full of water and a sandbag containing our NBC (Nuclear, Biological, Chemical) suits and another with our extra rations, which we dragged along with us. On top of all that, I had my M203, which is an M16 rifle with a grenade launcher attachment with a maximum range of 400 metres. That was another 12lbs when loaded. Some of the other guys on the patrols had opted for the FN Minimi 5.56mm light machine gun, which weighs even more. With the extra ammunition, medical packs, survival kits and anti-personnel mines, our total weight was in excess of 250lbs. No soldier can operate with that kind of load on his back. We couldn't even operate our weapons, because they were attached to a sling around our necks and dangled in front of us.

As it turned out, we didn't need much of the kit we had packed. We had taken vehicle camouflage nets to cover our OPs, because we thought we were going to dig in. We were advised to pack thermal sheeting, which is quite heavy, because there was a concern that Iraqi helicopters or aircraft equipped with thermal imaging cameras might fly overhead and discover our position. But by the time we inserted, the Iraqi air force had been pounded into submission, along with many of their bases. There was a lot of other stuff that we didn't need.

The kit we did need, we didn't have enough of. Each patrol had a Magellan GPS device: at the time they were fairly hi-tech, but the GPS function on a standard phone is probably more advanced these days. The Magellan was about the size of an old brick car phone. You turned it on, got the 'lat and long' (latitude and longitude) and then marked your position on the map. We were limited to one per patrol, which was far from adequate.

Also in short supply were the TACBEs (Tactical Beacons), a newer version of the SARBEs the Regiment had used in Borneo and elsewhere. We had two of these in the patrol, one on a British frequency and the other set to an American frequency. I had one, and the patrol commander had the other. The TACBEs were personal locators that transmitted a distress signal when you pulled out a pin on the side of the device. An AWACS (Airborne Warning and Control System) aircraft, flying overhead, would constantly monitor for the signal. The TACBEs had a two-way, press-to-talk facility, allowing you to speak to pilots, but the range was very limited.

There were, seemingly, problems with almost every piece of kit. We had been issued KITE sight image intensifiers, able to pick out a target at a distance of more than two hundred metres. But no one had thought to provide us with the necessary rail systems – the mounting brackets that clamp on to a rifle, allowing the operator to clip on various attachments to the weapon. The only way we could use the intensifiers was as standalone sights, peering through them at the enemy. The KITE sights were great for night-time observation, but we couldn't fire at a target using them.

Our radio sets were equally flawed. They had the facility to send burst transmissions: long encrypted messages shrunk down and sent across in high-speed bursts. This counters any direction-finding equipment the enemy might have. The shorter the time you're on the air, the less chance there is of the enemy locating you. EMU (Electronic Messaging Units) had replaced the one-time pads, which at least saved us the hassle of encoding transmissions manually.

There was a problem, however. None of the seventeen radio sets we had been given worked properly. We were unaware of this at the time of our deployment, but we had been given the wrong frequencies to communicate to HQ. This was a disaster for us, because it meant that we didn't have a chance of getting through using our patrol radios. It's like telling someone your landline number, but giving them the wrong area code. You can dial that number all day long, but you're never going to get through.

Those radios should have been our lifeline. Instead, they were next to useless.

We were also given a Satcom phone, but then instructed to use it only when we sighted a Scud. The Iraqis, we had been told, had Direction Finding equipment that could pick up the electronic splash from the Satcom and locate it to within a range of ten metres. All of a sudden you start thinking, 'Well, what's the point of taking that thing with us?'

Our Bergens were unsuitable. Ideally, we should have been issued with rucksacks fitted with detachable daypacks. These are widely available in any outdoor clothing shop for around £150. Carrying these instead of our regular Bergens would have given us the option of separating the daypacks and taking vital rations, medical kit, water and supplies with us on the run. Instead, when we later came under heavy fire and had to get rid of our Bergens, we lost everything.

Other personal kit we carried included two morphine syrettes, blood money in the form of gold coins, and a document in Arabic with an individual serial number, offering a £5,000 reward for anyone who assisted the bearer. Personally, I couldn't see that going down too well with the fiercely loyal Saddam worshippers in Anbar province.

We spent our time at Al Jouf packing and repacking our Bergens, sorting out our kit. Some of what we didn't have, we acquired through bartering with the American Special Forces. Some of our boil-in-the-bag rations were swapped for the much tastier American MREs (Meals, Ready-to-Eat). We traded other stuff too, such as clothing and spare ammunition.

The Americans had an abundance of everything. I went up to one bloke and told him, 'Look, I've got no 203 grenades.'

The guy laughed and went off. He came back a few moments later, clutching a whole bandolier of 203s. 'Here,' the guy said, 'help yourself, buddy.'

During our stay at Al Jouf we had to put up with repeated Scud warnings. To begin with we rushed around in a mad panic, diving into slit trenches, fumbling with our respirators and NBC suits. After a few false alarms we thought, sod this. We were in a tiny airfield in the middle of nowhere. The chances of Saddam whacking us with a few rockets seemed incredibly remote.

On the evening of 19 January, we set off to insert by Chinook. We made it as far as Arar, near the Saudi–Iraqi border, before we had to abort. The pilot had learned that Coalition aircraft were heavily bombing the area we were going to cross, pummelling Iraqi positions. The Chinooks had to deconflict the area, to avoid the possibility of getting hit by the massive amounts of ordnance being dropped. The pilot had no choice but to turn around and return to base.

Three nights later, we finally deployed.

CHAPTER 19

Bravo Two Zero

The Bravo Two Zero mission was a disaster waiting to happen. We all knew it, even before we had set off. I remember going to see the squadron quartermaster and telling him, 'This is a one-way ticket. I'm not going to see you again.'

We broke every SOP going in terms of briefings, kit and intelligence, and it cost three men their lives. That mission should be studied in military colleges as a textbook example of what you should never do.

From the moment we landed, everything went wrong. Mistakes that had been made in the planning stages came back to haunt us at every turn. For a start, it was much colder than we had been led to believe. The temperature was below zero not only at night but also during the day. It was like the depths of an English winter, cold, wet and muddy, with a wind chill so fierce it sliced right through us. The landscape was like the surface of the moon, rocky and as flat as a pancake.

No one had told us it would be so cold in the Iraqi desert at that time of the year. Consequently, we didn't have any specialist winter clothing. We had Gore-Tex bivvy bags, our smocks and our normal soldiering kit, and that was it. This was a problem that affected all three squadrons, at least for a couple of weeks, until resupplies were able to come in and deliver thick Arab winter coats to the patrols.

At Swaihan, I had asked what the conditions were going to be like in Iraq. All I had been told was, 'We don't know.'

They could have easily approached the guys at Shell or one of the many Westerners who worked on the oilfields in Iraq and asked them about the weather. Or they could have picked up the phone and called someone at *National Geographic* to find out. There were plenty of information sources. But it was all about opsec (operational security). No one wanted to discuss any aspect of the mission with anyone outside the Regiment.

The ground didn't conform to the imagery we had studied. At Swaihan, we had been given black-and-white satellite photographs that had been misinterpreted. We had been looking at them, thinking the dark areas were the high points of the terrain, when in fact they were the low points. When we got to the site we had selected for our OP, we then discovered that we couldn't dig, because the entire area around the wadi was bedrock. With no cover in sight, we laid up in a small cave beneath an overhang at one end of the wadi, rigging up a defensive perimeter using a few mines we had managed to scrounge off some of the SBS lads at Victor.

The next day, things went from bad to worse.

A recce party the following evening discovered that the MSR we had been tasked to watch was only a series of muddied tracks. It was nothing like the modern metalled road we had been expecting. There were no fibre-optic cables running alongside the dirt tracks, so that was yet more nonsense. We had brought specialist cutting equipment with us for no reason.

We would later learn that it would have been impossible for a TEL vehicle to have driven along those tracks. We didn't know it at the time, but there was no chance of a Scud coming down there.

More frighteningly, at first light we had spotted an anti-aircraft (AA) gun emplacement a few hundred metres from our position. We later identified a second AA position. That was a big shock. We knew that the Iraqis didn't just stick those things out in the middle of nowhere. They had to be guarding something fairly important, although we didn't know exactly what. It could have been a military installation or an armoured division. We never had the chance to find out.

We attempted to send a report back, but none of the radios were working. We didn't know then that we had been given the wrong frequencies. At the time, we merely assumed that we were in a patch of dead ground and couldn't get a signal.

On the second afternoon, a young goatherd approached the wadi and caught sight of our patrol. As soon as the boy ran off to raise the alarm, we got on the radio again and started communicating over the emergency Guard Net, which is an open frequency. Luckily it was being monitored by a young signaller based in Cyprus. We sent an urgent message through in plain language Morse code, telling the signaller who we were and giving him our call sign. We explained that our patrol had been compromised and we needed immediate extraction or relocation with a new radio.

Contacting the Guard Net is like phoning the operator. It's unsecured. Anyone can do it. We were hoping that the signaller would contact the Regiment and pass the message on, telling them that we had been in touch. It was a long shot, but better than nothing.

Later, after I returned home, I was told that this message was not acted upon because it had been corrupted. That is not true. I know that message was clean, because the signaller confirmed it over the net after we had sent it. There was some other reason that help wasn't sent, but it had nothing to do with the quality of that message.

What happened next has been extensively documented. After a bulldozer approached our position, we realised that we had definitely been compromised. We began to move out of the area and head back to the LZ to await our emergency extraction, in accordance with the lost comms procedure. Before we could leave, however, we came under heavy fire from Iraqi militia forces occupying the high ground.

During the initial contact I dug out my TACBE personal locator and screamed into it, desperately trying to alert any Coalition pilots flying overhead to our predicament. There was no reply. It turned out that the nearest AWACS aircraft was some 350 miles away. The TACBE has a 'line of sight' of around

75 miles, if you're lucky. We were never going to raise anyone using those TACBEs.

As darkness fell, we managed to break contact and regroup, but only after ditching our Bergens and all our equipment to increase the pace. We made for the LZ, confirmed our location using the Magellan and waited for the helicopter to extract us.

That chopper should have arrived at 2000 hours. As the minutes ticked down, I absolutely knew that it wasn't going to come in. In the still darkness of the desert, we would have heard the distinctive sound of the rotor blades from quite a distance. With a few minutes to go until the helicopter was due to arrive, the land-scape remained eerily quiet. The RAF doesn't do late. Those guys would have been there right on the button. A few minutes past 2000 hours, it was obvious that help wasn't coming. From then on, we were on our own.

We now had a decision to make, so we agreed to head for the Syrian border. The Iraqis were still tailing us, so the plan was first to head south and make it look as if we were legging it to Saudi Arabia. Then we'd box in, heading west and then north again before eventually crossing over into Syria.

After walking for some time in the pitch black, our patrol got split up. I was in one group, with Stan and Vince Phillips. After several failed attempts to make contact with the rest of the team, and with the Iraqis still following us, the three of us decided to move on.

We spent the day laid up in the ruts of a tank track and moved on again that night. The weather was horrific. It rained and snowed all day and a vicious wind was blowing, numbing us to the bone. It was like being on top of a mountain with a storm sweeping in. We were wet and freezing cold and I felt sure that we were all going to die.

At some point Vince became separated from us. We tried look-ing for him by tracking our footprints back through the snow, but by then both Stan and I were coming down with hypothermia. Eventually, we had to abandon the search. Vince died of hypo-thermia that night. His body was later found by the Iraqis.

That left two of us. We only made it through by walking on.

You've got only one choice in that situation. If you sit down, you're definitely going to die. If you keep on walking, there's the slightest chance that you'll make it. That's what kept us going.

In the early hours we found a ditch to lie up in, but the next day we were compromised by another goatherd. Stan wanted to go off with him, reasoning that he might be able to find a vehicle to get us across the border. I was adamant that this would be a mistake. I would have preferred to kill the guy. Despite my protests, Stan decided to leave with the herdsman. That was the last I saw of my friend. They walked for several hours until they came to a cluster of buildings. After a brief gun battle with Iraqi forces, Stan was arrested and taken away for interrogation.

Meanwhile, the other group of five hijacked an Iraqi taxi with the aim of driving it into Syria. Taking one of the Iraqis with them, they drove westward and made it as far as a vehicle check-point (VCP) before they were compromised. The guys had debussed from the vehicle some way short of the VCP while the Iraqi drove up to the checkpoint, having arranged to meet him on the other side. Instead the driver sold them out to the VCP and the Iraqis came looking for them. The group had no choice but to head back into the desert. They continued on foot towards the border, until they got contacted by enemy forces.

During a series of firefights, Bob Consiglio was shot dead after single-handedly holding off a large Iraqi force for half an hour. The patrol commander and another soldier were separately captured by the enemy before they could make it across the border.

The remaining two men, Dinger and 'Legs' Lane, made it to the Euphrates and tried to get across on a canoe, but couldn't release the vessel from its moorings. With the enemy closing in, they attempted to escape by swimming across the river. The water was freezing cold, and Legs began to struggle as he came down with hypothermia. Dinger dragged him out of the water onto the far bank and found a place to hide, but Legs was already in a very bad way and slipping in and out of consciousness. Despite Dinger's best efforts to save his companion, Legs later died of hypothermia.

Dinger himself was captured by a crowd of locals and taken to a police station. The survivors were imprisoned, badly beaten and interrogated before being released after the end of the war.

I spent the next five days lying up and another six nights on the run before I finally made it across the border to Syria.

The hardest part of my escape was having to go static during the daylight hours. Lying still for twelve hours at a time in the appalling cold and wet was really rough. Every part of my body was numbed. I'd fall asleep and wake up five minutes later, shaking violently.

Each day I'd stare at the ridgelines of distant grey hills and mountains, calculating roughly how far I would be able to walk the following evening. I'd wonder what I might encounter, whether I'd make it or get captured. At other times I slipped into a vivid dream-like state. I'd hear the voices of the other guys talking right next to me. They seemed so real that I started to think that they were really there. Then I'd open my eyes and find myself utterly alone. That was a real kick in the teeth.

Some critics have suggested that we would have been better off making for Jordan after being compromised. That wasn't an option for us, for several reasons. The Jordanian border was further away, and we were out of water after using up our supplies during our escape from the wadi. The nearest source was the Euphrates, so that's where we had to get to. If we had tried going in any other direction, we would have died of dehydration.

Other countries were further away, and even harder to get to. The bulk of the Iraqi forces had assembled along the Saudi border in trenches and emplacements. Other troops were watching the border with Jordan very closely. In addition, we knew that Syria had stated that they would hand any downed Coalition pilots back to our side. It was by far our best option.

We also got a lot of flak for going in on foot instead of taking vehicles. The truth is, the Land Rover 90s were not up to the job. If we had taken them with us, we would have been compromised a day earlier. The anti-aircraft emplacements near the MSR would have spotted the dust clouds rising from our wagons from miles away. They would have shot us up long before we could turn around.

The intelligence shortcomings were staggering. We didn't know what the border looked like around Syria or Jordan or Saudi Arabia. Our knowledge of the ground at the MSR was severely limited. When I asked for a Harrier jump jet with a mounted camera to fly over the area that they were sending us into, I got laughed down. But if we had done that, we would have known that the road we were supposed to watch was a track and totally unsuitable for a vehicle the size of a Scud launcher. We would have picked up the enemy AA positions as well. Lives could have been saved.

From start to finish, the mission was a rush job. The only way I can describe it is that we behaved like a bunch of school kids itching to get into a fight. No one stopped to think of the consequences if it went south.

The CO eventually ordered a search-and-rescue mission on 26 January, four days after our insertion and two days after our patrol had been compromised. The first attempt was called off after bad weather, but a second mission on 27 January managed to fly over the escape route to Saudi Arabia – not realising that we had boxed in and headed for Syria instead. Further attempts to mount a search were made until the head shed learned that I had made it across to Syria and it was clear that no one in our patrol had struck out towards the Saudi border.

I hated it at the time, but the decision not to send in a helicopter as soon as we had been compromised was the right call. The Regiment had only three Chinooks at our disposal for operations in Iraq. Resources were badly stretched. Sending them in was a risk. They had no armaments and the loadies were equipped with SA80 assault rifles, which were close to useless. If they had been attacked or shot down, what were the aircrews supposed to do?

Any rescue operation would have involved a large group of guys throwing up a cordon around the LZ to secure the area. That also carried risks. In Afghanistan in 2005, a quick reaction force was dispatched to rescue a US Special Forces recce team that had been compromised. One of the MH-47 Chinooks was shot down by an RPG (rocket-propelled grenade) fired by Taliban forces, killing all sixteen passengers and crew.

Sixteen men died in an attempt to save a handful of blokes on the ground. You can argue the rights and wrongs of that decision, but personally, I would have preferred to go through what I did and walk two hundred miles to safety, rather than have a large force of guys come in to rescue me, only for them to get taken out.

There are other possible reasons why our message wasn't acted upon. For all the head shed knew, we might have been captured by the Iraqis and forced to send it under duress. Or the Iraqis might have killed us and sent the message themselves. It hadn't come in on the right frequency, and it had been tapped out in plain language. It might have looked suspicious.

My only gripe is that if the Iraqis had come at us from another direction and we had to fight through them to get to the RV for extraction, we'd have taken casualties. And it would have been a waste, because the chopper wasn't coming anyway. If that was the situation, they should have just told us.

Of the two other eight-man teams from B Squadron that inserted into Iraq on the same night as our patrol, 22 January, one team returned home. The other never made it off the chopper.

The commander of one of the teams, Andy, disembarked from the Chinook with his men and vehicles and laid up in the darkness. At first light Andy looked around him, realised there was no cover in sight and decided to head south, back to the Saudi border. He carried on, despite radio messages telling him to link up with elements of D Squadron in his vicinity. Andy insisted that the radio wasn't working properly and that these orders were never received. The patrol was rumbled on several occasions before they finally made it back to Saudi Arabia.

The commander of the third patrol decided against inserting. As the pilot approached their LZ, he explained to the commander, Pete, that a highway they had passed some time ago was still visible on the horizon. Which meant that there was no deviation in altitude or dead ground in which to hide. Hearing this, Pete told the pilot to put the Chinook down so he could go outside and have a look for himself.

The tailgate lowered, Pete got his night-sight up and running and scanned the landscape in front of him. It was totally flat. Realising that his men would be horribly exposed if they deployed into this area, he got back on the chopper and sent a message back to HQ, telling them that he was flying back to base and asking to be relocated in a new area.

On his return, a handful of senior members in the Regiment accused Pete of cowardice. They were going around Hereford, making snide comments and making his life difficult. This was totally unfair. I knew Pete. He was a stand-up guy, and out of the three Bravo patrols he was the only commander who made the correct decision. And yet he was getting negativity from a few blokes in the upper echelons who hadn't been there at the time. Tellingly, none of the other guys criticised Pete. They all understood that he'd done the right thing.

Pete eventually decided to leave the Regiment. That was a real shame. He had made a brave call in Iraq, one that had undoubtedly saved the lives of his men – and yet it cost a good soldier his career.

For those of us who did go ahead with the mission, the attitude of the head shed towards our potential capture or death was baffling. None of the British embassies in Syria, Jordan and Saudi Arabia had been alerted to the fact that eight SAS soldiers were missing and might show up unannounced at any moment. When Syrian security forces finally handed me over to the embassy in Damascus, the staff had no idea that the Regiment had been deployed.

Shortly after I returned to Al Jouf, the Regiment CO took me to one side and said that I would be sent down to Victor to get kitted up before redeploying to Iraq. I stood there, nodding like an idiot, and said, 'Yeah, okay, Boss.'

You should have seen the state of me. I'd lost thirty-eight pounds in body weight in seven days and eight nights on the run. I could hardly walk a hundred metres or climb a set of stairs without getting out of breath. My feet didn't have any skin on them. I had no toenails. All my gums had receded from the effects of drinking radioactive waste I had mistaken for water when I'd stumbled upon a nuclear processing plant. I had liver and kidney disorders. Blood disorders. My head was all over the place. And they wanted me to go back in as if nothing had happened.

The mistakes we made on Bravo Zero Two will hopefully never happen again. Lessons were learned, thankfully. Changes were made to the SOPs for escape and evasion scenarios, in the event of a patrol getting split up. The details of these procedures remain top secret, but it was one of the only good things to come out of that failed mission.

Our resistance-to-interrogation techniques had to be radically changed after we found out what had happened to Stan and the other prisoners. Up until the Gulf War, it was standard practice for SAS soldiers to invent detailed cover stories in the event of capture by the enemy. That approach worked until the guys came up against Saddam's interrogators.

One of the lads, Dinger, stuck to his line that he was from the Parachute Regiment. The Iraqi officer questioning him insisted that he was Special Forces, but Dinger kept faithfully to his story. Then the officer asked him, 'Who is your commanding officer?'

Dinger had been in the Paras before passing Selection, so he knew the answer. He gave the Iraqi the name of his CO. The officer's face lit up.

'I know him,' he said. 'We went to Sandhurst together. His wife's name is Claire and they've got two nice kids, haven't they?'

That threw Dinger. He hadn't been expecting that reply. You go into an interrogation expecting to be grilled by someone you've never met before. Instead, you find out that they know someone you know. It completely changes the dynamic.

The interrogators took a different approach with Stan. His cover story was that he was an army medic who had been on a rescue mission. Stan had a background in dentistry, so the Iraqis brought in a patient and a local dentist and said, 'Tell us what's wrong with this man.'

Stan examined the patient. Then he made his diagnosis.

The Iraqi dentist listened carefully and nodded. 'Everything this man has just said is absolutely correct,' he told the officer.

That still didn't satisfy his interrogators. They asked Stan where he had been a dentist. Luckily, he was able to remember the phone number for the duty sergeant's room at a place where he'd done some work. Then the Iraqis brought in a telephone and told him to dial the number while they listened in. An orderly answered the call, much to Stan's relief.

None of this mattered anyway. The Iraqis knew exactly who these guys were. They had retrieved the abandoned Bergens from near the wadi. They knew how many soldiers were in the patrol, how many of us were still on the run. They had found Vince's body. They were asking the other prisoners about me, referring to me by name. They wanted to know where I was going, what route I would be using to escape.

We now realised that inventing detailed cover stories was pointless. It was too easy for any trained interviewer to check out a soldier's story and poke holes in it. (This is doubly relevant today, with the digital fingerprints everyone leaves online.) You may as well take the beatings or the torture and wait for someone to rescue you.

The critical thing is to hold out for between twelve and twenty-four hours. If you can withstand the punishment for that long, any sensitive information you are holding on to will automatically become useless. By that time, the head shed will know that you have been captured and will have taken measures to change any pre-set codes for the encryption devices. Any other patrols at risk of being compromised will also be extracted as a precaution.

These were valuable lessons for the Regiment. It's just a travesty that three men had to die so they could be learned.

Communications are key to any SAS operation. Whether that is sending information back about a target or telling HQ that you've been attacked, the ability to get in touch with the command centre and tell them what's going on is crucial. We didn't have that in Iraq, and it cost us dearly.

Despite all these problems, I would have still got on that chopper if we had been told, 'There is no forty-eight-hour lost comms procedure. No one will be coming to rescue you. If you get bumped, that's it.' That might sound crazy. But the bottom line is, you're in the SAS. That comes with special privileges – and big responsibilities. You know that at some point in your career, you're going to be asked to do something that is extremely dangerous. You'll have to risk your life, and on some operations there's a good chance that you won't be coming back home.

But you still do it, because the mission is critical. Stopping the Scuds was vital to the Coalition war effort. No one else was capable of going in, so it was down to us to get the job done. If you want to wear that famous beige beret with the winged dagger, then you've got to be prepared to lay down your life. That's what it means to be in the Regiment. You're following in the footsteps of the first guys who volunteered for the SAS. Men who parachuted into the desert in the Second World War, knowing that there wasn't any rescue plan, that the only way out was to steal a German vehicle or walk.

The alternative is to be a coward and say you can't do it. Then you've got to live with yourself, knowing that you weren't up to it. For an elite soldier, that's a special kind of hell.

Whenever anyone asks, 'Why did you get on that chopper?' my answer is: Because I was in the Regiment. Looking back now, almost thirty years later, I can honestly say that I wouldn't have done anything differently, once we got into contact on the ground. And I would have still carried out the mission, knowing all the risks. It just would have been nice to know that the weather was going to be terrible.

CHAPTER 20

Behind Enemy Lines

While I was on the run, A and D Squadrons were pushing deeper into Iraq.

The two columns from D Squadron had been the first to cross, slipping across the border near an ancient fortress on 20 January 1991. The troops in A Squadron were delayed after they had trouble finding a crossing point through the high sand berm the Iraqis had constructed along the border. They eventually made it over the following night, slipping through a narrow gap in the wall next to a Saudi fort.

Each fighting column moved in single-file snake formation, with the Unimog all-terrain truck in the middle. In the A Squadron patrols the motorbike outriders rode on the flanks. If they got bumped, the vehicles would line up alongside one another and open fire simultaneously, like the cannons on a warship. To avoid detection they drove at night, with the driver in the lead Pinkie using NVGs to guide the rest of the column.

An hour or so before first light, the patrols would loop back on themselves and find a defensive position to set up their LUP, ideally at a feature such as a depression or the side of a wadi. They'd get the vehicles tucked into the side of the high ground, throw the cam nets over the top and basha up. L9 bar mines were laid around the LUP in case of approaching enemy vehicles. These are pressure-activated devices, about a metre long and shaped like wooden railway sleepers. Because they're longer than traditional anti-personnel mines, they're ideal for blowing up tank tracks.

Patrols spaced out their vehicles as far as possible to create a 360-degree defensive ring around their position. The threat wasn't only from the enemy, however: with the air war in full swing, there was always the chance of being mistakenly targeted by passing Coalition aircraft. One such incident took place when one of the D Squadron columns pitched up at an LUP. The soldiers parked two of their Land Rovers nose-to-tail before throwing one of the cam nets over them. At first light an A-10 tank buster flying overhead spotted the wagons and, because they resembled a large mobile platform, the pilot wrongly identified them as a mobile Scud launcher.

The sleeping troopers were suddenly jolted awake by an earth-shattering explosion. An AIM-9 Sidewinder missile had slammed into the ground very close to the Pinkies, throwing up a shower of debris, dirt and rocks. One of the startled soldiers grabbed hold of his emergency radio and screamed at the A-10 pilot. 'Stop! Stop shooting! We're British Special Forces!'

There was a pause before the pilot's voice came over the radio. 'Was that a direct hit?'

Miraculously, the patrol suffered no serious injuries. They were saved because the Land Rovers had been stationary for several hours. The Sidewinder is a heat-seeking missile; when there is no available heat source to latch on to, it goes for centre mass. As a result, it ended up hitting the patch of ground between the two Pinkies. If either of those vehicles had their engine running, a lot of the guys would have been killed. Patrols took to spreading Union Jack flags over their wagons, to reduce the chances of a possible blue-on-blue.

After about a week, around the time I had reached the Syrian border, A Squadron had penetrated about seventy miles into Iraqi territory. Further north and to the west, D Squadron was also making inroads. All four columns were maintaining comms with HQ, building up the intelligence picture, so they were constantly updated on enemy positions and troop movements.

One of A Squadron's patrols got their first taste of action when a Russian-built GAZ-69 truck approached their LUP in a wadi, apparently mistaking the soldiers for friendlies. The lads scrambled to take up concealed firing positions beneath the cam nets and looked on as the GAZ pulled up a short distance away.

Two figures debussed from the front cab. One of the Iraqis was dressed in the uniform of a high-ranking officer. As he stepped towards the LUP, one of the soldiers emerged from behind cover and coolly approached the Iraqi. The officer opened his mouth and said something in Arabic. He was only a couple of metres away from the SAS man when he realised his mistake. The soldier went to open fire but suffered a stoppage and dropped to the ground and the other guys in the patrol opened up. In the hail of bullets that followed, both the officer and the driver were killed, along with a third man concealed in the back of the wagon. A fourth Iraqi was taken alive.

The guys took the surviving Iraqi prisoner, gathered up the evidence of the firefight and bugged out of the LUP, having learned that a large formation of Iraqi forces was nearby. On the orders of the Squadron OC, the column then doubled back on itself and headed for an RV close to the border with Saudi Arabia, where a resupply could be made, and the prisoner handed over for further interrogation.

They took the GAZ with them, along with the bodies of the slotted Iraqis: they were operating in an area crawling with enemy units, and the discovery of their dead colleagues would have surely compromised the patrol.

The lads made several unsuccessful attempts to dispose of the bodies. Their main problem was the terrain. It was the same flat, hard bedrock we had encountered further to the north. You can't dig into it more than a few centimetres. The nature of the ground meant that they couldn't give the Iraqis a proper burial and after a few attempts to dig into the bedrock they gave up, deciding it would be easier to get rid of the corpses when they handed over the POW.

The column drove for several hours before reaching a suitable

LZ at a point close to the Saudi border. An hour before first light, the chopper arrived at their position and the loadies began taking out all the resupplies for the patrol: spare fuel for the vehicles, extra rounds and rations, along with several thick Bedouin winter coats the Regiment had acquired. It would have been better if they had sent everyone in with the proper clothing to begin with, but at least someone at the camp had belatedly addressed the cock-up.

There was another surprise waiting for the soldiers on the chopper: the Regimental Sergeant Major, a blunt Yorkshireman. He promptly took the Squadron OC to one side, told him that he was being relieved of his command and ordered him to get on the Chinook with the Iraqi POW. To the astonishment of the patrol, their commanding officer had been sacked, in the middle of an operation. His replacement was the blunt RSM, a far from popular officer, disliked by many of the soldiers.

The head shed later claimed that the OC, an SBS officer who had been cross-posted to the Regiment, had been removed from his position because he wasn't being aggressive enough. They felt he was stalling. But there's an old saying in the Regiment that goes back to the Second World War: Always trust the man on the ground. It's alright sitting behind your desk at the base and telling someone they should be more aggressive, but it's the guy in the field who has to make the decision.

Perhaps the OC was guilty of being cautious. Certainly, his decision to head back to Saudi Arabia instead of pushing on wasn't wildly popular. Maybe if there had been more air cover and support, the officer might have felt he was able to go out more aggressively. But if the RSM genuinely believed that the OC was doing a bad job, there were plenty of other officers who could have taken over. In a war, the place of the RSM is most definitely not on the field of battle.

The guys from A Squadron continued on their way. The stolen GAZ vehicle, along with the three dead Iraqis they had tried to bury, was later rigged with explosive charges and blown up.

A few days later, the other half of A Squadron discovered an

Iraqi military installation. A three-man team consisting of their squadron sergeant major Bob, Steve and a friend of mine, John, went forward in one of the Land Rover 110s to do a night-time CTR, using a MIRA night-sight to guide them on their approach.

They had punched through the defensive perimeter and were rolling past slit trenches when the recce team heard the metallic scrape of barbed wire snagging on the Pinkie tyres. Suddenly, an Iraqi soldier sprang into view out of the darkness. John gave him the good news with a burst from the GPMG. This alerted the surrounding forces and the darkness was illuminated by muzzle flashes as the Iraqis opened up. Rounds hammered against the Land Rover, throwing up bright orange sparks.

The soldiers returned fire as the driver attempted to reverse out of their position, but they were massively outnumbered by the enemy. Bob leapt down from the Pinkie and tried to free the stricken vehicle from the tangle of barbed wire. As he did so, a bullet struck him in the upper leg. The round shattered his hip, tearing through his thigh, calf and ankle.

The other lads abandoned the bullet-shredded Pinkie and raced over to Bob. They hauled the wounded man to his feet and carried him as they hurried away on foot, hoping to lose the Iraqis in the darkness. Every so often John would stop, turn and put down a burst on their pursuers, but soon their situation was looking grim. Bob was in a seriously bad way and it was clear that he couldn't go on any further. With the Iraqis converging on their position, Bob gave the order for the others to leave him behind.

'Are you sure, Bob?' John asked, believing that he was close to death. 'Do you want us to finish you off?'

'No, no,' Bob said. By now he was delirious from the amount of blood that he'd lost. 'I'll be okay. I'll hold them off until the squadron can rescue me. You two go on.'

John and Steve left their colleague with a 66mm rocket and carried on into the night. Bob was discovered the next morning by a group of Iraqi soldiers. Despite the fact that he was slipping in and out of consciousness, he had tried to fire the rocket at the enemy's position before he was captured. He was taken away and an Iraqi surgeon who had previously worked in a London hospital operated on his shattered leg.

Bob spent the rest of the war in captivity. He was interrogated, beaten and tortured, before he was released with the other prisoners at the end of hostilities. When the doctors in the UK examined his leg, they said that they couldn't have done a better job themselves. Luckily for him, Bob had ignored the advice the Regiment CO had given on the eve of the war to 'save the last bullet for yourself'.

John and Steve were on the run for the next twenty-four hours. They were eventually rescued by their patrol when they contacted the pilot of an A-10 flying overhead using their TACBE. The pilot took their coordinates and directed the rest of the guys from A Squadron on to their position.

At around the same time, D Squadron had a contact of their own. One of their units had been compromised by a sizeable attacking force after they had basha'd up close to an enemy position. A heavy firefight broke out and after repulsing the enemy, the lads made a run for it in their wagons. One group got separated from the others after their Land Rover refused to start and they ended up bugging out on foot. One of the soldiers was badly injured after a bullet went through his chest. The lads eventually made their way to Saudi Arabia, driving across in a wagon they had bought from a Bedouin encampment with their survival coins.

After a couple of weeks, and in spite of these setbacks, the A and D Squadron half-column patrols began to carry out a number of successful attacks. Their targets included a series of towers that the intelligence cell believed were being used to direct the Scud missiles. The guys started cruising around the desert and destroying these facilities, until a few Iraqis were taken prisoner and revealed that the towers had nothing to do with the Scuds. They were in fact beacons used to communicate with Iraqi aircraft. By that point, there was no air force to speak of.

Around the same time, news of our missing patrol had been picked up by the other squadrons. The failure of Bravo Two Zero, along with the other two aborted B Squadron patrols, shifted the focus for the remaining SAS forces in Iraq. Both squadrons now went out on Scud-hunting operations, going after fixed launch sites and mobile Scud convoys, although they still had permission to look for other opportune targets to hit.

They had some success in destroying the Scuds. Whenever a column discovered a launcher, they would light it up with a Laser Target Designator (LTD) and call in Coalition aircraft to blow it up. In one attack, D Squadron stumbled upon a pair of Scud TELs going through their pre-launch programme. The guys hurriedly got on the radio and called in fast air. Coalition aircraft arrived in the nick of time, dropping their payloads and destroying the missiles and their launchers. When the guys returned the following day, they discovered that there had been at least seven Scuds in the convoy.

One of the big problems with calling in airstrikes was the delay between identifying the target, getting on the comms, pinging across the coordinates and waiting for fast air to come in. Sometimes it could take sixty minutes or longer before the jets arrived. By that time, the Scud might have fired or moved on to another location. The lads came up with some creative solutions. In one instance, a D Squadron patrol pinned down a convoy of Scuds they had spotted, fixing the vehicles in place until the F16s showed up to pound them into oblivion.

Aside from the Scuds, the squadrons also found success in destroying sections of the Iraqi military's fibre-optic cable network. Dems teams rigged explosive charges to the service shafts that were staggered at regular intervals along the lines. The resulting explosion would rip apart the access shaft and the cable running beneath it, devastating the enemy's communications.

As they pushed deeper into Iraq, the patrols gradually became more settled in their environment. They hit a bewildering variety of targets, ripping up army camps and airfields, tearing into enemy convoys.

The tactics for hitting static targets were simple but effective, in the best tradition of the Regiment. Fire support groups (FSGs) would form up at a baseline, along with the 81mm mortars. The mortar crew would put a stonk in, and then the assaulters would move forward. As soon as they had sight of the enemy they would engage. Meanwhile the FSGs would pour in a barrage of covering fire to the left and right, using the vehicle-mounted GPMGs, Browning .50s and Milan missiles.

Attacks almost always took place at night, allowing the guys to approach unseen before hitting the enemy hard. NVGs were scarce, although visibility during contacts wasn't a problem. Firefights were often at close range, with assaulters usually firing at targets no more than twenty or thirty metres away. With all the tracer rounds coming in and the shadows cast by the moonlight, the soldiers could easily distinguish their targets. Once the target had been destroyed and the enemy wiped out, the patrol would pull back to the baseline before melting away into the darkness.

It didn't take the SAS long to realise that the Iraqi conscripts were nowhere near as good as we had been led to believe. Once the guys got in among them, they tore the enemy up. Whenever they got into a contact, the patrols saw that they were dominating the fights and could easily roll over the enemy. Even when they were massively outnumbered, the Iraqis took most of the casualties. The D Squadron marauders grew so confident that they started rattling around the desert in broad daylight, reasoning that it was easier to look for targets in the day rather than sticking to night-time patrols.

If the Iraqis had possessed light armoured vehicles such as the FV101 Scorpions the British Army used, they would have been all over the SAS. But because their vehicles were slower than the Land Rover 110s, the guys were able to break contact if they got bumped and had to make a run for it.

Even the notorious Republican Guard wasn't all it was cracked up to be. We had been told that these guys were the cream of the crop, Saddam's most feared troops. I actually walked right past a load of Republican Guard soldiers while I was on the run. These guys should have been on stag at night, guarding an anti-aircraft position. Instead they were huddled up in their sleeping bags, nobody bothering to keep watch. They were poor quality.

To begin with, they couldn't believe that British Special Forces were operating inside their country. In one incident, one of the columns from A Squadron was crossing a main highway in the desert. As they started to drive across, the lads spotted a military convoy bowling towards them from further down the road. The Iraqis stopped and waved at the patrol, assuming they were friendlies.

Instead of panicking and driving away, they calmly waved back, finished crossing the road – and then turned left and headed up the road, directly towards the convoy. The Iraqis were still waving as the Pinkies drew parallel with them. Then the guys opened up, walloping the enemy. Only the risk-takers of the Regiment would dare to pull off such a bold move.

Considering the weather, the lack of cover, the patchy intelligence and the fact that they were operating with minimal support in enemy territory, casualties were remarkably light. Aside from the three men who died in our patrol, the Regiment only suffered one other fatality in Iraq, when one of the men in A Squadron, David 'Shug' Denbury, was killed during an attack on an Iraqi convoy.

It could have been far worse. In one operation, A Squadron came up against an unexpectedly large enemy force when attacking an enemy communications complex codenamed Victor Two. The patrol, under the command of the RSM who had taken charge in the field, had been given orders to blow the place up, including the two-hundred-foot-tall mast at the heart of the site. Air power alone couldn't destroy the base, since much of the specialist equipment was believed to be located underground.

After carrying out a close target recce, the squadron went in the following night. An airstrike had hit the base several hours prior to the assault, damaging the main buildings and the outer defensive perimeter, but the microwave tower remained intact. The guys pushed on with their plan to destroy the tower, communications equipment and anything else that had survived the bombing.

Approaching stealthily, the assault group and dems guys slipped through a breach in the perimeter and moved towards their targets. They were covered by a fire support team at a baseline a few hundred metres from the complex, armed with Milan missiles, grenade launchers and heavy machine guns. Another team provided close fire support from the Pinkies using the twin-mounted GPMGs.

The squadron had been told that the base was lightly guarded by a handful of guards and personnel. The assault group was compromised when two of the guys crept forward to silence the occupants of a guard truck parked close to the main tower. When the startled driver reached for his rifle, one of the SAS soldiers, who had attempted to get the young Iraqi to remain quiet, had no choice but to open fire. His colleague also opened up, spraying the truck with bullets and killing the other Iraqi inside.

In the next instant, the soldiers came under intense fire from all directions. Instead of a small number of guards, A Squadron found themselves up against a force of at least three hundred Iraqi soldiers.

Under covering fire from the two fire support groups, the dems team hurriedly placed their charges on the legs of the tower. They fired their percussion-cap timers and then sprinted back towards their wagons, racing to get clear as tracer rounds zipped past them. Moments later, there was an earth-shuddering boom as three of the four explosives detonated, and the tower came crashing down like a snapped sailing mast.

There was no time to admire their handiwork. The assault group rushed back to the support vehicles and immediately came under fire from another group of Iraqis who had formed up along a nearby tank berm. The guys managed to fight their way out, some riding in the wagons, others hurrying along on foot, eventually reaching the Emergency RV a mile or so away from the installation.

In the confusion of the firefight, the main fire support team had become separated from the rest of the squadron, believing that the dems team guys were still inside the compound. They bugged out several minutes later, after one of the signallers finally managed to raise them over the radio. One of the motorbike outriders risked his neck by racing back into the teeth of the fighting to fetch his comrades, leading them to the Emergency RV.

After three weeks of operations, the patrols were running low on supplies. The Regiment organised a massive convoy to go across the border and replenish the squadrons. With the Iraqi air force decimated, it was considered safe enough to send in a resupply by vehicle rather than aircraft. Ten trucks would make the journey and RV with both squadrons, with a dozen guys from B Squadron providing the muscle, riding in Land Rovers and motorbikes. A team of REME (Royal Electrical and Mechanical Engineers) fitters accompanied the convoy, along with a technician from 264 Signals who could make repairs to the comms equipment. The resupply party was led by a widely respected SAS veteran, Bob Shepherd.

The convoy crossed the border in mid-February, driving at night with their headlamps off to make themselves less visible to any enemy forces. After a journey of almost two hundred kilo-metres across rough terrain, they reached the RV at a wadi and over the next few days the formations came in to stock up on fresh food, water, clothes and ammunition. Vehicles were repaired, spare fuel was distributed, and stories exchanged between the various patrols. The resupply team even boiled up some water in forty-five-gallon drums so the guys could have a scrub.

After weeks of getting in among the Iraqis, the resupply was a big morale boost to the formations and a chance to have a rest before heading out again. They even found time to call a meeting of the Sergeants' Mess in the Iraqi desert. Several days later, the convoy returned across the border – minus its leader, Bob Shepherd. A true soldier to his core, Bob hated the idea of missing out on the war. So he had decided to join up with D Squadron, going off with them for the rest of their patrol.

For the next few weeks, A and D Squadrons continued to search for Scuds and other targets, blasting up enemy camps and airfields right up until the beginning of the ground offensive. They were so successful that in the days before the Coalition forces attacked, they were eventually told to go static. There were no more targets left for them to rip up.

A Squadron pulled back to the Saudi border to await further orders. They stayed there right until the end of the war. D Squadron remained in the field for a while longer, attacking Iraqi installations and ambushing forces along the supply routes.

On 24 February, Coalition land forces rolled across the border into Iraq. Four days later, the US announced that Kuwait had been liberated and declared a unilateral ceasefire. The ground war had lasted barely a hundred hours. Soon after, A Squadron was finally recalled. D Squadron returned later on, in early March, having spent an incredible forty-two days behind enemy lines.

The war had ended with a shameful episode, when Coalition aircraft bombed a column of Iraqi forces retreating from Kuwait to Basra. Hundreds if not thousands of military personnel were killed, and thousands of vehicles were destroyed over the course of the bombardment. It was wholesale slaughter – and totally unnecessary. The enemy was already on the run. The mission to liberate Kuwait was all but over. There was no need to batter the Iraqis from the air.

At the time, the attack was justified because the Coalition wanted to destroy Saddam's military machinery. We certainly achieved that. Their army was completely devastated after the Gulf campaign. Our forces had inflicted long-lasting damage on Saddam's ability to wage war, leaving his military in tatters. And yet a decade later, we were told that Saddam was an urgent threat again, possessing huge stockpiles of deadly weapons. The claim was laughable. It would have taken the Iraqis decades to recover from the pasting we had given them in 1991.

The SAS achieved some great victories in the Gulf. Both A and D Squadrons took part in classic wartime operations and helped to reduce the Scud threat, taking out more TELs than anybody else. Without their actions, many more Scuds would have landed on Israel and Saudi Arabia, potentially dragging the Israelis into the war and breaking up the fragile Coalition. The patrols caused massive amounts of damage to Iraqi lines of communication, vehicle convoys and encampments.

Sadly, the efforts of A and D Squadrons were overshadowed, to an extent, by what happened to our patrol. Those guys were out there day and night, doing the kinds of missions that would have made the likes of David Stirling and Paddy Mayne very proud. And yet if you stop someone in the street and ask them about the SAS in the Gulf War, they'll usually say something like, 'Oh, yeah, Bravo Two Zero.'

For me, that is a real shame. The other squadrons are the real success story of the war. They spent up to six weeks operating behind enemy lines, dominating the ground, winning firefights and generally wreaking havoc.

The guys from B Squadron who went out with the resupply also did a really important job, allowing the lads in the field to stay operational during the final weeks of the war. It's those guys people should be talking about. Not us.

As for the survivors of Bravo Two Zero, the Regiment didn't seem to know what to do with us. There was no debrief after the war, which is a sure sign that something is wrong. Instead, they gave each of us a thousand pounds to go on holiday and disappear. It was the Regiment's way of saying, 'Get out of the way for a couple of weeks, until everything settles down.'

We were given a free holiday. The other squadrons got nothing.

It was the same deal with the medals. Some of the missions that A and D carried out were incredibly brave, and yet there were guys who didn't even get a lowly Mention in Dispatches. Meanwhile, B Squadron was awarded more medals than anyone else. It seemed as if the British Army was trying to keep us happy, getting us to stay quiet by throwing us a few gongs.

Personally, I would have been happy never to have received a medal. I didn't even want to go down to Buckingham Palace to receive it. I was in Zaire when someone told me, 'The investiture is next week. You'll have to go back for it.'

'I'm not interested,' I said. 'Have them send it up to Hereford.'

The next day, a message came back. I was on the next flight out. That was that.

Over the next eight years, the SAS started looking at areas to improve, in light of what had happened in Iraq. This led to the creation of the Force Projection Cell (FPC), which was formed of a representative from each Troop.

The Cell was a small, dedicated team that looked at everything to do with insertion techniques and equipment, making sure they got the guys into the places they were supposed to be. They studied methods of entry, SOPs, escape and evasion procedures, how to recover personal kit and hardware that had been left behind in the field.

There's an argument that without our experiences in the Gulf, and the changes that the Regiment later went through, the soldiers wouldn't have the kit and machinery that they do today. The guys these days have a much better support system, in the form of reinforcements and air cover. The comms have improved immeasurably. That's probably the biggest difference. As every SAS man knows, as soon as communications go wrong, everything starts to fall apart. Our patrol proved that.

CHAPTER 21

War in the Balkans

Zaire, 1991

In the decade after the Gulf War, the Regiment reverted to its cycle of team training jobs and counter-terrorism work. At the same time, small groups of SAS soldiers were sent out to a string of low-intensity conflicts in the Balkans, Africa and elsewhere. Working alongside green army troops, NATO forces and UN peacekeepers, they took on a variety of roles, sometimes working as unofficial mediators and bodyguards. But the guys also found time to engage in classic SAS activities, running counter-sniper ops, rescuing hostages and snatching war criminals. In the process, they developed some of the tactics the Regiment would later use to deadly effect in Iraq, Afghanistan and Syria.

In 1991, the Regiment kept itself busy on the ground in Africa, taking part in diplomatic jobs in various hot spots. In May, a small team went out to Ethiopia to rescue members of the Ethiopian royal family following the overthrow of the Marxist junta led by President Mengistu.

Four months later, I was part of an eight-man team posted to Zaire (now the Democratic Republic of Congo) to help evacuate the British Embassy in Kinshasa. Colonel Mobutu Sese Seko had been running the show for twenty-six years, but unrest against his rule was spreading. Soldiers hadn't been paid, inflation was through the roof and people were dying of starvation. To keep the army onside, Mobutu had given them free rein to loot mansions.

276

First of all, the officers would go in and nick any valuable paintings, furniture and fittings. Then the soldiers went in. Then the civilians. By the time they had finished, the property would have been stripped bare. Fireplaces, air-con units, electrical wiring – anything that could be ripped out. Demonstrations were taking place outside the British Embassy and it looked like the staff would have to leave at any moment.

It was a familiar story in terms of weaponry and kit. We wanted claymores, smoke grenades and 203 grenades, along with explosives and anti-personnel mines to guard the embassy. The Foreign Office refused. They said we could take our pistols and MP5 submachine guns and nothing else. It felt like the Gulf War all over again.

To begin with, we were supposed to be in Zaire for three days. We ended up staying for several weeks as Whitehall dithered over whether to go ahead and evacuate the embassy. Meanwhile the situation in the country was getting steadily worse. There was rioting and looting in the streets. Food was scarce. Lepers had resorted to waiting outside the back of the hospital, carrying off dead bodies and foraging for amputated body parts. People were dying from starvation.

While this was going on, we were sending daily situation reports back to Hereford and Whitehall, but nobody at their end seemed very keen to get us out. The ambassador had several heated conversations with the ministers, begging them to let us leave, but they were adamant that we weren't going anywhere. I was certain that if things kicked off, given our lack of gear, the embassy would be quickly overrun and we'd start taking casualties. Later on, we found out why the evacuation kept being pushed back. The Foreign Office had recently dropped several million pounds on a big refurbishment of the embassy and they didn't want to lose it.

Our emergency escape plan involved crossing a busy road, heading down an embankment and taking a Gemini inflatable boat across the fast-flowing Congo River (then known as the Zaire River) before heading to Brazzaville. Then we found out that the boat had a leak, which meant we had to go out every twelve hours to pump it up.

While this was going on, I had befriended a couple of guys from US Special Forces, who were doing the same job over at the American embassy. They had recognised me from a briefing I had given their lads during the Gulf War. At the time they were getting ready to go in and scope out a chemical plant in Iraq I had passed through during my escape. The Americans had bombed it and US SF were tasked with doing a damage assessment of the site. These guys had spotted me in Zaire and we got chatting. I asked them what their extraction plan was.

They told me they had a Galaxy Starlifter transport aircraft on standby in Brazzaville. They had two UH-60 Black Hawk helicopters, plus a Little Bird chopper that would come in and evacuate the ambassador. Once they got the order to evacuate, the team would be back in the US within twelve hours.

'What's your evacuation plan?' one of the lads asked.

I pointed to our leaky boat. 'That, over there,' I said. 'That's it.'

'What the hell!'

By that point the Portuguese, French, Germans and Israelis had all shipped out. The Americans soon followed. Even the South Africans ended up leaving. Those guys are stalwarts – when they start evacuating, you know it's serious. Before they left, they told me, 'You guys really want to get out. It's going to go badly wrong.'

My tour there finished abruptly when I had to come home to receive my medal at Buckingham Palace. The rest of the team stayed on for another four weeks. They got the ambassador out safely in the end, and the staff later returned once the situation had calmed down, but it could have been a very different story.

The widespread pillaging and violence of Zaire, however, was nothing compared to the atrocities the Regiment would encounter in its next deployment.

Bosnia and Herzegovina, 1994

On 25 June 1991, four months after the Coalition had rolled over Saddam's forces in Iraq, Croatia and Slovenia both declared their independence, triggering the breakup of Yugoslavia – and setting the Balkans on the path to war.

The following March, Bosnia and Herzegovina also formally announced its independence. Civil war quickly engulfed the region as long-simmering tensions between the Croats, Serbs and Muslims rose to the surface, turning on one another in an orgy of unspeakable violence and brutality. A United Nations Protection Force (UNPROFOR) comprising almost forty thousand troops was sent in, but they did little to stop the fighting between the rival forces. Soon they were joined by NATO forces providing air support and enforcing no-fly zones across the area.

In early 1994, small teams from A, B and D Squadrons were posted to Bosnia, under the cover of British Army liaison officers attached to the UN peacekeeping mission. Negotiations between the ethnic Croatians and Muslims in Bosnia were at a delicate stage and the Regiment was brought in to help map out the frontlines as part of the deal that was being brokered between the two parties.

The involvement of the Regiment had much to do with the appointment of General Mike Rose as the head of UNPROFOR. A former CO of 22 SAS, the general wanted guys on the ground he could trust to gather intelligence, marking out all the defensive positions, military bases and heavy weaponry on each side. The SAS teams would then feed this information back to Hereford as well as the command group, giving the general another source of information to rely on. In a politically charged environment, where everyone is telling you a different version of events, secondary intelligence sources are crucial. They can tell you who's being honest, and who is lying to your face.

The task called for guys who could operate in some of the most dangerous terrain in the Balkans. It was only natural that he'd turn to the Regiment for the job.

The SAS has repeatedly demonstrated a truth of modern warfare: no matter how good your aerial surveillance is, you still need eyes on the ground. A drone might identify a hundred soldiers at an army base, but it can't tell you the morale of those guys. Whereas a handful of experienced SF operators, inserted into that location, can tell you what state the troops' kit is in, whether they're well-dressed and well-fed, what the mood is like. All the tiny details that can't be gleaned from the air.

Getting access to the frontlines wasn't going to be easy, however. All the routes in and out of the disputed areas were heavily guarded by Croat, Muslim and Serb forces. But the SAS soldier is crafty. He has a slyness about him that has been drilled out of the green army infantry.

Wearing their UN blue berets, carrying standard-issue SA80 rifles and driving around in white-painted Land Rover 110s, the lads approached the roadblocks bearing gifts of whisky and sleeves of cigarettes. Accompanied by army interpreters, they'd hand over the goods and pretend to be friendly with the local troops, shooting the breeze with them over coffee and shots of homemade fruit brandy.

What the Croats and others didn't realise is that the SAS men were subtly interrogating them, teasing information out of them. They thought they were having a casual chat with a couple of UN advisers. Instead they ended up volunteering information about the locations of their anti-aircraft weaponry, tanks and trenches.

In addition to their mapping tasks, SAS teams posing as UN observers were ordered to gather intelligence from the besieged Muslim enclaves in the area. The Serbs were running a systematic campaign of 'ethnic cleansing' in eastern Bosnia, driving out or murdering hundreds of thousands of Muslims. Their forces had encircled these safe havens, setting up blockades at all the entry points and blocking access to foreign media and neutral third parties. Food convoys weren't getting in and the people trapped inside were being starved to death. There were also reports of atrocities being committed against the civilian populations. The Regiment was tasked with sneaking inside to find out what was happening.

Once inside the safe havens, these small groups would establish OPs and gather information on the enemy armour and artillery positions, feeding everything back to the UN via tactical satellite communications (tacsat). At the same time, they went out to recce and establish LZs for food supplies to be dropped in and bring much-needed relief to the beleaguered citizens.

Where possible, they would look to identify the units and individuals responsible for any war crimes that had been committed against local residents. The thinking was, if they could get evidence of atrocities inside the enclaves to the outside world, they could apply international pressure to the Serbs and force them to end the sieges, or at least allow convoys to get through. If the towns came under attack, they would call in airstrikes and direct ordnance on to the Serbian positions. (The Bosnian War was unique in that it was one of the very few occasions when Western powers fought on the same side as a Muslim population.)

One six-man team inserted into the besieged town of Goražde in April 1994. The Muslim community there had been holding out for several weeks despite being repeatedly pounded by Serbian artillery and tanks. As their forces closed in on the town, the SAS team went in and set up an OP on the rooftop of a bank, reporting on the Serbian positions and directing NATO airstrikes.

Several days later, the team was ambushed by Serbian forces while driving around in their UN-style, white-painted Land Rovers. With Goražde coming under renewed attack, it looked like the Serbs might roll in at any moment and the guys had gone out to look for a possible LZ to extract from the town. The Serbs opened fire on them, despite the fact that they were supposedly neutral forces and were travelling in UN-marked vehicles. One officer took a bullet to the shoulder. A second man, Fergus Rennie, was shot in the head by a sniper.

The soldiers pulled back to the town under intense tank and artillery fire and called for an immediate casevac. Fergus was airlifted out of the town by helicopter and flown to Sarajevo. Sadly, he died of his injuries shortly after arriving at the hospital.

Meanwhile, the wounded officer was treated on the ground in Goražde. He managed to get out of the town that night with the rest of the team, escaping through the mountains under cover of darkness before being extracted by helicopter. They were joined by a British pilot whose Sea Harrier jet had been shot down by the Serbs during an airstrike on their positions earlier that same day.

I was at home when I heard the news about Fergus. The guard room rang me up to tell me what had happened. His death hit me very hard. Fergus had been a student of mine on Selection and he was an excellent soldier, absolutely brilliant, with a very bright future in front of him in the Regiment. He was the first SAS soldier I had passed who had been killed. And I had very nearly failed him.

We had been doing a NavEx in the jungle when I had told the students to move off before first light. This is a good way of testing the guys to see who packs their kit properly in the darkness. If you don't, you'll lose stuff and end up leaving traces of your presence for the enemy to discover.

Predictably, when I returned to the camp site at dawn, I found bits of rope and string and other items lying around the place – along with an EMU device that someone had forgotten to pack. I was prepared to fail someone else for leaving that EMU at the camp, but when Fergus confessed to the crime, I decided to let him off.

If I had failed him, he would still be alive today.

I was racked with guilt after his death. That's what capped it for me. I had been weighing up whether to leave the Regiment, but when I heard the news about Fergus, I thought, I've had enough of this.

Eighteen soldiers had died during my time at Hereford. Their deaths were saddening, but you know that's the risk you take when you join the Regiment. You go to the funeral, mourn their passing, and then you move on. But Fergus was different. He was the first student I had lost, and somehow that made it much tougher. Even today, I still find it difficult to process.

The war in Bosnia was a nasty, brutish conflict. Many of the soldiers found it hard to believe that a community could become so bitterly divided within such a short period of time. A lot of these guys had done tours in Northern Ireland, but the violence in the Troubles was nothing compared to the horrors they witnessed in the Balkans. You had foreign fighters coming over to take part as well. Volunteers from Greece fought alongside the Serbs, mujahideen from the Middle East and North Africa took the side of the Muslims.

British, French and German mercenaries also got involved. Some of them went to fight for ideological reasons, or for a thirst for adventure. Others just wanted to kill. Things didn't end well for many of them. Two Britons who had gone over were caught by the mujahideen. The captured men were skinned alive and then 'necklaced' – car tyres filled with petrol were placed around their necks and set on fire.

One atrocity followed another as the region descended into chaos. Even aid workers were targeted. On one occasion, a Bosnian Army roadblock near Gornji Vakuf ambushed a convoy of relief vehicles coming in from Italy. The caravan was loaded up with supplies to deliver humanitarian aid to the stricken population, but that didn't matter to the Bosnians. They robbed the trucks of their supplies, siphoned fuel from the tanks and shot dead two aid workers and a journalist who had been travelling with the caravan.

These were the types of horrific acts that were being perpetrated in the Balkans.

From time to time, a few of the lads took matters into their own hands. A handful of SAS soldiers had been tasked to bodyguard General Rose while he was in charge of the UN's military forces. One of the guys, 'Geoff', was known to go out into the streets during his downtime and look for Serbian snipers to kill. At around this time the Serbs had been indiscriminately murdering civilians and Geoff had decided to do something about it.

He would set up urban OPs and search for targets, looking for likely firing positions such as blocks of flats, watching to see when the shooters exited the buildings. Unofficially, and using his own initiative, Geoff dropped quite a few snipers in Bosnia.

A few years later, once things started to calm down, the

Regiment took on a more proactive role in the Balkans – hunting Serbian war criminals.

The Regiment had gone after war criminals before, picking up Nazi officers in Germany during the dying days of the Second World War. Now they were back at it, lifting HVTs (high-value targets), setting ambushes and carrying out hard arrests. Backed by American intelligence, SAS snatch squads went out to capture a number of suspects indicted by the war crimes tribunal in The Hague.

The Regiment got the gig because the guys in US Special Forces units, although extremely professional and well-trained operators, didn't have the experience of making hard arrests. Whereas the SAS had been doing it for decades in Northern Ireland. But capturing these men would not be easy. The environment they were going into was far more dangerous than anything they had done in Ulster, with the targets living in areas where much of the population was fiercely loyal to the Serbian cause. In many cases, the suspects were being shielded by powerful figures in the political establishment and the security forces. Several of them were closely involved with local organised crime gangs.

In July 1997, the SAS moved to arrest their first target. Simo Drljača had been a feared paramilitary leader during the Bosnian War whose men had been instrumental in a campaign to 'ethnically cleanse' the town of Prijedor. Thousands of civilians had died in a number of concentration camps in the area. Now Drljača was about to get his comeuppance. Intelligence had established that the Serb spent most of his downtime fishing at a lake not far from Prijedor.

The snatch squad set up an OP at the lake and went on hard routine, watching the target for several days. Once they had confirmed the identity of the target, the team moved forward to make the arrest. As they approached their quarry, Drljača drew his weapon and opened fire, wounding one guy in the leg. The team instantly returned fire, killing the target.

While Drljača was making his last stand, another SAS team apprehended his partner-in-crime, Milan Kovacevic, arresting him at the hospital where he worked. He surrendered without a fight. A simultaneous snatch had been necessary to grab Kovacevic before anyone tipped him off. Drljača was a very well-connected individual. If the guys had gone after Kovacevic separately, someone might have told him that the Regiment was coming for him. He would have almost certainly gone to ground, as many other war criminals did.

The following September, the Regiment carried out a much riskier operation. Their target, Stevan Todorović, was a former Bosnian Serb police chief who had committed a range of war crimes in the town of Bosanski Šamac. US intelligence experts had tracked Todorović to a log cabin in a remote wooded area in the mountainous region of western Serbia. Arresting the suspect would mean crossing from Bosnia into another sovereign country, kidnapping him and smuggling him back across the border while avoiding any of the main crossing points. The guys would be inserting into an area they didn't know, in an environment that was extremely hostile to British forces. If it went wrong, they wouldn't be able to seek any help from the locals.

In the dead of night, a four-man snatch team grabbed Todorović from his cabin. They blindfolded the Serb, tied him up and manhandled him into the back of a waiting vehicle. From there the team drove north to the banks of the Drina River and crossed over to Bosnia on a Zodiac inflatable boat. Once on friendly soil, the suspect was airlifted to another location before being flown on to The Hague. Todorović later pled guilty to a number of charges and was sentenced to ten years in prison.

Over the next few years, the Regiment successfully captured several more suspects. These operations did more than bring vicious Serbian war criminals to justice. They also gave the soldiers vital experience in lifting targets from treacherous foreign environments. Years later, they would carry out similar operations in Iraq, but on a much bigger scale.

The Balkans conflict was a difficult campaign for the SAS. Coming off the back of the Gulf War, where they had been given free rein to cause as much damage as possible, they were suddenly having to work under very tight restrictions. In a complicated warzone, they had to take on a more varied role than in previous conflicts.

One minute they were gathering intelligence on the frontlines. The next, they were calling in air cover to protect food convoys. At other times they were bodyguard dignitaries or hunting down war criminals. Only a unit with the diverse skillsets and experience of the SAS could carry out so many different jobs.

Despite some successes, the Balkans had been a relatively low-key engagement for the Regiment, compared to the huge multi-squadron deployment in Iraq. At the beginning of the next decade, however, the guys would be back in the thick of the action.

CHAPTER 22

Operation Barras

Sierra Leone, 2000

At the beginning of the twenty-first century, Sierra Leone was one of the most impoverished, lawless and violent states in the world. Throughout the 1990s, the country had been ravaged by a series of vicious coups, led by the armed rebels in the Revolutionary United Front (RUF). Backed by Liberian President Charles Taylor and funded by the profits gleaned from the lucrative trade in 'blood diamonds' (diamonds mined in conflict zones, used by dictators and rebel militias to finance wars), the RUF waged a war of terror against the government and the civilian population, capturing villages and massacring the locals in an unrelenting orgy of violence, rape, looting and murder.

Among the RUF's recruits were child soldiers in the 'Small Boys Units', some of whom were as young as seven or eight. These kids were ordered at gunpoint to kill people from their own villages, often including their own families. Young girls were kidnapped and taken as sex slaves.

Others were subject to appalling mutilations. The rebels cut off the lips, noses and ears of their victims, gouged out their eyes or hacked off their genitals. Many more had their arms or legs amputated, including young boys and girls. In one of the RUF's most infamous campaigns, people were offered the choice between a 'long sleeve' and a 'short sleeve.' If the answer was 'long', the person's hand was cut off at the wrist. If they said 'short', the rebels would hack off their arm at the elbow.

In May 1999, a ceasefire had been brokered between the rebels and President Ahmad Tejan Kabbah. A few months later, a force of 13,000 UN soldiers was brought in as part of the UN Mission in Sierra Leone (UNAMSIL). But the poorly trained peacekeepers were either unable or unwilling to stop the RUF and the rebels were soon stirring things up again. In early May 2000 they attacked a number of UN bases, taking hundreds of peacekeepers hostage, and within a matter of days the rebels were closing in on the capital, Freetown.

Panic spread through the city. The RUF had already laid siege to the capital during a number of bloodthirsty rampages in the late 1990s, pillaging, raping and killing indiscriminately. In 1997, an ex-SAS soldier, Will Scully, had almost single-handedly kept a huge force of rebels at bay as they attempted to storm the Mammy Yoko Hotel, where hundreds of civilians had sought refuge. Now it seemed as though Freetown was about to fall to the murderous rebels once again.

British commanders launched an operation to evacuate British, European and Commonwealth nationals trapped inside the city. A force of troops, led by 1st Battalion, Parachute Regiment, was sent in to oversee the evacuation. Once they arrived, 1 Para moved rapidly to secure Lungi International Airport and the area around the Aberdeen Peninsula, including the Mammy Yoko Hotel. In a matter of days, the troops had begun pushing into the interior, dominating the ground and halting the rebel advance.

That was swiftly followed by the creation of a British Army training team to bring the ranks of the Sierra Leone Army (SLA) up to scratch. These teams were broadly doing the same kind of work that the Regiment had done in Oman in the 1970s. Based at Benguema Camp, a Sierra Leonean army base several miles outside Freetown, the training teams would teach recruits to the SLA about basic infantry tactics so they could go out and destroy the rebels. Only once the RUF and the other rebel groups had been crushed could there be any hope of a permanent peace in Sierra Leone.

Three months later, however, the British Army was sucked into a new crisis. On Friday, 25 August 2000, eleven soldiers from the Royal Irish Regiment training team were ambushed and taken hostage while on a vehicle patrol near the small village of Magbeni. Their captors were a feared rebel group known as the West Side Boys.

Even among the hardcore rebels of Sierra Leone, the West Side Boys had a terrifying reputation. A motley crew of former soldiers, rebels and thieves, they had fought alongside the armed rebels in the RUF before turning on the Sierra Leone Army and the UN. The Boys, who called themselves the 'West Side Niggaz' after their obsession with US gangsta rap, lived in the jungle, looting and killing as they pleased. Led by 'Brigadier' Foday Kallay, they were a law unto themselves.

Some of them wore female wigs. Others dressed in colourful T-shirts, flip-flops and combat fatigues. Many wore lucky charms that they believed made them bulletproof. They got drunk on potent palm wine, smoked marijuana and took heroin. To fund their lifestyle, they preyed on vehicles travelling along the main road towards Freetown. When they weren't nursing hangovers, they were indulging in their favourite pastimes of torture, beatings, rape and murder.

This was the group of psychopaths, bandits and lunatic killers lying in wait for the Royal Irish patrol as they made their way back to their base.

Accompanied by their Sierra Leonean Liaison Officer (LO), the soldiers had taken an unplanned detour towards Magbeni when they were suddenly confronted by a throng of angry members of the West Side Boys. After a heated exchange, the soldiers found themselves boxed in. Realising that they were heavily outnumbered and with no chance of escape, they reluctantly obeyed their commanding officer's orders to lay down their weapons. The disarmed soldiers were then dragged from their vehicles and roughed up before being taken to the Boys' head-quarters at the nearby settlement of Gberi Bana.

The rebels' leader, Foday Kallay, now saw a golden opportunity to hold the British government to ransom. The soldiers were taken hostage and placed under armed guard and the Boys began issuing their demands.

Sixteen days later, the crisis would result in the Regiment's most famous hostage-rescue operation since the Iranian Embassy Siege.

The Regiment was alerted to the situation more or less immediately. At the time, D Squadron was elsewhere on the African continent, doing squadron and troop-training exercises. They were the logical choice for the mission, and seven days after the ambush, the squadron arrived in-country and headed over to the British Army camp at Waterloo, twenty miles due east of Freetown.

They were joined by twenty-four men from the SBS, plus infantry reinforcements in the form of A Company, 1 Para. The guys were up against an enemy force of at least six hundred rebels in Sierra Leone: far too many for one or two Sabre Squadrons to tackle. At the time the SAS was severely understrength, so it made sense to bring in operators from other parts of the UKSF family and back them up with a force of motivated, highly trained soldiers. The extra 150 men from the Parachute Regiment would go a long way towards levelling the odds.

From the outset, things didn't look good for the Royal Irish soldiers. They were being held in a well-defended stronghold in the jungle, surrounded by hundreds of heavily armed rebels. The Boys' camp consisted of two ramshackle villages situated along the banks of the Rokel Creek River. To the north was the smaller settlement at Gberi Bana, a scattering of crude mud huts and concrete dwellings. Around two hundred rebels lived in Gberi Bana, including the leader Foday Kallay and his subordinates.

This northern settlement is where the soldiers were being held.

During their imprisonment they were routinely threatened, slapped about and subjected to mock executions. Their unfortunate liaison officer had it even worse. He was separated from the others, confined to a hole dug in the ground and urinated on by his sadistic captors. Every so often he was dragged out of his pit and beaten senseless.

The majority of the West Side Boys, four hundred or so, lived in the village of Magbeni, on the south side of the Rokel river. The settlements were defended by twin ZPU 14.5mm anti-aircraft guns, mortars and landmines placed around the fringes of the camp. It was believed that the mortars at Magbeni were within range of Gberi Bana, which meant that any operation to rescue the hostages would have to deal with the rebels in both settlements.

The rebels themselves were well-equipped, armed with AK-47 assault rifles, RPGs, grenades and stolen British SLRs. They also had a number of technicals – pickup trucks with heavy machine guns mounted to the rear cargo areas. Whichever way the lads in D Squadron decided to go in, they were going to come up against some serious opposition.

The situation facing the SAS in Sierra Leone was on a much bigger scale than anything they had attempted before. At the Iranian embassy, the guys had been tasked with rescuing the hostages from a single confined building. Now D Squadron had to figure out how to assault two entire villages. In 1980, they had been up against six Iranian–Arab gunmen with a clear political motivation. In 2000, they were going up against several hundred drug-crazed bandits and deserters, who seemed more interested in drinking and killing than anything else. Under Foday Kallay, the soldiers had been brainwashed into believing they were impervious to enemy fire.

That attitude would make the West Side Boys dangerously unpredictable in a firefight. On the flip side, those habits of smoking ganja, drinking and partying don't bode well for when you're going to come face-to-face with the ultra-professional SAS.

The first priority in any hostage-rescue operation is to get eyes on the stronghold. In Sierra Leone, that meant inserting guys into the jungle to run OPs on the two enemy camps at Magbeni and Gberi Bana.

Very soon after they had set themselves up at the camp at Waterloo, two small SAS teams were inserted via the Rokel Creek River. Once ashore they moved into their positions along the perimeters of the camps and set up their OPs. A friend of mine, Bill Draper, was part of the team tasked with observing the enemy settlement to the north at Gberi Bana.

Going on hard routine, the guys began feeding information back to the camp and the command centre in Freetown, updating them on the enemy's morale, the routines of guards and sentries, the locations of different individuals, and the positions of weaponry and equipment around the camp. Everything that D Squadron needed to build up a complete picture of the stronghold.

From that moment on, once the SAS had got in there and put eyes on their camp, the West Side Boys were on a hiding to nothing. They didn't know it, but they were living on borrowed time.

By this point the rebels had already made contact with the British Army. Negotiations were led by Lieutenant-Colonel Simon Fordham, CO of the 1st Battalion, Royal Irish. He was supported by a pair of trained Metropolitan Police negotiators. According to Damien Lewis in his gripping account of the mission, *Operation Certain Death*, a couple of Regiment guys were also added to the negotiating team. There was a clear logic to sending in two SAS men to help, as Lewis points out. 'Both men,' he notes, 'were skilled in hostage-negotiation tactics.'

The negotiators did their best to try and resolve the situation peacefully, but that was always going to be difficult with a group like the Boys. The negotiations did produce some early results. At a meeting to demonstrate proof of life, one of the captured soldiers managed discreetly to pass a pen lid to the negotiators, with a drawing of the layout at Gberi Bana secreted inside. Even more useful was the release of five of the hostages in exchange for a satellite phone – a seriously impressive achievement by the negotiators under the circumstances. The freed soldiers would provide crucial details to the SAS as they started making preparations for the assault.

Back at the camp, the guys set about creating a life-size facsimile of the West Side Boys' headquarters, based on satellite imagery, the briefing given to them by the freed Royal Irish soldiers and the information they were getting from the men in the two OPs. Using the same procedure as at Prince's Gate, the model of the stronghold would allow them to practise assault drills, making sure that they were familiar with every square inch of the village at Gberi Bana.

The guys quickly realised that going in by land was impossible. The rebel headquarters at Gberi Bana was surrounded by a tangle of thick jungle and swamps. An attacking force moving through that terrain would be knackered before they had a chance to get stuck into the enemy. A river assault was also out of the question: any boats navigating the murky waters of the Rokel Creek would run aground on the many sandbars lurking beneath the surface. Which meant the guys would have to insert by air. And that was far from ideal. 'The option of an airborne assault had nothing going for it,' writes Damien Lewis in *Operation Certain Death*. 'It was completely lacking in either stealth or surprise.'

The Regiment used a bold combination of tactics for their assault in Sierra Leone. It brought together elements of jungle warfare, CQB and counter-terrorism tactics – backed up by highly trained troops on the ground and air support.

The plan involved flying D Squadron into Gberi Bana using a pair of Chinooks, bringing the guys directly on to the target. Once in position, the men would fast-rope down from the chopper, with one team going for the hostages while the others cleared the surrounding buildings of rebels and secured the LZ.

At the same time, the soldiers in 1 Para would deal with the larger rebel force in Magbeni, to the south of the Rokel River. A third Chinook would bring in an initial detachment of Paras, dropping them into an area of swampland to the west of Magbeni. They would advance to a strip of forest on the edge of the village, with one section securing the LZ while the others waited at the treeline for the chopper to return with the remaining platoons. Meanwhile, three Lynx attack helicopters would strafe both villages, taking out the heavy machine guns and fixing the rebels in place until the rest of A Company could be brought forward.

The Paras would hit the village hard, going through the place like a dose of salts. The rescued hostages, along with any casualties, would be extracted to the Royal Fleet Auxiliary vessel *Sir Percivale*, which was anchored in Freetown harbour. With the villages cleared of rebels, the remaining SAS, SBS and Paras would then be airlifted out of the camp.

There were risks at every stage of the plan. The Chinooks would be exposed to dangerous ground fire during the insertion phase. If the rebels heard the choppers coming in and realised they were about to be attacked, they might blow the choppers out of the sky before the teams could fast-rope down. Once they were on the ground, the assaulters would be massively outnumbered by the defending rebels.

There aren't many military forces in the world that would risk inserting into a camp teeming with rebel fighters. Most would probably consider it suicidal. But the lads in D Squadron were gambling that the West Side Boys wouldn't expect an aerial assault. Which meant they would have a small window in which to insert before the rebels could react. To maximise their chances of success, the assaulters would come in at first light, when the rebels were likely to be hungover or asleep. By the time they realised what was happening, the SAS soldiers would already be on the ground and getting stuck into them.

In early September, the negotiations hit a brick wall. The West Side Boys were becoming increasingly aggressive at the meetings and the British negotiators felt that the rebels were merely stringing them along. All the signs indicated that Kallay and his men would kill the hostages, once they believed they had extracted as many concessions as they could – a view supported by the mock executions the Royal Irish soldiers had been forced to endure. The final straw came when the Brits learned of a plot to ambush the negotiating team. 'That particular trap was barely avoided,' notes Richard Connaughton in his account of the operation, 'but it meant an end to playtime.'

It was time to act.

On Friday, 8 September 2000, a decision was made by Tony Blair's government to give the go-ahead for the assault, code-named 'Operation Barras'. On the Saturday, the assaulters made their final preparations for the imminent attack. According to Damien Lewis, this included the delivery of a truckload of alcohol to the rebels. 'Knowing the West Side Boys' predilection for booze,' he writes, 'the plan was to get them well lashed the night before the assault went in.'

In the early hours of the following morning, Sunday 10 September, the team went in.

Shortly after 0530 hours, the three Chinooks carrying the guys from D Squadron, elements of the SBS and half of 1 Para set off for their respective targets. They were accompanied by the three Lynx helicopters and a seventh aircraft, a Russian Mi-24 Hind gunship, whose aircrew included a former SAS soldier, Fred Marafono.

Fred had been the SSM in B Squadron during my time in the Regiment. After leaving Hereford he had gone to work on 'the Circuit'; in the mid-1990s he had been recruited by Executive Outcomes, a South African-based PMC (private military contractor) outfit. At the time, EO had been hired by the Sierra Leone government, which was in danger of being overrun by the RUF. For a while the mercenaries had been brilliantly effective, using a handful of old Soviet gunships to push the RUF back into the countryside.

After EO's contract was cancelled, Fred and a few other guys had decided to stay on in Sierra Leone, doing what they could to take the fight to the rebels. Fred was a true soldier, a warrior to his core, and he would have been chuffed to bits at the chance to take part in an SAS operation once more.

Flying low to make themselves less vulnerable to anti-aircraft fire, the choppers stealthily made their way along the route of the Rokel River towards the stronghold. On the ground, Bill Draper and the other guys in the OP team at Gberi Bana had crept forward in the darkness and were now within spitting distance of the prisoners' hut. As soon as the choppers arrived they would open up, dropping the guards to give the lads on the Chinooks valuable seconds to fast-rope down. Until the very last moment the OP team was in communication with the choppers, updating their colleagues on the rebel numbers and positions.

As the two Chinooks with the sixty-odd men of D Squadron on board came in over Gberi Bana, the stillness of the dawn was abruptly shattered. The choppers hovered over their LZs in the exact positions that had been marked out by the planners. Everything was done according to their training, right down to the direction the choppers' noses were facing, so that every member of the assault group was able to orientate themselves as soon as they hit the ground.

On board the Chinook, the guys in D Squadron would have been mentally rehearsing the firefight in their minds. It's like a Formula One racing driver waiting on the starting grid before a big race. Before that green light, they're going over the course in their minds, visualising each turn. It's the same before the SAS goes into an operation. You're thinking about the first building you need to attack, how many rooms are inside, how many guards sleep there, what's behind that hut and to the left and right of it. All of the familiarisation work you've done on the replica at the camp is transferred from being in your head to actually seeing it on the ground. From the moment you get off that chopper, you know exactly where to go and what to do when you get there.

As the Chinooks hovered overhead, the guards outside the prison building were evidently stunned. They stood there, gawping at the choppers as if transfixed. In the next instant, Bill Draper and the rest of the OP team opened fire, walloping the rebels.

By now the first guys were spilling out from the Chinooks, fast-roping from two ropes at the rear and two either side. The SAS are trained to descend differently from the rest of the British Army. Instead of using their legs, they grip the rope between thick-gloved hands and make an ultra-rapid descent. It's all about speed, getting down and into the action as quickly as possible.

As the SF guys came screaming down the ropes, disaster almost struck. Some of the Boys, having recovered from the initial shock of the assault, managed to return fire at the British helicopters. Two RPGs were reportedly fired at the Chinooks as they hovered overhead, but both narrowly missed their target.

The crews on all three helicopters were ballsy guys. They had to flare their choppers over the villages and hold them in position, exposing themselves to potentially lethal fire while their passengers debussed. Without the skill of the RAF pilots, the assault could have gone disastrously wrong.

In a matter of seconds, the guys in D Squadron were out of the choppers and on the ground and hitting targets, covered by Bill Draper and the rest of the OP team. The assault groups were packing some heavy-duty firepower for the raid on Gberi Bana, including GPMGs, Minimis, LAW 66mm rocket launchers, grenades and Diemaco C7 assault rifles. The latter is a derivative of the tried-and-trusted M16 used by the SAS until the late1990s, with a few minor technical modifications. But it's still just as effective in a firefight.

The rescue group headed straight for the prison hut to locate the hostages. At the same time the other teams worked their way through their designated sectors, clearing the buildings and brassing up any rebels they encountered.

The West Side Boys were completely overwhelmed. They were hardened fighters, but they had never come up against an elite SF unit before and had no idea of what the SAS was capable. Now they were finding out. The hard way.

There was a lot going on at this point. The Lynxes were tearing up the other side of the river, blasting up the rebels at Magbeni to protect the Chinooks. The Hind gunship was also mixing it up, firing rockets at selected targets. On the south side of the river, the first platoons from A Company, 1 Para inserted into an area of swampland to the west of Magbeni. One group of lads remained at the LZ to guard it, while the rest of the soldiers waded towards their designated baseline. Meanwhile the Chinook flew back to the camp at Waterloo to collect the rest of A Company.

Within a few minutes, D Squadron had rescued all six hostages. The Sierra Leonean LO was not among them; he was discovered in another hut, alive but badly beaten and weakened from lack of food. The assault teams now regrouped and advanced north to secure the LZ on the outskirts of Gberi Bana, driving the rebels back towards the jungle. Twenty minutes after the firefight had begun, all seven hostages had been extracted and flown to *Sir Percivale*.

By that point D Squadron had already taken its first casualties. Brad Tinnion, a patrol medic, had been hit in the lower back by a stray 7.62mm round during the early stages of the battle. He was casevacced and flown to the hospital ship for emergency surgery, but died shortly after. His death was a blow to the rest of D Squadron, but it highlights the close proximity of the opposing forces in Gberi Bana. There was a lot of metal flying around, a lot of bullets and shrapnel, with several guys getting fragged by the grenades being posted and the RPGs the rebels were firing at them from the treeline.

The Boys were putting up a determined fight. They were poor soldiers, but a combination of drinking, hard drugs and voodoo magic made them fearless even in the face of overwhelming fire-power. Their fierce resistance took the Brits by surprise. One section of SAS men had been stationed aboard *Sir Percivale* as a reserve force, ready to join the main group if casualties started coming in. As the first assaulters flew in early that morning, these lads held in reserve were thinking to themselves, they'll annihilate the rebels; we'll never get involved. Then one of the Chinooks returned with the SAS casualties on board and the reserves were told to get ready to depart. That woke them up. All of a sudden, they were having to go into a hot DZ (Drop Zone).

By now the rest of the force from 1 Para had been brought forward to join their colleagues at Magbeni. The Paras also took casualties when an enemy mortar exploded in their midst, wounding several infantrymen and their commanding officer. They quickly recovered, keeping up the momentum of the advance as they swept from west to east through the village, tearing into the rebels with a ferocious barrage of 66mm rockets, grenades, GPMGs and small-arms fire.

By 0800, the Paras had cleared the village.

The remaining rebels had been pushed into an area of jungle beyond the villages using 'Directional Fire' tactics. To DF the enemy, you drive them into an area that has already been marked off. Once they're in the kill zone, the mortar teams can get straight to work, hitting them with the heavy stuff. Anyone caught inside that kill zone is turned into mincemeat. You keep pounding them until there's nothing left.

As soon as the mortar crews started putting down stonks on the West Side Boys, it was game over. The battle raged for a few more hours as the rebels counter-attacked, but each time they were easily repulsed. Against a force of elite British SF, infantry and air power, they never stood a chance.

By mid-morning the fighting was over. The three stolen Land Rovers were airlifted out of the camp, while the dead bodies were loaded on to the Chinooks, along with the handful of prisoners the assaulters had taken.

Among the captured rebels was the self-styled 'Brigadier' Foday Kallay. The West Side Boys' feared leader had been found cowering pathetically under some bedding in one of the huts in Gberi Bana. He was plasticuffed, marched over to one of the helicopters and dumped on top of a pile of bullet-riddled corpses.

'You might think you're the West Side Boys,' Bill Draper told him in his Cockney accent. 'But we're the bloody SAS.'

At around 1100 hours, the last members of the assault group were airlifted out of the camp. By then the surviving Boys had fled deeper in the jungle, having seen their mates get wiped out.

Officially, twenty-five rebels died in the raid. Another eighteen were captured. The real number was far, far higher. One thing was for sure: the Regiment, along with the Paras and the SBS, had given the Boys a lesson they wouldn't forget in a hurry.

Operation Barras had been a stunning success. All seven hostages were safely rescued. The West Side Boys had been battered. Their leader had been captured, their weapons and equipment destroyed, and their fighters driven from their jungle hideout. The Boys' defeat at Gberi Bana and Magbeni essentially finished them off as a fighting force.

On the British side, one SAS soldier had died, another man was seriously injured, and eleven others were wounded. The death of Brad Tinnion was a sad loss for D Squadron, but the total casualties were far lighter than had been anticipated. That is a testament to the training, skill and fighting determination of the SAS. Using a combination of tactics, and supported by a sizeable infantry force, the lads had shown that they could overcome formidable obstacles to carry out a hostage rescue against a much larger, well-armed foe.

The concept of using attack helicopters in support of the Regiment was brilliantly innovative. So was the idea of moving at breakneck pace, using speed instead of stealth to get straight onto the target and overrun the enemy. But it was the success of the Paras in Sierra Leone, fighting alongside the lads from the Regiment, that would have the most far-reaching impact – eventually leading to the creation of a brand-new SF unit, the Special Forces Support Group (SFSG).

SFSG was officially created in 2006. The whole of 1st Battalion, Parachute Regiment, was permanently attached to SFSG and made up the bulk of its fighting strength of approximately eight hundred men. Other elements were brought in from the RAF Regiment and the Royal Marines. The role of the SFSG is to provide a highly motivated infantry support team for SAS operations. Deploying alongside the Sabre Squadrons, they can put up a defensive cordon and take part in the fighting, freeing up the SAS to carry out the precision strike.

Conceptually this was a huge leap forward. In the past, the SAS had lacked proper backup in the field. If we were caught out, as my patrol had been in Iraq, there was no one else we could rely on to come and help us out. Now, for the first time, the Regiment could focus on the strategic parts of an operation, doing the tasks that required their specialist skills – explosive entry, room clearances, CQB tactics – while the SFSG teams put down rounds and made the area safe to operate in.

The SFSG guys are excellent soldiers in their own right, trained to an incredibly high standard. That's important in terms of supporting the Regiment on operations. The SAS soldier knows he can rely on the SFSG to put down accurate covering fire or bring in a mortar crew to hit a target several miles away.

A few years later, during the Iraq War, when the four Sabre Squadrons were being over-worked, SFSG even took over the counter-terrorism team for a while. They were very, very good. These guys were training to a consistently high standard, putting in the hard work, following the drills to the letter. Nobody could have done a better job.

By the time the SFSG had been formed, the Regiment had already been sucked back into the vortex of war in the Middle East – a conflict that would see them pioneer a new type of special forces warfare.

CHAPTER 23

Manhunters

Afghanistan, 2001

On the morning of 11 September 2001, terrorists hijacked four passenger airliners and carried out a series of devastating attacks on American soil. That evening, in a televised address, President George W. Bush vowed to hunt down those responsible, marking the beginning of a war on terror that would bog down the West in conflicts in Afghanistan and Iraq for the next decade. The Regiment would be heavily involved in operations in both theatres, stretching its resources to breaking point as the guys came face-to-face with a deadly new threat, unlike anything they had tackled before: the rise of Islamist militant groups. To defeat them, the SAS would have to learn a whole new way to soldier.

Over the past two decades, the SAS has become increasingly important in the fight against global terrorism – both at home and abroad. In Iraq, working alongside US Special Forces, they were pushing the envelope on a daily basis, doing things that hadn't been attempted before, harvesting high-grade intel to target insurgent networks with ruthless efficiency.

It's the type of work the guys are ideally suited for: fighting unconventional wars against emerging threats, and coming up with new tactics, has been the Regiment's MO for the past seventy years. With their experience of counter-insurgency ops and their anti-terrorism training, the lads have shown that they have the capability to do what conventional forces can't, going in and hitting the terrorists hard, degrading their upper ranks.

In a world where the general public in Britain has become war-weary, putting 'boots on the ground' and suffering casualties is politically unacceptable, the SAS's ability to deploy covertly makes them highly valued by their political masters. Rapid advances in technology and surveillance measures have made them more effective than ever before. In Iraq, the scale and quality of the information the guys were getting helped them to bring down one of the most feared terrorist networks the world had ever seen.

The first target for the West after 9/11 was Afghanistan. The Taliban, who controlled most of the country, had provided a safe haven for the mastermind behind the attacks, Osama bin Laden, and the al-Qaeda terrorist network he had cultivated. Under their reclusive one-eyed leader, Mullah Mohammed Omar, the Taliban had presided over a brutally repressive regime since coming to power in the mid-1990s, banning TV and music, destroying ancient monuments and forbidding women from travelling alone or getting an education. So it was no surprise when Omar refused an ultimatum from the Americans to hand over bin Laden and his fellow perpetrators. A US-led invasion was inevitable.

On 7 October 2001, Coalition aircraft carried out a series of strikes on Taliban targets, destroying anti-aircraft emplacements, radar installations and command and control sites. Within a few days they had established complete air dominance, paving the way for the ground phase to begin. Anti-Taliban forces did most of the fighting, supported by Coalition airstrikes, US SF teams and CIA operators. By early November the anti-Taliban forces, mainly comprising Northern Alliance militiamen, had seized vast swathes of territory from the enemy. On 12 November they rolled into the capital, Kabul, and the remaining Taliban and al-Qaeda fighters fled into their spiritual stronghold at Kandahar, in the south of the country.

While this was going on, the Regiment had been largely side-lined from the main action. A and G Squadrons had deployed to Afghanistan in mid-October, but instead of getting involved in the operations to hunt down bin Laden, they spent most of the war doing reconnaissance tasks in the north-west of the country. It was only after the fall of Kabul that they were finally given a juicier assignment.

In November, both Sabre Squadrons took part in an assault on a suspected al-Qaeda opium processing plant located to the south-west of Kandahar. Opium production had theoretically been outlawed by the Taliban, but the trade continued to thrive after the ban, fuelled by the stockpiles of opiates inside the country and the increasing price of heroin – which was itself rising due to the destruction of poppy fields inside Afghanistan. The lucrative profits from the business were channelled back into financing terrorist operations against the West; destroying the production facilities was crucial in order to deprive al-Qaeda of funds and curb their ability to carry out attacks.

Four SAS soldiers including the RSM were wounded during the assault, which took place in broad daylight due to the restricted availability of US air support. After a heavy firefight the men cleared out the facility and searched for intelligence before bugging out.

The success of that raid may have led to the involvement of the SAS in an assault on the Tora Bora caves complex the following month. In early December, Kandahar fell, signalling the collapse of the Taliban. Mullah Omar escaped from the city before he could be captured and went into hiding. He was never seen or heard from again until Afghan security chiefs announced in 2015 that he had died two years earlier while living in exile in Karachi.

Meanwhile the remaining al-Qaeda and Taliban resistance retreated into the mountainous caves of Tora Bora, twenty kilometres from the border with Pakistan. Originally used as a refuge by the mujahideen during the Soviet–Afghan War, the complex was a formidable defensive position, an intricate network of natural caverns and bunkers with only a handful of navigable tracks going up and down. Hundreds of enemy fighters were believed to be bottled up inside.

It was the job of a motley force of anti-Taliban militias to flush the enemy out before they could slip away across the Pakistani border. The fighters, numbering 3,000 men, were backed up by US air power and Special Forces. Soldiers from both A and G Squadrons were flown in to take part in the operation, along with a handful of SBS operators. Their job was to direct US airstrikes on to targets and assist in the assault on the caves complex, engaging targets and seizing ground until the enemy had nowhere left to go. The guys from A Squadron led the assault, during which two men were injured, one in the leg and the other in the arm.

The battle raged for two weeks as American B52s pounded enemy positions, while the assaulters moved further up the mountain, clearing the caves and killing pockets of al-Qaeda fighters. The ferocity of the airstrikes and the aggressiveness of the SF-led assault teams eventually forced the defenders to retreat deeper into the mountains, but instead of pressing home their advantage, the Afghans agreed to a ceasefire with their trapped enemies. The defenders used the negotiations as a delaying tactic, buying time to sneak away, fleeing the mountain at night and crossing into Pakistan.

Although there was never conclusive proof that bin Laden had been at Tora Bora, it was a well-known mujahideen hideout and there was a reasonable chance that he may have been among the resistance forces holed up there. Either way, bin Laden evaded the global manhunt for another decade until he was finally eliminated by US Special Forces, after being tracked to a compound in Abbottabad, Pakistan.

The Regiment's first involvement in Afghanistan had been short-lived. Fifteen months later, they would deploy to Iraq for a much longer campaign – hurtling them into the world of hi-tech, non-stop counter-terrorist warfare.

Iraq, 2003–05

The dust had barely settled on the battle for Tora Bora when the US turned its attention to its next target: Saddam Hussein. In January 2002, two months after the defeat of the Taliban, President

Bush gave his State of the Union address to Congress, denouncing Iran, North Korea and Iraq as part of an 'axis of evil'. Throughout the second half of 2002, the Bush administration began publicly making the case for toppling Saddam, although the decision to invade had almost certainly been made much earlier.

To back up their argument, White House officials claimed that Saddam had got his hands on, or was about to acquire, all kinds of terrifying biological, chemical and nuclear weapons – completely ignoring the fact that we had reduced the Iraqi military to rubble in the Gulf War, and the country had been economically crippled by sanctions ever since.

That didn't stop the hawks from arguing the case for getting rid of Saddam, however, and by early 2003 war against Iraq was an inevitability.

The air campaign began on 20 March 2003, after a deadline for Saddam to pack his bags and leave or suffer the consequences elapsed. The night before, the Coalition had planned to launch a series of decapitation strikes, aimed at eliminating the upper echelons of the Ba'athist regime. But when US intelligence officials learned about the potential whereabouts of Saddam and his sons, Uday and Qusay, they authorised a bombing attack on the target. The tip-off was based on misinformation, however, and Saddam remained at large as cruise missiles rained down on Baghdad, smashing targets across the capital. At the same time, ground troops surged across the desert from Kuwait, using lightning speed and aggression to overrun the enemy.

By that point, the Regiment had already been in the desert for a few days. They were part of a massive deployment of Special Forces units sent in ahead of the main invasion, including US and Australian soldiers. Tactically, this made much more sense than it had in the Gulf War, where SF patrols had only infiltrated into Iraq after the airstrikes had begun. Instead of teams having to rush across the border, they could insert before the air war, keeping a low profile until the bombs start dropping. Then they could start hitting targets.

Operating mainly in the Anbar region of western Iraq and in

the Kurdish north, the SF teams were tasked with capturing key targets including oil facilities and fixing the Iraqis in place. The oilfields were particularly important. Saddam's army had set fire to hundreds of oil wells in Kuwait in 1991, acting as a smokescreen to cover their retreat. The clean-up took months and cost billions of dollars, and the Coalition was keen to avoid a repeat scenario.

While this was going on, B and D Squadrons were in Anbar as part of the British SF deployment, Operation Row. They were going out in their Pinkies, tooled up and searching for targets to rip up, just as we had done in the first Gulf War. At the same time, the patrols were setting up OPs, seizing airfields, hitting enemy facilities and calling in airstrikes on strategic targets. These operations were intended to divert Iraqi forces away from Baghdad and the frontier, forcing them to commit resources to hunting down the raiding parties. The Regiment was the natural choice for this work, given their training and the vast experiences they had gained in the Iraqi desert twelve years earlier.

In a poignant moment, the guys from B Squadron took a break from the fighting to leave a memorial near the Euphrates for Bob Consiglio, one of the soldiers who had died during our ill-fated Bravo Two Zero mission.

The Iraqi regime collapsed with almost unbelievable speed. At the beginning of April, allied forces had captured Saddam International Airport (renamed Baghdad International Airport, BIA). A few days later they were sweeping into the capital. On 9 April 2003, just three weeks after the invasion began, Baghdad fell. Locals and American soldiers gathered in Firdos Square to tear down a statue of Saddam, in scenes broadcast across the world. Saddam's rule was over, with around 150 fatalities on the Coalition side.

On 1 May, President Bush stood on the deck of the USS *Abraham Lincoln* and triumphantly declared that combat operations in Iraq were over. It looked as if the Regiment's role would be limited to a handful of blokes hanging around Baghdad, bodyguarding security service personnel.

But even as the politicians were congratulating one another on a job well done, a new and violent insurgency was brewing.

In late May, the Coalition Provisional Authority (CPA) disbanded the Iraqi armed forces and intelligence services, presumably because they feared that the senior ranks were stuffed full of Saddam loyalists. Instead of weeding out any pro-Ba'ath elements, however, the authorities decided to scrap the forces entirely and start over.

This was a disastrous decision, because it suddenly put hundreds of thousands of trained Iraqi soldiers and police officers out of work. These disaffected individuals promptly took up arms with the nascent insurgency, providing it with all the manpower it needed to step up operations against the Coalition and Shi'ite Muslims. Many of these guys would end up fighting for Islamic State several years later.

While the insurgency was building, the SAS took on a new role in Iraq. From 2003 onwards, it essentially became a manhunting unit. In Iraq, and later in Afghanistan, hearts and minds was put to one side as the soldiers went on a relentless search for terrorists, arresting or eliminating targets. In the process the Regiment became an indispensable tool in the fight against terrorism.

The soldiers were initially restricted to going out on ops for old Ba'ath party members, known as Former Regime Elements (FREs). Later on, their mission was expanded to include other threats to the Coalition. The deployment consisted of a single Sabre Squadron, based in a house in the Green Zone, a heavily fortified area in the centre of Baghdad, living next door to US Special Forces. To begin with, the Regiment had access to a number of Chinook helicopters. Later on, the Chinooks were replaced by Lynx and Puma choppers. The Regiment would also be able to call on other support elements in Iraq, such as the newly formed SFSG. In addition, there was a locally raised unit of surveillance assets. Squadrons initially did four-month rotations, although that was later extended to six months.

The Brits were part of a much bigger US SF operation in Iraq, known variously as Task Force (TF) 121, TF-145 and TF-88. The name changed frequently to disguise its role in operations. The task force included teams from various units within US Special Forces and was supported by airborne elements. Each team within the task force had a designated colour name and area of operations. The SAS was based in Baghdad and initially codenamed Task Force Black.

Although they were staying next door to the Americans, the lads were kept at arm's length from them operationally and instead relied on British security services for intelligence on potential targets. At the same time, the CIA was ramping up its activities, identifying high-value targets to go after, along with other persons of interest. They were busy setting up a complete intelligence network, recruiting touts, processing sources and paying people to hand over information.

But while the search continued for Saddam and his inner circle, the task force soon turned their attention to the growing insurgency.

Between late 2003 and early 2004, the violence in Iraq increased dramatically as former soldiers, hardened criminals and foreign fighters waged a bitter war against the Coalition forces. In August 2003, a suicide bomber drove a truck filled with explosives into the UN headquarters in Baghdad, killing twenty-two people, including the UN's special representative in Iraq, Sergio Vieira de Mello.

The following March, guerrillas in Fallujah ambushed a pair of SUVs escorting a catering convoy and killed four American security personnel working for the private contractor, Blackwater. An angry mob surrounded the bullet-ridden vehicles, torched the bodies and dragged one of them through the streets. Two of the mutilated corpses were strung up from a bridge across the Euphrates, to delirious cheers from the crowd of onlookers.

Iraq was becoming a crucible of terror. Each day brought fresh reports of bombings, slayings and shootings. The arrest of Saddam Hussein, found in a spider hole in Tikrit the previous December, did nothing to stem the violence spreading like wildfire across the country. Coalition troops were getting shot and fragged by IEDs on a daily basis. Suicide bombers attacked Shi'ite holy sites in Karbala and Baghdad, killing hundreds.

Among the individuals and groups wreaking havoc across the country was a Jordanian terrorist called Abu Musab al-Zarqawi. A violent former criminal who had grown up in the industrial city of Zarqa, he had spent his youth drinking and brawling before he travelled to Afghanistan to fight alongside the mujahideen. Somewhere along the way, the young al-Zarqawi underwent a religious transformation, turning from a petty criminal into a hardline Islamist militant. On his return to Jordan, he was arrested and sentenced to prison for terrorist-related activities.

Following his release in 1999, al-Zarqawi travelled to Afghanistan once more to meet with senior figures in al-Qaeda. With their support and financial backing, he set up a terrorist training camp in the west of the country. After the fall of the Taliban, he had floated around the Middle East for a while before ending up in Iraq, where he began building up his own network of terrorists.

From April 2004 onwards, insurgent militias in Iraq started kidnapping foreign nationals. Over the next few years, hundreds of contractors, journalists, aid workers, pacifists, engineers and truck drivers were taken hostage. Some of these individuals were freed after their countries agreed to pay a ransom. Others were sold on to jihadist groups for a profit. A few were murdered in gory videos – and al-Zarqawi's group led the way with this grisly new tactic.

In May, his group posted a video online depicting the killing of Nicholas Berg, a twenty-six-year-old radio technician from Pennsylvania, who had gone to Iraq to look for employment. In the grainy footage, Berg can be seen sitting in front of five masked figures, dressed in an orange jumpsuit with his hands bound behind his back. One of the masked men reads a long, rambling message to the camera in Arabic, before drawing a knife and beheading his helpless victim.

This pattern of taking hostages and filming their horrific murders would later be adopted and taken to a new level by the eventual successor to al-Zarqawi's group, Islamic State.

More gruesome murders followed. Some were committed by al-Zarqawi's network, but other groups were responsible as well. In June, one gang executed an interpreter from South Korea, Kim Sun Il, after capturing him near Fallujah. In August, twelve Nepalese labourers were kidnapped and shot dead in cold blood. A sickening video showed the victims lying face down in the sand as a masked man walked among them, casually emptying single rounds into the backs of their skulls. Eleven of the labourers were killed this way. The twelfth had his throat slit by another hooded figure.

Earlier that month, an Italian journalist, Enzo Baldoni, had been abducted near the city of Najaf, a hundred miles south of Baghdad. His captors later sent a videotape to the Al Jazeera news channel depicting his murder.

In September, al-Zarqawi's mob struck again with the kidnap of three Western contractors, Eugene 'Jack' Armstrong, Jack Hensley and a British man, Ken Bigley. The group had threatened to kill the hostages unless a number of unspecified female prisoners held by the authorities were released. After the deadline passed without any concessions, Armstrong and Hensley were executed within twenty-four hours of each other. Bigley was murdered at the beginning of October.

In the same month, al-Zarqawi pledged allegiance to bin Laden and changed the name of his organisation to 'al-Qaeda in the Land of Two Rivers'. In Coalition circles, it became known as al-Qaeda in Iraq (AQI). By now al-Zarqawi had shot to the top of the Coalition's most wanted list, with the Americans slapping a $25 million bounty on his head.

Under his leadership, AQI would transform into a terrorist group like no other before it. Al-Zarqawi and his murderous gang carried out a spate of suicide attacks and car bombings, kidnapping foreigners and blowing up markets with alarming frequency. They even targeted Shi'ite mosques in an attempt to trigger a violent sectarian war. Their goal was simple: cause as much carnage as possible. Stopping him became the number-one priority for the task force.

While the Americans turned their attention to al–Zarqawi and his lieutenants, the SAS was mostly left to hunt down former Ba'athists, with Whitehall concerned about the treatment of detainees at the American-run detention facilities. (This was at a time when the scandal at Abu Ghraib, with graphic pictures of prisoners being tortured and degraded, was all over the news.) This arrangement persisted until late 2005. By that point, the Americans were running a sophisticated, ultra-modern setup, going out on high-speed operations, carrying out lightning raids on targets, lifting suspects and processing them, then acting on any information they provided. It was counter-terrorism on steroids, jacked up and more intense than anything that had ever been done before, with teams often going out on multiple raids on the same night.

This revolutionary approach was the brainchild of General Stanley McChrystal, who had been appointed to head up the Joint Special Operations Command (JSOC) in late 2003. During his time in Iraq, and later in Afghanistan, McChrystal would become a massive fan of the SAS and its capabilities – even using the guys to lead hostage-rescue operations ahead of US Special Forces.

By then, the SAS had already taken part in a high-profile assault to rescue two of their own. On 19 September, a pair of SAS men were stopped at a roadblock in Basra by Iraqi police. The soldiers were part of a second, smaller SAS detachment based in the southern port city, tasked with doing reconnaissance patrols and protecting security service personnel. The two men had been running a surveillance operation that day. They were driving a knackered old motor and dressed as Arabs and had weapons concealed in the vehicle.

A confrontation with the police led to shots being fired. One Iraqi was hit before the soldiers accelerated away. After a short chase they were caught by uniformed officers and rather than get into a prolonged gun battle, the SAS men attempted to defuse the situation by laying down their guns. Under the circumstances, they had no choice. If they had opened up on the police, dropping dozens of the people they were supposed to be working with, that would have caused a political storm back home.

The two soldiers were arrested, beaten and driven to a police station in the middle of Basra. They were now in an extremely perilous situation. The local security forces were deeply corrupt and riddled with Shi'ite insurgents. There was every chance that the police officers might try to hand the hostages over to one of the rebel militias. If that happened, it wouldn't be long before the soldiers' heads were parted from their shoulders.

Some of the lads from A Squadron, plus a team of guys from SFSG, flew down from Baghdad and went on standby for a rescue assault, while British forces threw up a defensive cordon around the police compound and tried to negotiate for the release of the captured soldiers.

A heaving throng of Iraqis quickly swarmed over the arriving Brits, pelting them with rocks and bricks and petrol bombs. One of the armoured Warriors burst into flames, leading to one of the defining images of the war as a soldier leapt from the turret of the burning vehicle, his body wreathed in flames.

As the situation worsened, the soldiers were smuggled out of the police station and taken to a nearby property. The SAS now had good reason to believe that the police officers were bartering with terrorists to hand over the hostages. Once that happened, any hopes of rescuing the two men would evaporate.

Realising that they had to act immediately, British commanders sought authorisation to launch a rescue operation. But when the request went up to the top brass at Northwood, in the north-west of London, no approval was forthcoming. In his gripping account of the SAS in Iraq, *Task Force Black*, Mark Urban writes that the major on the ground couldn't get hold of the Chief of Joint Operations on his mobile. 'It later went around the SAS that the senior officer had switched it off because he was playing golf.'

The failure to green light the operation very nearly led to a mutiny within the ranks of A Squadron. The feeling among the guys was very much, 'Screw this. We're going for it anyway.' There was no way that the rest of the lads in A Squadron were going to leave their mates in the lurch. They knew the hostages were in dire straits. If they didn't go in and get them out, they would either be moved on, or tortured and chopped up on video. In the end, the decision was made to go in to rescue the soldiers – with or without Whitehall approval.

Later that evening, A Squadron and their support elements sprang into action. One team took part in a diversionary raid on the police station, using Challenger tanks and Warriors to bull-doze through the compound walls, flattening several prefabri-cated buildings. At the same time, the second team carried out an explosive entry on the house, using the noise and chaos of the police station assault to distract the enemy. They quickly located the hostages but found no sign of the abductors, who had already bolted.

CHAPTER 24

Defeating AQI

Iraq, 2006–09

The success of the Jamiat operation possibly led to the Regiment being given the lead role on another hostage-rescue job. On 26 November, a team of four Christian pacifists was seized by gunmen in a Baghdad suburb and taken hostage. Their kidnappers, a previously unheard-of group called the Swords of Righteousness Brigade, demanded the release of a number of prisoners from American and Iraqi jails.

In early March 2006, one of the captives, Tom Fox, an American peace activist, was shot dead. His body was later discovered by Iraqi police beside a railway line in western Baghdad. The other three hostages – Briton Norman Kember and two Canadians, Jim Loney and Harmeet Singh Sooden – were still being held by the kidnap gang, despite repeated appeals for their release from across the political and religious spectrum.

By now Whitehall had taken the leash off and the SAS was becoming increasingly integrated with the Americans. With British hostages being kidnapped and resources being stretched, Whitehall was no longer in a position to keep the Regiment semi-independent of the wider task force. From now on, the SAS would join the US SF teams in helping to tackle the urgent threat from AQI. Acting on premium-grade intelligence, the lads were going out on multiple raids per night, lifting HVTs and gathering vital intelligence. They were also given a new codename, following the media exposure the unit had received after the Basra rescue op. From now on, they would be known as Task Force Knight.

The usual format was that they would get briefed on a target pack and go out that evening by helicopter to make the arrest. Coming in low, only a few feet above the rooftops, the chopper would move into position above a road or garden near the target. Then the guys would fast-rope down before making their final approach on foot. Using the helicopters allowed them to cut around Baghdad much faster and avoided the risk of getting fragged by IEDs on the ground.

Once they were in position, the raiders went into door-kicking mode. This is where their counter-terrorism training gave them a decisive edge. The team would breach the door either by blowing off the hinges with a sawn-off shotgun or through the use of explosives. If they encountered a metal door, the breacher would step forward, with the charges set and ready to go. He'd stick one on the door and detonate it, blasting it open. The team would then sweep inside to clear the building. They were going in 'weapons hot', their guns raised and ready to engage any hostiles.

Buildings were systematically cleared and secured and the survivors rounded up. Evidence was collected and bagged up, interpreters were brought forward and the identity of the targets confirmed. They were then blindfolded and marched out to the waiting helicopter, which would have found a safe place to land nearby. Detainees were then taken back to base, where they would be processed and interviewed by US interrogation teams. Meanwhile the guys would move straight on to their next target, often getting briefed in the air.

This was extremely risky work, light years ahead of what the guys had been doing in Northern Ireland with the SMU. Back then, the SAS had been conducting maybe two or three operations a month, working on ops that might last anywhere from twenty-four hours to several days, in an environment where they had the backup from the security forces and the green army, going into locations that had been pre-recced by the Det. In Iraq, the soldiers were heading directly from one target to the next, so there wasn't the time to give them a full intelligence picture of the building and its layout.

What the guys were accomplishing was incredible. They were operating in a hostile environment where people had access to RPGs and could easily have downed the chopper they were flying in. The targets they were going in to arrest were mostly ex-military types, former police officers or veteran terrorists. They were heavily armed and knew how to use a weapon. In many cases, they would be lying in wait, knowing that someone was coming for them. Yet the Regiment lads still went in there, hit the targets, captured them and barely had time to catch their breath before the next briefing was coming in.

Over the next few years, the SAS carried out many hundreds of raids in Iraq. And it produced results.

In late March, B Squadron lifted an Iraqi detainee on one of the many raids they had been carrying out while searching for Kember and the two captured Canadians. Under interrogation, the Iraqi spilled his guts and confessed that he knew the whereabouts of the hostages: a house in a western suburb of Baghdad.

The guys knew they had to move fast before word got back to the kidnappers and they moved location. That morning, B Squadron and a support team approached the target location. Shortly before they were in position, a phone call was placed to the kidnap gang. The gist of the message was: *The Regiment is coming for you. If you want to live another day, leave now. And don't lay a finger on the hostages.*

Making that call to the captors was a bold move. It could have backfired – there was a chance that they might panic and execute the remaining hostages – but the team would have been counting on the fact that the kidnappers did not appear to be as fanatical as al-Zarqawi's gang and would choose freedom over certain death.

It worked. The kidnappers fled moments before the SAS crashed through the door. Norman Kember and the two

Canadians were located in a room on the first floor of the building, handcuffed but otherwise unharmed.

Kember was criticised in some quarters for a perceived slowness in thanking his rescuers. The head of the British Army, General Mike Jackson, voiced his unhappiness when he told *Channel 4 News* that, 'there doesn't seem to have been a note of gratitude for the soldiers who risked their lives to save those lives.' In fairness, Kember did later thank the soldiers during an interview with the BBC. In keeping with his Christian beliefs, he refused to testify against his kidnappers when they were arrested by Iraqi police later that year.

The Regiment is often maligned as a bunch of violent, racist thugs. That couldn't be further from the truth – and missions like this prove it. The soldiers I know are committed to saving lives, no matter the race, religion or beliefs of the persons in danger. In Norman Kember's case, the guys put their lives on the line to save someone who was totally opposed to what they stand for.

With the hostages freed, the SAS now turned its attention to al-Zarqawi and the leadership of AQI. Here, too, the Regiment would play a decisive role. In April 2006, the guys carried out a bust on a house in the town of Yusufiyah that led to a major breakthrough.

After a fierce battle with the defenders, leaving several of them dead and a number of SAS men wounded, the team seized various items from the property, including a rifle with al-Zarqawi's fingerprints and DNA on it. They knew the gun belonged to the AQI chief, because they had discovered video footage at the same address, showing al-Zarqawi posing with it. Amazingly, the team later found out that the man himself had been in a nearby house at the time of the raid.

There was more. The following month, they discovered that al-Zarqawi had a confidant, an Islamic cleric and spiritual adviser called Sheikh Abu Abdul Rahman. Through intelligence, the task force was able to stick surveillance on the Sheikh and started to build up an understanding of when and where he met al-Zarqawi, and his security precautions before each meeting.

On 7 June 2006, a British surveillance team including men from 22 SAS stealthily tracked Rahman as he drove out of Baghdad and headed north into the countryside. In the early evening he pulled into a safe house situated on the edge of a date palm grove, not far from the city of Baqubah.

At the same time a Predator drone circled overhead, relaying live footage of Rahman's movements to HQ. As the HQ team looked on, the adviser was seen talking with a figure who had the same height and build as al-Zarqawi. Shortly after that individual was positively identified as the AQI terrorist chief, a decision was made to eliminate him.

A nearby American F-16C fighter jet dropped two laser-guided bombs on to the safe house, destroying the building and killing Rahman, three women and a child. Iraqi police discovered al-Zarqawi's body amid the smouldering ruins and debris.

Incredibly, he was still breathing in spite of his terrible injuries. His torn, ragged body was lifted on to a stretcher while US medics tried in vain to save his life. The Jordanian, realising that he had been captured, attempted to throw himself off the stretcher in one last pathetic attempt to escape. A short time later, he finally died of his injuries. The second most wanted man in the world, after bin Laden, was no more.

The years working with the Americans in Iraq were a game-changer for the SAS. From 2006 until the end of their deployment three years later, they were pushing the envelope on a daily basis. Mark Urban notes that in one six-month period in 2007, A Squadron 'mounted raids almost nightly, during which it arrested 335 people and killed 88.'

The task forces as a whole were averaging in excess of ten raids a night in 2006. They were carrying out counter-terrorism ops on an unprecedented scale, hunting down AQI targets, gathering information and making hard arrests that resulted in either the death or capture of insurgents. They were doing so many raids each night that the terrorists couldn't replace the men they had lost quickly enough.

It was through working with the US SF teams that the soldiers now started getting their hands on the latest kit. All of a sudden, the SAS and the top brass realised that their equipment and comms setups were out of date and no longer suitable for the type of work they were doing. The British started taking a closer look at the systems and kit US Special Forces were using. That was an eye-opening experience, seeing the kinds of gear that the Americans had access to, compared to the stuff the SAS had been relying on.

Everything changed. The guys were given the latest NODs (night optical devices) for improved night vision. Their uniforms changed as they took to wearing US-manufactured Crye Precision kit, which comes with built-in knee and elbow pads, making them ideal for house assaults. This kit isn't cheap – a single pair of combat trousers costs hundreds of pounds – but it lasts. Their body armour now included groin protectors so the soldier's undercarriage wouldn't get blown apart if he stepped on an IED.

At around this time they also began wearing lightweight Kevlar ballistic helmets, with rails on the side for mounting a variety of cameras and lights. They could also mount strobes that emit an infra-red light when you switch them on, marking the soldier's position and making it easier for helicopter crews and gunships to identify them as friendlies.

Comms gear improved massively. The guys started carrying personal radios with earpieces attached and a boom mic for hands-free communication with the rest of the team on encrypted frequencies. Their weapon systems were also upgraded. Their primary weapon was the Diemaco C8 rifle, the M16 derivative. Guys would sometimes have two optics on the gun, a night optic and a day scope. Lasers were mounted on the left-hand side of the weapon for fixing targets, with torches attached on the other side.

All these attachments make it difficult for an operator to grip the handguard. To get around this problem, vertical foregrips were added to the underside of the rifle, allowing the soldier to operate the weapon in a two-handed grip. SAS soldiers also regularly carried other tools of the trade including Heckler & Koch HK417 rifles, Knight's Armament M110 7.62mm sniper rifles and FN SCAR-Hs.

The upgraded equipment was accompanied by a move away from carrying heavy loads of kit, towards a more lightweight soldier. The guys quickly realised that when you're going out on house raids every night, you don't need a lot of the kit that we used to hump around. So they ditched it.

The result of this thinking was that the SAS soldier's kit was stripped right back. All the survival kits and spare ration packs were junked – anything that wasn't absolutely necessary for their raids got left behind. The theory was, the lighter the soldier, the more mobile you become. And the quicker you can storm a house and clear it out. The guys carried tourniquets for medical dressings, spare magazines for their weapons and very little else. The old loose webbing pouches that we used to carry were set aside. Instead the men now carried everything on their chest – clips, comms gear, the works.

They also started working with members of the newly formed Special Reconnaissance Regiment (SRR). Created in 2005, a year before SFSG was officially founded, the SRR carried out the same type of role as the Det had done in Northern Ireland, running mobile and technical surveillance. They were going into areas that the SAS couldn't operate, using their ability to work undercover to identify key individuals and high-value targets. Once a target had been scoped out, the Regiment lads would then go in, carrying out their role as the door-kickers to arrest or take down the enemy.

The guys in the SRR are every bit as brave and smart as their Det forebears. One operator I know of was tasked with carrying out close reconnaissance on a block of flats somewhere in the Middle East, a few years after the end of the Iraq War. Several targets were believed to be living in one of the flats, but intelligence chiefs didn't know which one. The SRR operator, a swarthy-looking individual, disguised himself as a street beggar and lurked around the target location, begging for money from passers-by until he was able to identify successfully the apartment housing the terrorists. The whole time he was there, no one suspected a thing.

For the next two years, the SAS and their colleagues in the other task forces continued to make inroads into AQI, severely disrupting its ability to function. By whittling away the insurgents' middle and senior ranks, they deprived the enemy of a lot of bomb-making experience and terrorist know-how. Moreover, it had the effect of spreading fear throughout the rest of the network. Once word got around that the SAS was coming after them, it had a sobering effect on the terrorists. They knew what the lads were capable of. Not many of them would have been inclined to put up a fight when the soldiers came bursting through the door.

One unfortunate side-effect of the Regiment's success was the additional strain being placed on its manpower, with the guys now doing six-month rotations. At the same time, they were facing a decline in recruitment.

At the turn of the century, the only unit in the British Army doing any real fighting was 22 SAS. In the past, anyone in the regular infantry who had wanted to soldier properly would probably attempt Selection at some point in their career. But with the onset of draining, long-term conflicts in Afghanistan and Iraq, the green army was doing as much fighting as the Regiment, if not more so. Infantrymen who might have been prospective recruits to the SAS started asking themselves why they should go through the hassle of Selection when they were already doing good soldiering, knowing that at the end of their six-month tour they would be back home and spending time with the family.

In contrast, SAS soldiers were having to operate almost continually, with little chance of a break between rotations. Once they got back to Hereford, they had hardly any time to spend with their families. They had to go straight on refresher courses, as well as their Troop training and Squadron training. That six months goes by very fast. Then they would be on the SP team for several months. After that, they were getting posted around the world on team training jobs. Then they became the stand-by squadron, which could mean getting deployed anywhere in the world at very short notice. Then it was back to Iraq, starting the cycle all over again. It became exhausting. A lot of soldiers looked at what was required of them at Hereford and thought, I'm not doing that.

For the SAS men in Iraq, the work was non-stop. As well as the operations in Baghdad and Basra, teams of guys were also working in more isolated parts of the country. They were going out in half-squadron formations, sometimes to capture targets. On other missions they were locating and destroying groups of AQI fighters forming up in the desert. In addition, the Regiment carried out operations to combat Iranian influence inside the country. The Iranians were suspected of providing arms and training to insurgent groups, with the aim of destabilising the Iraqi government.

The high-risk nature of the missions the soldiers were conducting inevitably meant that they took casualties. In November 2006, a staff sergeant was fatally wounded during a house assault in Basra. The following April, an SAS man and an RAF sergeant lost their lives when their Puma helicopter was involved in a collision with another chopper.

In November, two soldiers were killed in a second helicopter accident, when their Puma crash-landed in a field outside Baghdad. The men were trapped beneath the wreckage as it burst into flames. Their colleagues frantically tried to free them, but the chopper was quickly consumed by fire and the soldiers had no choice but to abandon any rescue attempt. Despite this tragedy, the rest of the team pushed on with their mission to target an Iraqi insurgent, demonstrating the commitment, resilience and focus of the SAS soldier.

In March 2008, the Regiment carried out a raid in Saddam's former stronghold of Tikrit. The team stormed the building after calling on the two men inside to surrender. As they swept into the house someone opened fire, fatally wounding one of the assaulters. The other injured men pulled back while the insurgents were hammered by fire from supporting aircraft, killing both targets and a number of civilians including three children.

Despite these losses, by late 2008, AQI was on the ropes. The remorseless pressure applied to the insurgents and their foreign facilitators effectively wiped out their ability to plan and carry out operations. By the time the Regiment's deployment came to an end in May 2009, the AQI's management structure had either been killed, captured or driven underground into hiding. At around this time the American task forces also started winding down their operations, until the final withdrawal of US forces in December 2011.

According to Mark Urban, the SAS killed or detained 3,500 individuals during their time in Iraq. That is a staggering number of terrorists taken off the streets. In total, the JSOC task force killed around three thousand insurgents and captured three times that number. By the time the SF teams pulled out, there were believed to be fewer than one thousand AQI fighters left in the country, according to the Brookings Institution's February 2012 Index on Iraq. Their ranks had been decimated.

The surge of 2007, when the US committed an extra twenty thousand troops to Iraq, undoubtedly helped to stabilise the situation. The tactic of recruiting Sunni militias, many of them former insurgents, to fight against AQI also played a big part in stemming the tide of violence and chaos. But it was the task force teams who took the fight to the terrorists, at a time when they were causing mayhem.

The SAS and their American colleagues went out and did the business on an unprecedented scale, moving with lightning speed and pioneering a new type of counter-terrorism warfare. For the soldiers, it was a crushing workload, but their actions saved countless lives, both on the Coalition side and among the Iraqi civilians who had been getting massacred each day.

Despite their success, however, a hardcore of AQI managed to survive the campaign. They would emerge again in the years after the American withdrawal, gradually evolving into an even more terrifying and sinister organisation: Islamic State.

CHAPTER 25

Modern Warfare

Afghanistan, Syria, Libya, 2009–Present

While the Regiment had been going toe-to-toe with al-Qaeda in Iraq, the SBS had taken the lead in Afghanistan. This was a decision born out of necessity, since the squadrons were too thinly stretched to commit to sustained operations in both countries. But with the end of their deployment in Iraq in 2009, the SAS was now brought in to tackle the resurgent Taliban.

Violence had been steadily increasing across the country in the years since the SAS had taken part in the invasion. By 2006 the Taliban was firmly on the rise once more. Fuelled by the profits from the opium trade, and adopting the tactics used by the militias in Iraq, they began carrying out an increasing number of suicide bombings and IED attacks, undermining efforts to improve security and infrastructure. Allied troops were being killed and maimed with alarming frequency. Attempts to drive the Taliban back had been unsuccessful. The enemy was proving to be extremely resilient and showed no signs of giving up the fight.

History has a way of repeating itself in Afghanistan. Powerful countries have repeatedly come unstuck in that benighted country, and this time was no different. The West had failed to learn the lessons of the past and ended up getting sucked into a costly conflict we had no hope of winning, against an enemy that knows the land better than us and has vast experience of inflicting defeats on superior military forces. We were never going to win that war, no matter how many soldiers and drones we threw at the problem.

The Regiment's return was part of a strategic reboot in the country. At around the same time, General McChrystal was appointed the commander of the International Security and Assistance Force (ISAF) in Afghanistan. Bolstered by a surge in troop numbers authorised by President Barack Obama, McChrystal's approach involved going in and dominating the ground, clearing insurgents from a designated area and then holding it. Once that ground had been secured, the focus could then switch to civil and economic development and local governance, winning the hearts and minds of the locals. With the population on their side, the forces could then move on to clear another area of land, retaking the countryside bit by bit and driving the Taliban underground.

The role of the SAS was to go in and capture or kill high-level Taliban targets. To achieve this goal, they were building on the same tactics McChrystal had pioneered in Iraq, backed up by elements of the Special Forces Support Group and the Special Reconnaissance Regiment. Targets were identified using a combination of human and technical intelligence, surveillance and mobile phone intercepts. Once an individual had been established and located, the soldiers would insert into the Afghan village or compound at night to make a hard arrest. If the target resisted, they would be engaged.

The SAS did introduce some tactical innovations in Afghanistan. One important factor was the expanded use of dogs. The soldiers had first taken dogs with them on raids in Iraq, copying a trend started by American Special Forces teams, but they used them much more widely in Afghanistan, sending in specially trained dogs ahead of the entry team with cameras fitted to their heads to look for targets. Equally, they could go in and attack any armed insurgents who might be lurking inside, waiting to ambush the soldiers.

Many Middle Eastern countries have a cultural dislike of dogs, which makes them an even more effective tool for frightening and disabling enemy combatants. The Belgian Malinois, as I have said earlier, was the dog of choice for the SAS – a highly intelligent breed, ferociously loyal but with a mean bite on it. Once that beast clamps its jaws around your arm or leg, it won't let go.

Alongside the nightly raids against the Taliban, the Regiment continued to mount hostage-rescue operations involving UK nationals. In June 2012, a joint SAS–US SF operation was carried out to rescue a British aid worker, Helen Johnston, along with her Kenyan colleague and a pair of Afghan guides. Johnston and the others had been kidnapped in the remote province of Badakhshan in the east of Afghanistan while travelling on horseback. Their abductors promptly demanded a ransom of £7 million and the release of a number of men from prison.

Mobile phone signal intercepts and Predator drone surveillance had pinpointed the hostages to a pair of caves in a densely forested area of Shahri Buzurg, close to the border with Tajikistan. Fears for their safety intensified after the Brits learned that the kidnappers had been urged by a third party to put on a 'show of intent'. This was interpreted as a call to execute one of the captives, demonstrating to the negotiators that they meant business. Worryingly, some of the abductors were believed to have links to the Taliban and there was a concern that the gang might hand over the hostages to the group, once it became clear that their demands weren't going to be met.

It was time for the Regiment to move in.

The rescue team inserted at night by Black Hawk helicopters into an LZ several miles from the caves. Moving stealthily on foot, the SAS and US SF teams arrived at their starting points for their pre-dawn assault. Once they were in place, they launched a simultaneous attack, the SAS soldiers going for one cave while the Americans raced towards the other, posting flashbangs to disorientate the guards. The hostages were safely rescued and taken to the British Embassy in Kabul. Several insurgents were killed, with no loss of life among the rescuers or the captives. It had been a textbook hostage-rescue op.

By then General McChrystal had departed the country,

relieved of his command by President Obama in 2010 after a magazine article quoted the general criticising White House officials. He was replaced by General David Petraeus. Bin Laden was killed the following year, but the security situation inside Afghanistan remained dangerously fragile.

The Regiment hit the Taliban hard in Afghanistan. By early 2011, according to an interview General Petraeus gave to the *New York Times*, Allied SF units had captured or killed around three thousand insurgents. But in spite of the impressive numbers, the Taliban proved a harder nut to crack than AQI.

There are a number of reasons for this. For one, the Taliban had deep pockets. They were very well financed, with a steady income stream from the opium industry. They had vast experience of guerrilla warfare, and they enjoyed vital support from across the border in Pakistan, although the Pakistani government has always denied this. But perhaps the most important reason is the simplest: the Taliban had the numbers to absorb their losses and replace them, and AQI didn't.

At the height of their power, al-Zarqawi and his mob could call on around 12,000 insurgents. The Taliban had three times that number in 2010. Four years later, their ranks had swelled to 60,000. Decapitating an organisation that size is almost impossible for any Special Forces team, even if you're lifting dozens of targets each night. No matter how many insurgents the Regiment detained or killed, they were never able to disrupt the enemy to the point where they could no longer effectively function.

On 26 October 2014, British combat troops in Helmand handed over Camp Bastion to Afghan forces, marking the formal end of operations in Afghanistan. The pace of the American withdrawal was much slower, with a contingent of US troops remaining in the country for years to come. The British campaign, Operation Herrick, had lasted twelve years and cost the lives of 454 British soldiers.

In January 2018, the Taliban carried out a series of attacks in Kabul, killing more than a hundred people. In August they ambushed an Afghan National Army base, resulting in the deaths of forty-five soldiers and police officers. On the same day, a suicide bomber struck in Kabul, taking the lives of another forty-eight people. By that time the Regiment was already back in the country, working alongside Afghan security forces to tackle the continued insurgency.

By then, the guys were also having to tackle a horrifying new threat: the rise of Islamic State.

Islamic State, also known as ISIS (Islamic State in Iraq and Syria), ISIL or Daesh, arose from the shattered remnants of AQI. After licking its wounds for a couple of years, the surviving members regrouped in 2010 under a radical new leader, Abu Bakr al-Baghdadi, a former detainee at an American camp during the Iraq War.

In July 2012 the group, which also went under the name Islamic State in Iraq, launched 'Operation Breaking the Walls', a year-long wave of prison breakouts across Iraq. Hundreds of prisoners were freed, many of whom had been jailed for their involvement in AQI attacks during the Iraq War. With the ranks of the organisation topped up with a core of veteran fighters, al-Baghdadi moved into Syria in April 2013.

Syria was already in the grip of a full-scale civil war, following protests against the rule of President Bashar al-Assad. It was a complicated, messy conflict with moderate and Islamist rebel groups fighting against the Syrian armed forces. It was also the perfect environment for al-Baghdadi and his followers to realise their vision of establishing a strict Islamic state.

Rebranding itself as ISIS, the group swept aside the secular rebels and started taking control of territory that had been seized from the Syrian government, declaring Raqqa as its capital and imposing harsh Islamic laws on the population. In June 2014, the group achieved their biggest victory yet when they seized Iraq's second-largest city, Mosul, along with Saddam's old stronghold of Tikrit.

They promptly declared the establishment of a new Islamic caliphate, with al-Baghdadi as 'leader for Muslims everywhere'. The following month they captured oil and gas fields in Syria, massively boosting the group's coffers. An online propaganda campaign was established, using the power of social media to attract thousands of recruits from around the world. Slickly made videos were posted on the internet, depicting the beheadings of Western hostages.

Many of these videos featured a masked, black-clad figure with a London accent. He was later identified as a Kuwaiti-born British citizen from the Queens Park area of north-west London. His name was Mohammed Emwazi, but he would become known internationally as Jihadi John. Emwazi would soon become the focus of a major manhunt involving British and American intelligence.

At the same time, ISIS insurgents carried out an orgy of torture, rape and murder, committing atrocities against civilians and minority groups such as the Yazidis. Thousands of Yazidi women and girls were kidnapped and forced to become sex slaves. Men accused of being homosexual were flung to their deaths from the rooftops of tall buildings. Smoking, Western clothes and alcohol were outlawed. Local residents guilty of breaking the group's strict interpretation of Islamic law were publicly flogged, beaten, beheaded, crucified or stoned to death.

There seemed to be no limits to the group's ability to inflict terror. A Jordanian pilot who had been captured was doused in petrol and burned alive in a metal cage. Another captured soldier was run over by a tank. Teenage boys were murdered for the crime of watching a football match on TV. ISIS even recruited child soldiers into a unit known as the 'Cubs of the Caliphate'. With Western hostages being executed and ISIS's brand of terrorism inspiring fanatical followers around the world, it wasn't long before the Regiment was sent in to tackle them head-on.

They were coming up against a formidable enemy. Many of the insurgents were ex-soldiers and they were prosecuting a very different type of terror war, conducting military-style operations to capture towns and strategic targets. At one point, ISIS had tens of thousands of fighters and controlled an area of land roughly the size of Britain. They were raking in millions of dollars every week from crude oil, smuggling, extortion and ransom payments for kidnap victims. Tackling this organisation required a tactical shift for the Regiment, moving away from the raiding-type missions they had done in Afghanistan and Iraq. Once again, the guys would have to adapt in order to take on a terrifying new opponent.

Instead of kicking down doors and lifting targets, the SAS reverted to the tactics they had used in the first Gulf War, deploying in large-sized vehicle formations – except this time they were hunting terrorists instead of Scuds. Their mission was to roam the deserts of Syria and Iraq like a pack of wolves, sniffing out ISIS targets and blasting them up. There was no negotiation with these insurgents. The ISIS leadership was never going to stick their hands up and agree to discuss terms. The goal was to get in among them and eliminate as many of the enemy as possible.

By now the old Land Rover 110s had been consigned to history. The main fighting platform for the SAS was an upgraded version of the British-made Jackal MWMIK (Mobility Weapon-Mounted Installation Kit) armoured vehicle. These are long-range patrol vehicles that can absorb a direct hit from an RPG. The Jackals also have enough weaponry attached to them to carry out a fire-support role during an assault on a target. Their firepower includes two mounted GPMGs, 40mm grenade launchers and a .50 calibre heavy machine gun.

The Regiment also has access to an array of other vehicles, including heavily armoured Supacat HMT 400s and specialised armoured vehicles, which serve as the motherships for the fighting columns, carrying all the kit and supplies. When they need to blend in with the locals, the guys will cut around in white Toyota Hilux pickup trucks or locally sourced technicals, with machine guns mounted on the back. These days, the soldiers use whatever they need or can get their hands on.

Targets are identified through a painstaking combination of drone surveillance, technical and human intelligence and intercepted communications. Once a target has been identified at a particular location, such as an enemy camp or stronghold, the Regiment will go straight in to carry out an assault. Time is of the essence in such attacks: ISIS targets know they're being watched and are constantly on the move. There is no messing around and very little advance planning.

Attacks are based on firepower, speed and aggression, using infantry-type tactics to attack the enemy location. The guys in the armoured vehicles establish a baseline at a distance from the target, using the Jackals and Supacats as fire-support teams. They'll open up with all the heavy weaponry – the Browning .50, mortars, grenade launchers and Stingers. At the same time, the main assault force will move in and wipe out the enemy.

The Regiment was getting into a lot of scraps with ISIS – and dominating them. Tactically, these contacts were at the other end of the spectrum from what some of us had been doing in the first Gulf War. Instead of inserting small patrols to carry out OPs on a road, the soldiers were now going in to own that road and everything around it.

Some of these operations were carried out alongside US Special Forces. The Regiment retained its close relationship with US SF after the end of the Iraq War, going out on missions together to hunt down targets.

Alongside these operations, the Regiment was under pressure to go after the individuals running the ISIS propaganda machinery. This included targeting the infamous masked killers featured on the beheading videos. Priority was given to locating and eliminating Mohammed Emwazi, aka Jihadi John.

Snuffing out the insurgents' PR network was a vital part of the campaign to crush ISIS. The videos they had been distributing were designed to provoke a reaction, getting people to watch and share them. That in turn aided their recruitment, as the videos and the poisonous messages that accompanied them were spread across the globe. With each video, ISIS looked to make a bigger splash by ramping up the violence, making each killing more sickening and depraved than the last. It got to the point where people were becoming desensitised to it all.

In November 2015, intelligence traced Emwazi to a location in the ISIS stronghold of Raqqa. Sources have confirmed to me that the Regiment took part in the operation to kill Emwazi, inserting into a secure area outside the city. The team then launched a mini UAV drone fitted with a thermal-imaging camera and sent it into the target area under cover of darkness. Once Emwazi's identity had been confirmed, military commanders gave the order for a drone strike.

Shortly before midnight, Emwazi and his entourage emerged from the building and climbed into a waiting vehicle. Moments later, an overhead drone launched an AGM-114 Hellfire missile at the target and lit the car up, instantly killing Emwazi and the other three insurgents he was travelling with.

In July 2017, Mosul was retaken by Iraqi forces. Later that year, ISIS was driven out of its stronghold at Raqqa. By the following March, the terrorists were left with only a tiny fraction of the total land they had originally controlled. But despite these grievous losses, the decimation of their upper ranks and the successful strikes against the likes of Emwazi, ISIS remains a threat, having transformed itself into a stateless terror group.

In May 2019, the group claimed responsibility for a series of devastating suicide bombings in Sri Lanka that left more than 250 people dead. At the time of writing, the Regiment continues to run operations in Syria. The guys have got a full-strength squadron in the area, hunting down those members of the group still at large.

The Regiment has been tackling ISIS on the home front as well. In 2015, supporters of the group began launching terrorist attacks in Europe and the US. Deadly attacks in Paris, Brussels, Berlin, San Bernardino and Orlando killed hundreds of innocent people, and were either linked to the group or inspired by their propaganda messages.

In May 2017, twenty-three people died when a suicide bomber struck at an Ariana Grande concert in Manchester. Less than two weeks later, three terrorists inspired by ISIS carried out a vehicular attack in London Bridge, driving a van into pedestrians and stabbing others in bars and restaurants before they were shot dead by Metropolitan police officers.

Shortly afterwards, the on-duty Lead Assault Team (LAT) arrived from Hereford in their unmarked Dauphin Eurocopter, known as 'Blue Thunder'. The LAT is an immediate stand-by team based at the camp, under the command of a sergeant. Their task is to link up with the police CTSFOs (Counter Terrorist Specialist Firearms Officers) and provide assistance until the rest of the SP Team can arrive on the scene.

At the time they arrived, the immediate objective was to clear the area in case any more terrorists were still at large, other than the three men the police had shot dead. The LAT operators were tasked with gaining access to Southwark Cathedral by carrying out an explosive entry. Although the police CTSFOs are trained in EMOE (Explosive Method of Entry), the SAS are regarded as the best in the business and offered to breach the door themselves. The explosion reportedly damaged parts of the building including the door to the sacristy.

One consequence of the rise of global terrorism has been increased cooperation between the police force and the Regiment. In the 1980s and 1990s, other than a liaison officer, there was little interaction between ourselves and the Metropolitan Police. These days, the Sabre Squadrons work much more closely with Scotland Yard – to the point where the guys have reportedly borrowed one or two tactical innovations from the Met's anti-terrorist teams, such as the use of BMW touring bikes to get through heavy traffic and intercept mobile threats.

An armed police officer, riding on the pillion, is trained to shoot accurately while moving at fast speeds, allowing them to take down vehicles that might be carrying a bomb or used to target pedestrians. One guy from Hereford saw what the police were doing and promptly went back to the camp to teach the lads the same tactics. The SAS took the idea further and now have a fleet of souped-up motorbikes and cars, including Porsche Cayennes, fitted with sirens and blue lights to enable them to race through traffic.

The previous year, 2016, the Regiment had also been dispatched to Libya to combat ISIS, which had started to establish itself in the country, taking advantage of the chaos that had followed the end of Colonel Muammar Gaddafi's regime. By now the SAS had become more vital than ever to the British government and the security services. The global recession of 2008 had been followed by years of crushing austerity, cutting the military budget to the bone and reducing its ability to operate effectively.

The Army's political masters were terrified of getting dragged into another costly war after deep public disapproval of the conflicts in Iraq and Afghanistan. The only action they could take was covert, deniable ops, using Special Forces and the intelligence services. Now, when Downing Street needed to intervene in Libya, Iraq or Syria, they turned to the Regiment.

Libya's despotic ruler, Colonel Muammar Gaddafi, had been toppled by an uprising in August 2011, bringing to an end a dictatorship that had lasted for forty-two years. His life came to a grisly end when militia forces found him hiding in a drainage pipe in his hometown of Sirte, following a NATO attack on a convoy. Gaddafi was dragged out, beaten and shot dead.

His death left a power vacuum in Libya. The country soon descended into chaos and became a hotbed for terrorism as rival militias, tribes and Islamic extremists jostled for power. ISIS quickly identified the country as an ideal place to expand their network and have been active in the country since the beginning of 2014, when they seized the port of Derna in the east of the country. They made rapid progress, later capturing Sirte and moving towards Libya's oil crescent. By the time the SAS deployed, ISIS forces were closing in on the coastal cities of Tobruk and Brega.

Very little is known about what the Regiment has been up to in Libya. It's likely that the soldiers will have been working closely with security service personnel, bodyguarding them while they're moving around and dealing with various groups. The lads will also have been working alongside the Libyan security forces, training and equipping different units to combat the threat from insurgent groups. Soldiers will have conducted reconnaissance missions to see what kind of foothold ISIS had established in the country, and they may have assisted in going after targets.

One Libyan commander claimed in an interview with *The Times* in May 2016 that a team of SAS guys had attacked a truck bomb approaching a bridge in Misrata. According to the commander, the soldiers coolly fired a Javelin missile at the vehicle as it approached, destroying it before it could detonate and cause massive damage and loss of life.

This was not the only recent example of SAS men using their initiative to save lives. In January 2019, extraordinary footage emerged of an SAS operator charging into a luxury hotel in Nairobi during a terrorist attack. The soldier, a veteran SAS man, had been posted to Kenya as a liaison officer, training up local special forces.

He happened to be out shopping when gunmen from the hardline Islamist group al-Shabaab launched their attack on the exclusive dusitD2 hotel and business complex. Grabbing his ballistic body armour, Diemaco C8 assault rifle and Glock 9mm pistol, and with a balaclava pulled over his head to protect his identity, the soldier swept into the area where the firefight was going on, engaged the enemy and led several civilians to safety outside.

Twenty-one people died in the Nairobi hotel attack. It is very likely that more would have been killed if it hadn't been for that guy's actions. Very few individuals, military or otherwise, would have had the guts to charge headlong into a terrorist attack. It was another example of the incredible, everyday bravery of the SAS soldier.

CHAPTER 26

New Threats

At the end of the 1990s, the Regiment had moved out of its old base and taken over the facilities at RAF Credenhill. At the time, the existing camp in Hereford was small and cramped, overlooked by housing estates and with very little room to expand. As the unit grew, in terms of attached personnel and support staff, it had become clear that they needed a lot more real estate. There wasn't the scope to build at the existing base, so the SAS started looking around for a new camp to take over. They settled on Credenhill, which had been a flight training school until the RAF stopped using it in the mid-1990s. The base was renamed Stirling Lines, in honour of the Regiment's founder.

New equipment and facilities have been introduced into the training area at Pontrilas. The old Killing House was dismantled and replaced by a newer building, spread across several floors so that operators can get into the stairwells and practise moving up and down between the different floors. The soldiers now have access to a 200-metre gallery shooting range, built below the ground and set into the side of a hill, so that no one can spy on the soldiers from above.

There are gallery ranges, rooms for the dem teams to rehearse explosive entry techniques, rooms for the CT teams to train in CQB and 360-degree shooting. The walls are lined with rubber tiles and moving targets can be placed around the area, allowing the soldiers to practise advanced contact drills. Extractor fans suck out the lead particles and fumes in the air, which makes a big

337

difference when you've got a large group of guys putting down lots of rounds in a confined space.

The guys can also train for various other types of assault. There's a concrete mock-up of a passenger airliner for aircraft assaults and a range for advanced driving tactics to practise J-turns and shooting from a moving platform.

Other Regimental facilities have been improved or upgraded recently. During my time at Hereford, we had one PTI (Physical Training Instructor) and a physio. Today, the fitness and sports-science operation has been thoroughly modernised. The SAS now has a number of physios, specialists and dieticians. Soldiers are given targeted fitness programmes based on the type of training they're doing and their individual needs. There's even a separate team dedicated to rehabilitation, helping injured soldiers get back to fighting fitness.

There is now also a dedicated dog-handling team within the Regiment. Before, if we wanted to use dogs on an operation, we would have to bring along a handler from the Royal Army Veterinary Corps (RAVC). That was far from ideal – you're putting someone who isn't SAS-trained in a dangerous situation, close to the action. The Regiment eventually solved this problem by training up their own specialist dog handlers. Soldiers are now sent off to do courses with specialist K-9 units and are taught every aspect of dog training and handling.

But by far the biggest change has been the growth of the support units around the Regiment.

The fundamental size of 22 SAS hasn't really changed in the past few decades, but the support teams have expanded massively. SRR (the Special Reconnaissance Regiment) in particular has exploded in the past few years. Their Selection course used to last twelve weeks. Now it goes on for around eight months. In Afghanistan, Syria and elsewhere, those guys have become increasingly crucial to SAS missions.

The communications systems the soldiers use have improved immeasurably. Comms are now voice-based and one-to-one. In the past, when soldiers needed to send a message back to HQ, they had to encrypt it using a one-time pad to convert the contents into a random set of letters that only someone with access to the same key could decipher. Then that guy had to either tap the message out in long-form Morse code or send it across in a pre-recorded 'burst' transmission.

It was a fiddly and time-consuming process, taking about an hour to encode and send a message. Now, everything is done using clear comms on a secure frequency, which means that there is no longer any need for call signs. An SAS soldier communicating with Hereford or another patrol is essentially no different from two people having a conversation on Skype.

As any Special Forces soldier will tell you, communications are key to any successful operation. Good comms can mean the difference between life and death. If the comms aren't working and you find yourself stranded behind enemy lines, you're going to lose the fight and quite possibly your life.

The signals support for the SAS is unrecognisable from twenty years ago. In the first Gulf War, communications support for the Regiment was provided by a single squadron within the Royal Corps of Signals. Today, 18 (UKSF) Signals, which handles secure comms for all the Special Forces teams, is the largest regiment in the entire British Army. Signallers have to pass their own dedicated Selection course, known as the Special Forces Communicator (SFC) course, which lasts for six months and runs four times a year.

The signallers attached to the SAS are an extremely talented bunch. They can introduce different frequencies on to a particular net, allowing various patrols to talk effortlessly to one another and to base. This might not sound like a big deal, but this kind of straightforward communication has been difficult to achieve in the past. Now, the signallers can load multiple frequencies on to the soldier's phone or radio, allowing them to link up with units running on their own frequency systems, whether that's US SF, the RAF or other NATO troops.

Every SAS operator now carries a Regiment-issued mobile phone, which looks exactly like a regular touchscreen handset, with a few key differences. One of them is the inclusion of a distress signal disguised as a harmless-looking app. When you tap on the app, the phone transmits an emergency beacon to HQ. That signal will continue to broadcast even if the phone is put to sleep or turned off by the enemy. If a soldier is captured by insurgents or militiamen and he needs to alert HQ, he can activate this app and it'll constantly transmit his location. That makes it much easier for commanders to pinpoint where a soldier is being held and to mount a rescue operation.

Soldiers can also ping images back to base using specialist camera equipment and mini-drones, identifying targets in real time. Analysts at HQ can make a positive identification of a target within minutes, based on voice analysis, physical build and other key characteristics. The radio system the soldiers use also broadcasts their precise location at any moment in time, which cuts out mistakes when calling in an airstrike. A pilot approaching the target will know exactly where the friendlies are and where the hostiles are located, reducing the chances of a blue-on-blue.

The benefit of this extra support is clear. It gives the soldiers the freedom and scope to carry out more daring assaults. They can now go in hard in somewhere like Syria, taking on a well-defended ISIS position, safe in the knowledge that if things do go badly wrong, a helicopter will be there to pick them up and evacuate any casualties. They can call on air power to cover their withdrawal, and the SFSG can also come in, put up a cordon and lay down mortars on the enemy to stall their advance. Today, the SAS will not go on an operation unless they have fast-air coverage and helicopter extraction.

In part, this upgrade in support staff came about through closer cooperation with the Americans. The US military has always been very good at backing up their SF teams. They have grasped the fact that you have got this surgical instrument that can go in, hit a target and figure it out for themselves. But if anything goes wrong, you've got the muscle to come in and help them out of trouble.

It's taken a while, but we now think much more like the

Americans in terms of SF. There is a general acceptance that the Regiment is a prized military asset and needs to be properly supported if the guys are to go on high-risk missions. In the 1990s, we had a few mechanics and drivers, signallers from 264 Signals, cooks and a PTI. In every department, the number of staff has increased considerably.

It's no exaggeration to say that without the comms teams, the SRR and the SFSG, the Regiment wouldn't be able to operate in the way it does today. The types of aggressive operations they have been doing in places like Syria are only possible when you have the benefit of air support, real-time information, satellite imagery, reliable communications and the knowledge that if things go wrong, you've got guys who can come in and help you out.

In other ways, the SAS hasn't changed much at all. The demands of the soldier, what he must go through and what is expected of him on any operation remain as high as ever.

Continuation training is now heavily focused on counter-terrorism. Recruits spend a lot of time at the training areas in Sennybridge and Salisbury Plain, tearing around in upgraded Jackals, simulating squadron-sized assaults on ISIS strongholds. Both training areas have model villages featuring mock-ups of houses, allowing the guys to practise contacts with ISIS forces using live ammunition.

The Selection process has also grown massively since the 1990s. When I was helping to run SAS Selection back then, instructors were attached to a dedicated Training Wing. Now Selection is a regiment-within-the-Regiment. It is a huge organisation that has been slowly expanding over time. While the Sabre Squadrons have been fighting around the world and stopping terrorists at home, Selection has been growing like a tumour.

The new group is now responsible for the courses for all parts of the UKSF family, including SRR, SFSG and 18 Signals. Whether you're a signaller or a Para, whether you are going into surveillance or you're applying for Selection for 22 SAS, everything is overseen by the Training Wing Regiment, which is now called UK Special Forces Central Training (SFCT).

When the first modern SAS soldiers went out to the jungle in Malaya, they had virtually no backup. Now, the soldiers have got the cushioning they need. That has made a massive difference to the guys, giving them the freedom to be much more proactive.

The Regiment has always been full of risk-takers. That's just the way they are. A soldier will crash through a door, knowing there's a good chance he'll get clipped, if it means he has a chance of defeating the terrorist and rescuing the hostage on the other side. But now, if the worst happens and he gets shot, the support system is in place to rapidly extract him – and hopefully save his life.

In today's world, the SAS is in demand more than ever.

Attacks in Tunisia, Sri Lanka and Christchurch have shown that the menace of global terrorism is still going strong. I have no doubt that the SAS will be engaged in counter-terrorism ops for the foreseeable future, taking the fight to the enemy wherever they find them.

A covert unit within the SAS will continue to work closely with the security services, doing various training and bodyguard jobs overseas. That will, however, be the limit of their involvement. The SAS is not full of James Bond types. They are very well-equipped soldiers who work on high-grade intel and serve as the muscle on the ground, kicking in doors or hunting down select targets. That has been their role since the 1950s, and it won't be changing anytime soon.

Other threats lurk on the horizon. Our old enemies in Russia have been reasserting their ambitions in the past few years, seizing Crimea and dispatching agents to carry out assassinations overseas. The botched attempt to poison Sergei Skripal, a Russian double agent living in Salisbury, shows that they are unafraid of operating outside the traditional rules of the game. It may be that the Regiment gets brought in to train up rebel groups in the Baltics or eastern Ukraine, in the face of further provocation from Moscow.

If the US goes to war with Iran, we might well get dragged

into another conflict in the Middle East. And there is always the possibility that fringe groups in Northern Ireland might try to stir up trouble in that part of the country.

If the SAS gets called back there, I believe we would be going into a very different situation to the one that the Regiment operated in during the Troubles. The terrorist atrocities of the past twenty years have eroded any public sympathy for insurgent groups masquerading as freedom fighters. Any group looking to engage in terrorist activity would very quickly find themselves isolated on the international stage. The support that the IRA once enjoyed from the US and other countries simply wouldn't exist. And the Regiment would perhaps be given greater freedom to operate than in the past.

Wherever the conflict is, one thing is certain: the British Army will rely heavily on the SAS. They know that they've got something that works incredibly well – and they can't do without it.

Today, the soldiers are active in eight different countries. That is a frankly enormous commitment for a unit the size of 22 SAS. At present, one squadron is doing tours for six months at a base along the Iraqi–Syrian border. Other teams are operating elsewhere in the Middle East, in Latin America and around the world. In each location, the guys are working at a very high level. In some places, they are getting contacted on a daily basis.

The downside to this success is that the guys are very thinly stretched. Perhaps more so than ever. The problems that manifested themselves during the wars in Iraq and Afghanistan have not disappeared. Increasingly, the demands being put on the Regiment mean that the guys are at risk of burnout. For the soldiers getting bogged down in Iraq, Afghanistan and Syria, the six-month rotation doesn't really exist. They're so busy that they don't even have time to come back and take the courses necessary for promotion. Some of them actually ended up doing their courses while they were out in-theatre.

They were burning the candle at both ends. They didn't have time to switch off or let their hair down. One minute they had their noses in their books, studying for their range management courses. The next minute they were climbing into a Black Hawk helicopter and going out to arrest an insurgent target. After a while, some of the guys started to look like walking zombies. Inside Hereford, they started referring to the rotations they were doing as the 'Circle of Death'.

This situation has been exacerbated by the cuts made to the British Army. The smaller the armed forces, the smaller the pool of talent the Regiment can draw upon. You have fewer guys attempting Selection, which means fewer guys getting badged. Which puts even more pressure on the numbers in the squadrons. People talk about admitting more guys to the SAS, but you can't do that without lowering standards. It has been proven in the past that if you drop the standards required of the soldier, you erode the professionalism of the SAS. Do that for long enough, and the Regiment will cease to function effectively. It'll no longer exist.

There is no easy solution to this problem. The Army isn't getting bigger anytime soon, though. The Regiment will have to be savvy in terms of recruitment going forward.

Seventy years ago, when the SAS was fighting for its future, nobody could have predicted that it would be in such high demand now. It went from being a unit that was very nearly extinguished, to becoming arguably the most important regiment in the British Army. It achieved this because it had soldiers who, from the very beginning, had the courage to reinvent the way they were fighting. From the moment the SAS was re-formed, it has had a spirit of innovation and a willingness to experiment that set it apart from the rest of the army.

That spirit, forged in the sweltering jungles of Malaya, continues to this day – giving it a vital edge in the fight against the enemy.

In a world where threats are changing all the time, you need a bunch of guys who are extremely flexible and quick-thinking, able to shape their tactics depending on the ground and the nature of the enemy they're up against. That is what the Regiment has always specialised in. Today, they are more effective than ever, surrounded by an unrivalled support network and enhanced by rapid advances in technology.

When the Regiment first started taking on AQI, nobody had even heard of Twitter or Instagram. Almost nobody owned a smartphone. Now the Regiment utilises cutting-edge technologies to help it in its fight against insurgents and terrorists, conducting a revolutionary model of warfare. The advances have been mind-blowing, but it still comes down to the soldier on the ground, armed and ready to do the business.

No one can fully predict tomorrow's threat. Perhaps the next conflict will see the SAS reprise their role winning hearts and minds. Maybe they'll go back to running OPs and gathering intelligence, giving the head shed a definitive picture of the situation on the ground. They might be called upon to train up local fighters, as they did to such great effect in Oman. Or maybe they'll go back to hunting down enemies in the jungle.

Wherever trouble flares up, the men of 22 SAS will be ready to face down the threat, doing whatever it takes to fight – and win.

APPENDIX A

Norman Schwarzkopf: Letter of Commendation to 22 SAS Regiment

SUBJECT: Letter of Commendation for the 22 Special Air Service (SAS) Regiment

1. I wish to officially commend the 22 Special Air Service (SAS) Regiment for their totally outstanding performance of military operations during Operation Desert Storm.

2. Shortly after the initiation of the strategic air campaign, it became apparent that the Coalition forces would be unable to eliminate Iraq's firing of Scud missiles from western Iraq into Israel. The continued firing of Scuds on Israel carried with it enormous unfavorable political ramifications and could, in fact, have resulted in the dismantling of the carefully crafted Coalition. Such a dismantling would have adversely affected in ways difficult to measure the ultimate outcome of the military campaign. It became apparent that the only way that the Coalition could succeed in reducing these Scud launches was by physically placing military forces on the ground in the vicinity of the western launch sites. At that time, the majority of available Coalition forces were committed to the forthcoming military campaign in the eastern portion of the theater of operations. Further, none of these forces possessed the requisite skills and abilities required to conduct such a dangerous

operation. The only force deemed qualified for this critical mission was the 22 Special Air Service (SAS) Regiment.

3. From the first day they were assigned their mission until the last day of the conflict, the performance of the 22 Special Air Service (SAS) Regiment was courageous and highly professional. The area in which they were committed proved to contain far more numerous enemy forces than had been predicted by every intelligence estimate, the terrain was much more difficult than expected and the weather conditions were unseasonably brutal. Despite these hazards, in a very short period of time the 22 Special Air Service (SAS) Regiment was successful in totally denying the central corridor of western Iraq to Iraqi Scud units. The result was that the principal areas used by the Iraqis to fire Scuds on Tel Aviv were no longer available to them. They were required to move their Scud missile firing forces to the north-west portion of Iraq and from that location the firing of Scud missiles was essentially militarily ineffective.

4. When it became necessary to introduce United States Special Operations Forces into the area to attempt to close down the north-west Scud areas, the 22 Special Air Service (SAS) Regiment provided invaluable assistance to the US forces. They took every available measure to ensure that US forces were thoroughly briefed and were able to profit from the valuable lessons that had been learned by earlier SAS deployments into western Iraq. I am completely convinced that had US forces not received these thorough indoctrinations by SAS personnel US forces would have suffered a much higher rate of casualties than was ultimately the case. Further, the SAS and US joint forces immediately merged into a combined fighting force where the synergetic effect of these fine units ultimately caused the enemy to be convinced that they were facing forces in western Iraq that were more than tenfold the size of those they were actually facing. As a result, large numbers of enemy forces that might otherwise have been deployed in the eastern theater were tied down in western Iraq.

5. The performance of the 22 Special Air Service (SAS) Regiment during Operation Desert Storm was in the highest traditions of the professional military service and in keeping with the proud history and tradition that has been established by that regiment. Please ensure that this commendation receives appropriate attention and is passed on to the unit and its members.

H. NORMAN SCHWARZKOPF
General, US Army
Commander-in-Chief

APPENDIX B

The Regimental Clock Tower

The following lines are inscribed on the clock tower at 22 SAS HQ in Hereford. They come from a verse play, *The Golden Journey to Samarkand*, written by James Elroy Flecker (1884–1915).

> We are the Pilgrims, master; we shall go
> Always a little further; it may be
> Beyond that last blue mountain barred with snow
> Across that angry or glimmering sea ...

The rest of the verse continues:

> White on a throne or guarded in a cave
> There lives a prophet who can understand
> Why men were born: but surely we are brave,
> Who take the Golden Road to Samarkand.

Select Bibliography

This book could not have been written without consulting the following titles. The author highly recommends them for anyone wishing to know more about the SAS and Special Forces in general. All of the below are excellent books and well worth reading:

Cole, Roger & Belfield, Richard, *SAS Operation Storm*, Hodder & Stoughton, 2011.

Connaughton, Richard, *A Brief History of Modern Warfare*, Constable & Robinson, 2008.

Connor, Ken, *Ghost Force*, Cassell, 1998.

Cooper, Johnny, *One of the Originals*, Pan Books, 1991.

Cormac, Rory, *Disrupt and Deny*, Oxford University Press, 2018.

Crossland, Peter, *Victor Two*, Bloomsbury, 1997.

Curtis, Mike, *CQB: Close Quarter Battle*, Bantam Press, 1997.

Davies, Barry, *Joining the SAS*, Sidgwick & Jackson, 1998.

Davies, Barry, *SAS Combat Handbook*, Skyhorse Publishing, 2015.

Delves, Cedric, *Across an Angry Sea*, C. Hurst & Co, 2018.

Dickens, Peter, *SAS Secret War in South-East Asia*, Greenhill Books, 1991.

Doran, Geordie, *Geordie: Fighting Legend of the Modern SAS*, Sutton, 2007.

Firmin, Rusty & Pearson, Will, *Go! Go! Go!*, Weidenfeld & Nicolson, 2010.

Firmin, Rusty, *The Regiment*, Osprey, 2015.

Fowler, William, *Operation Barras*, Weidenfeld & Nicolson, 2004.

Fowler, William, *Certain Death in Sierra Leone*, Osprey, 2010.

Geraghty, Tony, *Who Dares Wins*, Little, Brown, 2002.

Hart-Davis, Duff, *The War That Never Was*, Century, 2011.

Horsfall, Robin, *Fighting Scared*, Cassell, 2002.

Hunter, Gaz, *The Shooting Gallery*, Orion, 1999.

Jeapes, Tony, *SAS Secret War*, Greenhill Books, 2005.

Jones, Tim, *SAS: The First Secret Wars*, I.B. Tauris, 2010.

Kemp, Anthony, *The SAS at War: 1941–1945*, Penguin, 2000.

Kemp, Anthony, *The SAS: Savage Wars of Peace, 1947 to the Present*, Penguin, 2001.

Ladd, James, *SAS Operations*, Robert Hale, 2007.

Large, Lofty, *Soldier Against the Odds*, Mainstream, 1999.

Lewis, Damien, *Operation Certain Death*, Arrow, 2005.

McCallion, Harry, *Killing Zone*, Bloomsbury, 1995.

McCrery, Nigel, *The Complete History of the SAS*, Andre Deutsch, 2011.

McFate, Sean, *Goliath*, Penguin, 2019.

Mackay, Francis, with Cooksey, Jon, *Pebble Island*, Pen & Sword Military, 2007.

MacKenzie, Alastair, *Special Force*, I.B. Tauris, 2011.

Neville, Leigh, *Special Forces in the War on Terror*, Osprey, 2015.

Neville, Leigh, *The SAS: 1983–2014*, Osprey, 2016.

Nicol, Mark, *Ultimate Risk*, Macmillan, 2003.

Packer, George, *The Assassins' Gate*, Faber and Faber, 2006.

Ramsay, Jack, *SAS: The Soldiers' Story*, Macmillan, 1996.

Read, Tom, *Freefall*, Little, Brown, 1998.

Rennie, James, *The Operators*, Arrow, 1997.

Riley, P.J. 'Red', *Kisses from Nimbus*, Clink Street Publishing, 2017.

Ross, Hamish & Marafono, Fred, *From SAS to Blood Diamond Wars*, Pen & Sword Military, 2011.

Ryan, Chris, *The One That Got Away*, Century, 1995.

Ryan, Chris, *Fight to Win*, Century, 2010.

Ryan, Mike, *Special Operations in Iraq*, Pen & Sword Military, 2004.

Scholey, Pete, *The Joker*, Andre Deutsch, 1999.

Scholey, Pete, *SAS Heroes*, Osprey, 2008.

Scully, Will, *Once a Pilgrim*, Headline, 1998.

Smith, Michael, *Killer Elite*, Weidenfeld & Nicolson, 2005.

Spence, Cameron, *Sabre Squadron*, Michael Joseph, 1997.

Spence, Cameron, *All Necessary Measures*, Michael Joseph, 1998.

Stevens, Gordon, *The Originals*, Ebury, 2005.

Taylor, Peter, *Brits: The War Against the IRA*, Bloomsbury, 2001.

Urban, Mark, *Big Boys' Rules*, Faber and Faber, 1993.

Urban, Mark, *Task Force Black*, Little, Brown, 2010.

Weale, Adrian, *Secret Warfare*, Hodder & Stoughton, 1997.

Winner, Pete & Kennedy, Michael, *Soldier I*, Osprey, 2010.

Wright, Lawrence, *The Looming Tower*, Allen Lane, 2006.

Websites

blackfive.net
britains-smallwars.com
cfr.org
dailymail.co.uk

defensemedianetwork.com
edition.cnn.com
eliteukforces.info
forces.net
theguardian.com
theindependent.co.uk
independent.ie
irishnews.com
militarytimes.com
nytimes.com
scotsman.com
specialoperations.com
statista.com
telegraph.co.uk
thestar.com.my
thetimes.co.uk
washingtonpost.com

Glossary

2iC – Second-in-Command
AA – Anti-Aircraft
ANC – African National Congress
AQI – al-Qaeda in Iraq
ASU – Active Service Unit (IRA)
AWACS – Airborne Early Warning and Control System
BAS – British Antarctic Survey
Basha – SAS term for a shelter
BATT – British Army Training Team
BCR – Battlefield Casualty Replacement
BDF – Botswana Defence Force
BFT – Army Battle Fitness Test
BG – Bodyguard
BIAP – Baghdad International Airport (formerly Saddam International Airport)
BMG – Browning Machine Gun
Casevac – evacuate a battlefield casualty
CFT – Army Combat Fitness Test
CO – Commanding Officer
COIN – Counter-Insurgency
CPA – Coalition Provisional Authority
CQB – Close Quarter Battle
Crow – Army slang for new recruits
CRW – Counter-Revolutionary Warfare Wing
CT – Communist Terrorist
CTR – Close Target Reconnaissance
CTSFO – Counter Terrorist Specialist Firearms Officer (UK police)
DA – Deliberate Action
DCM – Distinguished Conduct Medal
DF – Directional Fire
Dhobi – SAS slang for a wash
DPG – Diplomatic Protection Group (Metropolitan Police)

DRFLA – Democratic Revolutionary Front for the Liberation of Arabistan
DS – Directing Staff
DZ – Drop Zone
EFP – Explosively Formed Penetrator
EMOE – Explosive Method of Entry
EMU – Electronic Messaging Unit
Endex – End of Exercise
ER – Emergency Response
FAC – Forward Air Controller
FPC – Force Projection Cell
FRE – Former Regime Elements (Iraq)
FSG – Fire Support Group
GPMG – General Purpose Machine Gun
HAHO – High-Altitude, High-Opening
HALO – High-Altitude, Low-Opening
HE – High Explosive
HF – High-Frequency
HVT – High-Value Target
IA – Immediate Action
IED – Improvised Explosive Device
IMV – Infantry Mobility Vehicle
ISAF – International Security and Assistance Force (Afghanistan)
IRA – Irish Republican Army
ISIS – Islamic State in Iraq and Syria (also known as: Daesh, Islamic State, ISISL)
JSIO – Joint Services Intelligence Organisation
JSIW – Joint Services Interrogation Wing
JSOC – Joint Special Operations Command (Iraq)
Kampong – Malayan term for a tribal village
LAT – Lead Assault Team (counter-terrorism stand-by team)
LG – Life Guards (British Army regiment)
LMG – Light Machine Gun
LO – Liaison Officer
Loadie – Army slang for an RAF loadmaster, the person responsible for the
    cargo area on a military aircraft
LTD – Laser Target Designator
LUP – Lying-Up Point
LZ – Landing Zone
Medevac – medical evacuation
MiD – Mention in Dispatches
MM – Military Medal
MRE – Meals, Ready-to-Eat (US military ration packs)
MRF – Military Reconnaissance Force
MSR – Main Supply Route
MWMIK – Mobile Weapon-Mounted Installation Kit
NavEx – Navigation Exercise

NBC – Nuclear, Biological and Chemical (weapons or suit)
NCO – Non-Commissioned Officer
NOD – Night optical device
NVG – Night-Vision Goggles
OC – Officer Commanding
OG – Olive Green (shirt)
OP – Observation Post
OPSEC – Operational Security
PE – Plastic Explosive
PMC – Private Military Contractor
PSI – Permanent Staff Instructor
Psy-ops – Psychological operations
RAVC – Royal Army Veterinary Corps
RCL – Recoilless Rifle
Relish – Army slang for the Browning .50 Machine Gun
REME – Royal Electrical and Mechanical Engineers
RMR – Royal Malay Regiment
RSM – Regimental Sergeant Major
RTU – Returned to Unit
RUC – Royal Ulster Constabulary
RUF – Revolutionary United Front
RV – Rendezvous
SADF – South African Defence Force
SAF – Sultan's Armed Forces (Oman)
SAM – Surface-to-Air Missile
Sangar – temporary fortified position
SARBE – Search and Rescue Beacon
SB – Special Branch (RUC)
SBS – Special Boat Service
SEP – Surrendered Enemy Personnel
SF – Special Forces
SFC – Special Forces Communicator (Selection course)
SFCT – Special Forces Central Training
SFSG – Special Forces Support Group
SGTG – South Georgia Task Group
SLA – Sierra Leone Army
Slop Jockey – SAS slang for a cook
SLR – Self-Loading Rifle
SMG – submachine gun
SMU – Specialised Military Unit
SOE – Special Operations Executive
SOP – Standard Operating Procedure
SP – Special Projects Team (SAS counter-terrorism team)
SQMS – Squadron Quartermaster Sergeant
SRR – Special Reconnaissance Regiment

SRU – Special Reconnaissance Unit
SSM – Squadron Sergeant Major
Stonk – concentrated mortar bombardment
TA – Territorial Army
TACBE – Tactical Beacon
Tacsat – Tactical satellite communications
TEL – Transporter Erector Launcher
TEZ – Total Exclusion Zone
UAV – Unmanned Aerial Vehicle
UDA – Ulster Defence Association
UDR – Ulster Defence Regiment
UNAMSIL – United Nations Mission in Sierra Leone
USAF – United States Air Force
VCP – Vehicle Checkpoint
WP – White Phosphorous